PRAISE FOR *CUSTOMER-CENTRIC INNOVATION IN FINANCE*

"In this book Anette Broløs and Erin Taylor recentre the debate around humans and their needs against the backdrop of extensive data-driven innovation in finance and astutely recalibrate the thinking around the design and delivery of financial services. Using a wealth of examples, this must-read exemplifies how financial institutions can foster trust, enhance user satisfaction, and drive sustainable growth. A much-needed book in the current digital age!"
Anne-Laure Mention, Professor of Management, RMIT University

"Erin Taylor and Anette Broløs seamlessly deploy their thesis about using both qualitative and quantitative research methodologies to provide a comprehensive guide to solving human-centric problems and designing innovative financial products. As our world becomes increasingly complex, this book guides us through the intricate web of technologies, needs, channels, and models in financial services. It is an indispensable resource for industry professionals and advisors alike, offering a transformative perspective that aligns with the evolving reality of our changing world."
Tony Craddock, Director General, The Payments Association

"Erin Taylor and Anette Broløs tell us we need to 'hit the streets' and actually *talk* to people about their everyday lives and challenges if we want to build inclusive financial products and systems. *Customer-Centric Innovation in Finance* provides tools for understanding cultures of money and finance, as well as for fostering culture change in the organizations developing consumer financial products and services. A compelling guidebook to finance as, above all, a *human* practice, and a how-to for building a more just financial world."
Bill Maurer, Dean, School of Social Sciences, University of California, Irvine and Director, Institute for Money, Technology and Financial Inclusion

"This book on human-centricity is certainly needed in the overly quantitative field of finance and fintech."
Paolo Sironi, Global Research Leader in Banking and Financial Markets, IBM and Author

"Erin Taylor and Anette Broløs offer a rich and compelling ethnographic and data-driven account of how financial behaviour underlies the intimate dynamics of human relationships. This book is a must-read for those seeking innovative ideas and deep human insights revealed through the lens of financial behaviour."
Timothy de Waal Malefyt, Clinical Professor of Marketing, Gabelli School of Business, Fordham University

"Understanding customer trust, underpins financial services companies' ability to be successful. Given the fast pace of change in customer expectations, learning about how customers identify a need and determine the right product or service is more important than ever. Erin Taylor and Anette Broløs remind us that people make financial decisions, not technology and that technology enables people. This is a must read to learn how to stay connected to customers."
Lisa Frazier, COO, Judo Bank

"Money and finance are fundamentally about people and communities. *Customer-Centric Innovation in Finance* insightfully argues for qualitative as well as quantitative data and methods to be used in studying the topic of money, finance and innovation."
Ronit Ghose, Future of Finance, Citi

Customer-centric Innovation in Finance

Leveraging human insights to drive product innovation in the digital age

Erin B Taylor and Anette Broløs

KoganPage

First published in Great Britain and the United States in 2024 by Kogan Page Limited

2nd Floor, 45 Gee Street
London
EC1V 3RS
United Kingdom

8 W 38th Street, Suite 902
New York, NY 10018
USA

www.koganpage.com

Kogan Page books are printed on paper from sustainable forests.

ISBNs

Hardback 978 1 3986 1389 8
Paperback 978 1 3986 1387 4
Ebook 978 1 3986 1388 1

British Library Cataloguing-in-Publication Data

A CIP record for this book is available from the British Library.

Library of Congress Control Number

2024931849

Typeset by Integra Software Services, Pondicherry
Print production managed by Jellyfish
Printed and bound by CPI Group (UK) Ltd, Croydon, CR0 4YY

Anette would like to thank:

David Birch
for giving me the idea
to write a book

My family for
believing in me

Erin for making this
such an enjoyable
experience

Erin would like to thank:

Heather Horst
for getting me interested
in the anthropology of
finance many years ago

Todd Sanderson
for championing
our efforts to bring
qualitative approaches
to financial research

Anette for believing
in Finthropology

We would both like to thank
our cats for sitting behind us
as we write and not walking
across the keyboard too much

CONTENTS

List of figures xi
About the authors xiii
Foreword xv
Preface xix
Acknowledgements xxi
Abbreviations xxiii

01 **Human insights for finance: Why understanding customer behaviour has never been so important for financial services** 1
Understanding finance as human 5
Qualitative data is also data 9
Chapter outline 11
References 13

02 **Digital and social transformation in finance: What's at stake for customer-driven innovation?** 15
Financial services: From implementing technology to digital transformation 17
Changes in competition and business models 22
Changes in customer experience and expectations 27
Looking to the future: Change continues 31
Towards an uncertain future 36
References 37

03 **Technology and data-driven innovation in finance: Where do people fit in?** 43
Perspectives on innovation 43
Financial innovation practices 49
Customer-centricity and customer needs 56
Innovation is changing 63
References 64

04 Using behavioural science for decision-making and product development in financial services 69
What's wrong with economic man, anyway? 71
What do people want? 76
How do people make decisions? Some key factors 80
Bringing in complexity 88
References 90

05 Into the field: Understanding financial behaviour in context 93
Mobile money in Haiti 94
The launch of mobile money 100
Generating quality qualitative research 104
Socioeconomic humans 114
References 115

06 Innovating for a changing world: Using behavioural insights and qualitative data to develop new financial services 117
Stories 118
The importance of understanding the context 136
Where can qualitative studies contribute the most? 138
References 139

07 Financial inclusion: Myths and workarounds 141
Financial inclusion: Background and progress 142
Myths and realities 148
Human workarounds 155
Issues to consider 161
References 163

08 Designing for people: Learning from inclusion initiatives 165
Solutions for people on low incomes 166
Female finance 173
Migrants and refugees 178

Designing for people 184
References 186

09 **The future is in the field: Insights for services that don't exist yet** 191
The field is changing: Why start with customers? 192
Learning from innovation in payments 200
Researching for future innovation 212
References 213

10 **Organizing for customer-driven innovation: Analysis, tools and resources to use for innovation** 217
Doing user research in your organization 218
How to get started 219
Building the culture 223
Building a research organization 225
The toolbox 227
Research culture-centricity 239
References 242

Conclusion: A human financial world 245
A short summary 246
What would happen if...? 248
Where to next? 250

Appendix: List of company examples 253
Glossary 255
Index 259

LIST OF FIGURES

Figures

Figure 3.1 Three basic needs in financial choice **61**
Figure 5.1 Map of cash circulation routes in south-eastern Haiti **96**
Figure 6.1 What's in a bag? **120**
Figure 6.2 QCash – affordable loans for credit union members **131**
Figure 8.1 Designing financial services for women **176**
Figure 10.1 Persona of Anna Gomes, the rural entrepreneur **229**

ABOUT THE AUTHORS

Erin B Taylor, Managing Director and Founder, Finthropology

Erin is an anthropologist based in The Hague. She specializes in how people's financial behaviour is changing along with innovation in financial services. She holds a PhD from the University of Sydney, Australia, and has carried out ethnographic research in the Caribbean, South America, Africa and Europe. Erin is especially interested in how culture and group belonging influence people's actions and decisions.

Anette Broløs, Director and Founder, Finthropology

Anette is a fintech analyst based in Denmark. She is an experienced network leader working with strategic innovation and partnerships, and an experienced speaker and facilitator. She holds an industrial PhD in collaborative innovation and has a background in economics. Anette has extensive work experience in finance including consultant work on the implementation of PSD2 and six years as CEO of Copenhagen FinTech Innovation and Research.

FOREWORD

by David G W Birch

When I first began work in the fields of electronic payments and digital money, I thought that I was gaining an insight into the future of financial services by focusing on technology and innovation. It was only after a few years, during which I gained first-hand experience of both successful and unsuccessful population-scale product roll-outs, that I began to feel that the work of artists and social scientists was more critical to developing practical visions of the future than the work of cryptographers and computer scientists!

Like Erin and Anette, I found the work of Professor Lisa Servon to be seminal. For me it was eye-opening, and led me to a wider appreciation of the whole topic of financial transactions, financial services and ultimately financial health. In this book, they develop themes around inclusion and exclusion, money and wealth in ways that I found, and I am sure you will find, interesting and enlightening.

As we open up to new technologies such as artificial intelligence, decentralized finance, virtual worlds and the metaverse, these issues become ever more complex. The authors highlight virtual games (e.g., Roblox), mobile money and other examples from which we can learn, and they draw on valuable experiences from Starling Bank and Hiveonline, but their central message that more people-centric development is key.

We are no longer in the era of 'rational man' economics and must therefore draw more on the work of ethnographers and anthropologists to see how individuals use and want to use financial services. Collecting and collating the 'right stories' about financial services is therefore so valuable to those of us hoping to design the next-generation financial health infrastructure. In the coming connected world, it seems to me that stories about communities are especially valuable.

When the authors talk about design solutions for communities and not only for individuals, I really feel that they are on to something.

The transactional echo of McLuhan's global village demands different kinds of financial services in the future, services that emphasize relationships (particularly family and intergenerational relationships) and reputations, tribes and their transactions.

This is not a book about the future, though. It is a book about now and many of their insights are very timely indeed. Issues around central bank digital currencies and financial inclusion are important and deserve immediate attention, which is why I found the lessons from inclusion initiatives especially valuable. (The mention of digital identity as a fundamental component of future financial services warmed my heart, and I strongly agree with the view that we may see very new models of customer identity being developed in these new environments.)

While many of us (in the world of digital transactions) are comfortable with the topics of trust and risk, the emotional context for such transactions is harder to grasp yet just as important. The authors write:

> Many people don't recognize the role emotions play in their finances. As a result, they may go through their lives completely ill-equipped to deal with their finances and make them work for the wellbeing of themselves and their families.

As someone who has always been a poor money manager and a rather unsophisticated user of financial services, I cannot tell you how strongly this resonates with me! This is why when it comes to the particular topic of emotional wellbeing, the relationship between money and mental health is complex, but crucial for evolving a financial services industry that serves society as a whole.

Finally, I would like to highlight one question that the book raises and that remains unresolved. In a digital world, how do we teach children about money? Not merely the mechanics of it, but the emotional intelligence and wisdom required to manage it? I do worry that we are not building firm economic foundations for the next generation. Perhaps Erin and Anette can develop their insights here further in their next book.

David G W Birch *is an author, adviser and commentator on digital financial services. He is an international keynote speaker and recognized thought leader in digital identity and digital money. David is Principal at 15Mb Ltd, his advisory practice, and Global Ambassador for Consult Hyperion, the secure electronic transactions consultancy. He holds several board-level advisory positions as well as academic fellowships. He is the author of several books on digital money, payments and identity and is a contributor to magazines including* Forbes, Financial World *magazine and more. His website is https://dgwbirch.com.*

PREFACE

Welcome to the Finthropology Universe.

We, the authors of this book, met at a conference and immediately connected as we were both wondering why the innovation process in many financial institutions was still happening from the inside out (delivering new technology solutions to customers) rather than outside in (solving customer pain points). This was some years ago, and our wonder has continued as we have observed conferences, events and blogs talk about customer-centricity in financial innovation – mostly drawing on digital transformation and quantitative data.

We founded Finthropology with the intention of creating human insights for finance. We aim to help organizations to understand their customers' financial behaviour and innovate to meet their needs. With this book, we are happy to share with you examples of how surprising and enlightening spending time with customers can be. Our aim is not to suggest that qualitative studies are better than quantitative analysis. Our aim is simply to show that relying solely on data trail information is unlikely to fully illuminate the reality of customers' decision-making processes or how these impact upon their lives.

We hope you will enjoy our examples and perhaps consider starting to do your own qualitative customer research, following some of our suggestions in Chapter 10. And if you read this book because you already agree with our position, we still hope that the book adds to your ideas.

We are happy to hear from you.

ACKNOWLEDGEMENTS

Thank you to all of our clients and partners who have understood the value of what we try to do at Finthropology and who have allowed us to freely share our work. This book would not have been possible without you.

A particular word of thanks to Bill Maurer, Director of the Institute for Money, Technology and Financial Inclusion at the University of California, Irvine, for helping to launch us on this journey many years ago.

Thank you to Tessa Veldhorst (De Schaapjesfabriek), who created and updated the illustrations for the book, and for being a constant source of inspiration.

Many thanks to the European Women Payments Network (EWPN) for supporting the start of Finthropology.

A big thanks to our friends and connections for sharing your stories and experiences of human behaviour in finance.

Finally, we would like to thank Kogan Page for suggesting that we write this book, for supporting the value of a different perspective on customer-centricity, and for ensuring a smooth process throughout.

ABBREVIATIONS

AI	artificial intelligence
BIS	Bank for International Settlements
BNPL	buy now, pay later
CBDC	central bank digital currency
DeFi	decentralized finance
DLT	distributed ledger technology
ERP	enterprise resource planning
FDP	forcibly displaced people
FSP	financial service provider
KYC	know your customer
ML	machine learning
MNO	mobile network operator
mPOS	mobile point of sale
P2P	peer-to-peer
POS	point of sale
SME	small and medium-sized enterprises
UX	User experience

Human insights for finance 01

Why understanding customer behaviour has never been so important for financial services

Around the time of the Global Financial Crisis, anthropologist David Stoll was investigating a financial mystery in the Guatemalan town of Nebaj. Residents were struggling under the weight of unmanageable debt. How had they got themselves into this position? Stoll, who had been carrying research in the town since 1987, spent several years trying to get to the root of the mystery. Spending months at a time in the town, he was able to talk with many local residents and microfinance officers, as well as interviewing Nebajenese who had moved to the USA. His task wasn't easy, since he was asking people to talk about things that were considered shameful at best (debt), and were illegal at worst (undocumented migration). But eventually he was able to pull the story together, documenting it in his book *El Norte or Bust! How migration fever and microcredit produced a financial crash in a Latin American town* (2012).

Stoll learned that, for the past fifteen years or so, residents had been taking on microfinance debt to send migrants to the United States. Initially, those migrants encountered what they were looking for: jobs paying far higher wages than could be found back home in the Guatemalan mountains. They sent remittances back home, which their families used to build or buy new homes, sending real estate prices skyrocketing. But in 2007 work in the United States was drying up, and remittances were trickling in slowly. Suddenly, their families could no longer pay back the loans they had taken out to send their relatives across the border. They borrowed more money to try to make payments and delay default. In 2008, the US economy burst, making their situation even worse. Both bubbles burst, leaving many families with properties worth far less than they had paid for them, and an unmanageable amount of debt.

Several years later, in the United States, Professor Lisa Servon was attempting to uncover a similar mystery. She had learned that, in the wake of the 2008 financial crisis, low-income Americans were increasingly using payday lenders and cheque-cashing services. Why would people use such expensive services, when policy-makers and consumer advocates warned against it? To find out, she took a job for a few months in a cheque-cashing service called RiteCheck in the South Bronx, and then another stint at a payday lender in California called Check Center.

What Servon discovered surprised her – and many others. Before beginning her research, she had assumed that the kind of people who use cheque-cashing services and payday lenders would be people on low incomes who had not yet begun to use banks (the unbanked). Instead, she discovered that banking services were not well suited to serve low-income groups in need of small deposits and small short-term loans. She found that many left because they could no longer afford bank fees, such as charging fees for low balances or overdrafts. Rather than attracting interest, low-income bank customers were losing money, and not always in predictable ways.

Indeed, in her book about this study, *The Unbanking of America: How the new middle class survives* (2017), Servon notes that banks had closed the accounts of 6 per cent of Americans because their account had gone into the red. Cheque-cashing services and payday lenders in comparison built a thriving business by offering low-level, short-term deposits and loans for very high fees.

What do these stories have in common? In both cases, the researchers had to hit the streets to solve a financial mystery. Neither the Nebajenese in Stoll's study, nor the Americans in Servon's, could be easily understood using quantitative methods. Stoll, in his book, explains that doing a survey wouldn't have worked, because people would not have wanted to tell the truth. Instead, he had to spend time in Nabaj to earn people's trust. Servon tells a similar story about her ethnographic fieldwork.

Engaging deeply with people's lives and context can provide an understanding of complexity and answer questions that would be overlooked by more traditional surveys. They can be used to answer a wide array of questions that are difficult to answer due to lack of quantitative data, privacy concerns or the complexity of the problem. They may include: Why do many women lack confidence investing, even if they have plenty of knowledge or experience? If a government introduces a central bank digital currency, will their citizens use it? Why are customers of buy now, pay later services using many services rather than just being loyal to one? Why do surveys of rural villages in Laos indicate that both women and men have an equal say when it comes to making financial decisions, even though it's common knowledge that they do not? How does the switch from cash to digital banking affect how people budget their money?

All these questions come from research we have carried out in different countries. We could add many more to the list. The purpose of this book, however, is not to provide an exhaustive account of people's financial behaviour. Instead, we argue that, when faced with complex questions that don't readily lend themselves to quantitative analysis, qualitative methods can help to fill the gap – and sometimes in dramatic ways. Since methods like ethnography are open to encountering the unexpected, the insights gleaned can be stunning. They can help companies, not-for-profits and policy-makers ensure their solutions, programmes and policies reflect the realities of people's lives, rather than wasting time implementing innovations that are doomed to failure. And if people's practices are complex today, they are likely to be increasingly so in the future, as more financial services emerge with more ways to access them and combine them.

In financial innovation, it's important to consider real people, whether they are intended to be the actual users of your service, or may just be affected indirectly. In recent years, there has been a tendency towards greater customer-centricity, fuelled by the possibilities technology presents to provide people with more niche services. Indeed, the greater availability of customer data is an enormous help to map out what kind of financial decisions are being made by different kinds of people living in diverse places. In fact, the combination of technology and data has been the main driver of innovation for the past fifteen years at least. The internet, faster data management and the mobile phone have resulted in a stream of new service offers. Access to large customer data sets combined with artificial intelligence and machine learning are increasingly leading to data-driven innovation based on analysis of data and data patterns.

Quantitative data is powerful and we can't do without it. But it doesn't answer all our questions. Quantitative data is great at telling us what users are doing, but often doesn't give us much insight into *why* people do what they do. And if a service doesn't exist yet then there is no data to tell us how people use it.

This matters because the need to understand customers intimately has increased along with the rise of niche services and new providers that target specific groups rather than the general population. Not so long ago, new finance and technology companies needed substantial capital to get off the ground. With lower capital requirements, aspiring entrepreneurs can build new fintech services from the comfort of their own home, target specific customer needs and have reasonable expectations of success. It also puts pressure on large companies to meet their customers' needs. The development towards a more decentralized environment with Web 3.0 will push this further.

How can financial service providers ensure they understand their customers well enough to meet their needs? How can they avoid product failure due to misreading customers? How can they ensure their products and services don't cause more harm than good?

We believe that qualitative research can help fill the gaps of our understanding of current services and help us design future services. We don't advocate giving up on quantitative methods. Far from it. Rather, we advocate for using the methods that are right for the task at hand – and often this means a mixed method approach. There are quantitative initiatives out there that could benefit from using qualitative methods. And, equally, the reverse is true. Qualitative research also often misses out on critical information by not working with quantitative research.

We, the authors of this book, have training in anthropology (Erin) and economics (Anette). We both specialize in qualitative methods, though we also collaborate in mixed method projects. In this book we'll walk you through how to incorporate qualitative insights into your research and development. We'll demonstrate through many concrete examples how such methods have helped companies innovate. We'll also give you practical advice for embedding this approach into your own company's innovation practices.

But first, let's talk about how finance is inherently human-centric.

Understanding finance as human

Finance is not something we usually associate with human sentiments. While we covet it, at best we usually see it as a means to an end. Yet there is no doubt that money is associated with emotions. Whether it is the pleasure of receiving a crisp new bill as a birthday present, being proud to wave a large bill at the bar, feeling ashamed because of not understanding the risks and profits of investments or the despair of not understanding how money can be lost because of bank fees when it was deposited in the bank for safe keeping.

And sometimes we have decidedly negative attitudes towards money: we often see it as being out of our control. In our study of Swiss women (Broløs and Taylor, 2022), we interviewed well-educated women who felt they did not know enough about stock markets to be able to invest, even if they had plenty of investment experience. Danish academic Kirsten Bonde Sørensen (2013) carried out research in which she asked bank customers to explain their experience with money, and how they wished it would be. Most described how they felt unable to manage, and how they wished to be more in control of their spending and money decisions. We come back to this later in Chapters 3 and 4.

Yet this view of money makes little sense if we understand that the economy exists to serve people through helping them distribute wealth (however little that might be) and risk over shorter and longer timespans. Before formal financial institutions such as commercial banks and central banks developed, people organized their finances largely among themselves. They made agreements about how to pay each other, formed mutual insurance cooperatives, lent each other money and offered credit for purchases. They did all of this without the need for official intermediaries to set rules and regulations. Over time, advances in technology have evolved and changed solutions, reflecting societal development and the existing power structures.

The human origins of finance are well illustrated by the anthropologist David Graeber in his book *Debt: The first 5,000 years* (2011). Graeber explains how, since people in villages all knew each other, they would keep tallies of who owed what to whom in their heads. Over time, these turned into tally sticks or IOUs that could be cashed in or even used like money, so long as the next bearer trusted that the original issuer was good to pay his debt.

Insurance was also originally organized directly among people who knew each other. For thousands of years, humans have banded together to insure each other. Sometimes insurance was monetized, but not always. For example, insurance could be as simple as a community pitching in to rebuild a house that had burned down or feed a family if their crop failed. Everyone in the village knew they would be looked after: they had mutual assurance. In terms of more formal insurance, one of the earliest and most widespread forms was funeral insurance. Culturally, the death of a family member is one of the most emotionally distressing and financially devastating things that can happen. People want to ensure their loved ones have a proper burial, and that they can continue to support their families after losing an economically productive family member. And so, funeral insurance cooperatives formed everywhere (McFall, 2014).

But while the historical foundations of finance were certainly social, that does not mean they were equal. People everywhere need to acquire resources to survive. They need money, whether cash or digital, to pay the cashier at the supermarket. They need assurance that they will be looked after in the event of a catastrophe. They need loans to start businesses and buy homes. And they need to think about surviving in their old age. While this process was relatively egalitarian in foraging societies, and to a certain extent in small villages, human hierarchies have existed for thousands of years that have denied resources to many while bestowing them on a few. Indeed, formal financial services were initially developed for wealthy people.

This began to change around two hundred years ago, with the development of financial institutions for people living in poverty in Europe in the 1800s, such as cooperative banks and insurance providers offering services for ordinary people. These include the Scottish Widows Association (founded in 1815) and the Nutspaarbank, a savings bank for people living in poverty in the Netherlands (founded 1921). In the past few decades, the microfinance movement spearheaded by Muhammad Yunus's Grameen Bank has revived the notion of providing financial products for people living in poverty. However, as we will discuss in more depth later in this book, there are serious limits to the ability of financial tools to redress financial inequality.

Combining money and relationships also raises moral quandaries. In her renowned book *The Purchase of Intimacy* (2005), sociologist Viviana Zelizer argues that we all use economics to build and maintain intimate ties with other people. Along the way, however, we encounter quandaries as to how to strike a balance between using money to improve the quality of our relationships on the one hand, and overly quantifying them on the other. Any household that has tried to set a budget would realize that this balance is hard to maintain. Does earning more money than your spouse give you more rights? How should childcare contributions be compared to monetary income? To what extent should we worry about whether each household member makes an equal contribution?

The technologization of money is also adding new dimensions to our efforts to balance our socioeconomic lives. An interesting observation on the abstraction of financial transactions comes from Brett Scott, who in his book *Cloudmoney: Cash, cards, crypto, and the war for our wallets* (2022) notes how weird it is that we encounter scenarios in which we want to transfer money to a friend who we are standing right in front of, but rather than hand over cash we make a transaction on our phone, sending a signal that might travel hundreds of kilometres before arriving on our friend's screen.

And yet, money remains inherently social. Scott's scenario might sound strange, but there is nothing inherently antisocial about digitizing financial transactions. On the contrary, digital transactions provide the possibility for more social interactions in which money is used to express relationships. In China, people use an app to send digital 'red envelopes' to each other containing small amounts of money. This practice is a technologized version of an age-old custom of giving people gifts of cash placed in red envelopes. Far from denigrating the gift, these digital red envelopes became immensely popular. People began to send each other tiny amounts of money by way of a greeting.

In Kenya, M-PESA's television advertisements testify to the social nature of remittances, depicting a professional, urban man, dressed in a suit, using M-PESA to send money to his parents in the countryside. We see banknotes fly out of his phone and through the air. His parents watch it fly towards them as they stand in their field and are delighted when it lands in their phone. We may cling to the idea of money as a material thing, but the fact that this transaction is purely digital is not seen to interfere with its social purpose. As anthropologist Sibel Kusimba and colleagues (2013: 1) put it:

> Although mobile money technology is designed for person-to-person transfers, it is more accurately a tool of individuals who see themselves as parts of groups or collectivities, whether these be savings groups, groups of siblings and cousins, or extended families who amass contributions for public ceremonies.

Money and financial tools are also intricate in the financial relationships of people who have never met in real life, and who may never have communicated with each other at all. People donate to strangers' Kickstarter campaigns because they want to support the goal. These days, charities collect far more money digitally than by campaigning on the street. In the video game *World of Warcraft*, players use real money to buy in-game tokens to get further ahead in the game and increase their status.

However, we shouldn't forget that technology is fallible. Often, rather than using finance to facilitate social relations, people have to use their social relations to facilitate financial transactions. In Brazil, for example, if a software glitch occurs when one person is trying to send money to another using the payment service Pix, to find out whether the receiver actually got the money the sender has to call them to ask. Or residents of a rural village in Mexico, living far from a money transfer agent, rely on one local woman to collect money from their children living overseas. Or a professional woman living in Switzerland learns to use Google Wallet when her card payment fails at her convenience store.

Finance needs people as much as people need finance. How, then, can we ensure that finance and people are fit for each other? As financial services – and people's use of them – grows in complexity, how can we ensure we are innovating a system that works in the context of people's everyday lives? How can we ensure we recognize the critical role that people play in making the financial system work? And what kind of regulation of financial providers do we need to put in place?

Qualitative data is also data

Stoll and Servon spent months (or years in Stoll's case) getting to the bottom of their respective financial mysteries. Fortunately, complex human financial problems are not always quite so difficult to solve. Thousands of social scientists (this book's authors among them) have spent at least a century devising ways to research financial behaviour. Some of these problems may be understood fairly well by just doing a handful of interviews. Some are better suited to experimental methods or quantitative data analysis. Others call for spending time talking to people and observing their behaviour, whether in real life or online. As financial services have digitized, they have also innovated new ways to study financial behaviour. We expect that researchers will continue to innovate with methods, keeping pace with innovations in finance itself. We will discuss these themes throughout the book.

Before we move on to the rest of the book, we would like to make a clarification about quantitative research. Often we have heard people say, after hearing a research presentation based on qualitative methods, 'But it's just anecdotes! What can they possibly tell us conclusively about what people do?'

Such comments ignore the fact that qualitative data is also data. It makes no scientific sense to say that only numbers are trustworthy. True, qualitative studies will rarely (if ever) gather data from enough people to form a representative sample. This most definitely means that there are limits to how much we can generalize from qualitative research. However, qualitative research can both try to dive into a quantitative mystery and help build the right quantitative survey. Moreover, if a qualitative study is properly designed it is often reasonable to assume that the findings would also apply to a similar population. In the case of Stoll's research in Guatemala, understanding the experiences of one village can help us understand the financialization of migration in general. Similarly, Servon's ethnographic research sheds light on why a trend towards unbanking developed in America. In our study of payment choices in Brazil, we did interviews with 63 people on low incomes and also undertook observations. We feel that the insights we generated would probably hold for millions of other Brazilians. Why are we so confident? Because much of our data agrees with what has been found in larger surveys. Our new findings, on matters that are difficult to survey, add richness to the body of knowledge that already exists.

We would also like to point out that the idea that quantitative researchers do not use qualitative methods, or draw on qualitative research, is greatly overstated. Academics working in finance and business schools, for example, often analyse ready-made data sets but generally pay attention to the human activities that the data represents in order to make their analyses as reliable as possible. Sociologists and economists rely upon qualitative information to design surveys. Many quantitative researchers check whether the results of their analyses line up with real life.

Professionals working in the finance industry also rely on qualitative data to operate. Customer service representatives in banks collect feedback from customers to understand how well their business is serving their members. Fintechs scour Twitter and other social media fora to gauge customer reactions and get ideas for future features or services.

Even central banks – traditionally the home of conservative economics – depend on real-life observations. In his book *Economy of Words: Communicative imperatives in central banks* (2013), Douglas Holmes writes about how monetary policy committees sometimes have to make decisions quickly, such as to avert a financial crisis. Lags in quantitative data collection means that they cannot entirely depend upon it to guide their decisions. Instead, they consult with a spectrum of people in the economy, including shop owners, merchants and distributors. Central banks use this information to judge what direction the economy is moving in and make decisions based on it.

The problem, then, is not that the finance industry, or finance researchers, completely ignore qualitative data. The problem is rather that the power of qualitative data tends to be underestimated, and its methods are often not well understood. This means that qualitative methods may not be applied in situations where they would be most useful – particularly understanding complex human problems, and designing current and future services. It is this suite of problems that this book will address.

Chapter outline

This book consists of ten chapters and a conclusion. Throughout the book we blend discussions of how to understand people with perspectives on the broader financial system and its changes. We use stories extensively to illustrate our arguments.

In Chapter 2 we discuss the current digital transformation and the changes it is bringing to financial services and relate it to the parallel changes for consumers, other industries and society. We explain how digital transformation combines multiple technological changes in infrastructure, data management and innovation as well as both the competitive and regulatory environments. It requires a change in cultural mindset to encourage innovation, diversity and change as well as changes in skills to manage new technologies and an understanding of changes in customer behaviour and expectations.

Chapter 3 builds on Chapter 2's discussion of change in financial services. We dive deeper into the development of financial innovation and how it changes under digital transformation. We discuss the ways digital tools allow for new customer information and have caused a focus on customer-centric innovation.

In Chapter 4 we turn towards human behaviour, providing our perspective on why understanding people is so tricky. We look at different approaches to financial behaviour in the behavioural sciences and explain how our scientific understanding of people has changed over the past century. We explain why it's difficult to build models of human behaviour that reflect real life, walk you through some great research that offers better ways of understanding people, and touch on some of the implications for innovation in finance.

Chapter 5 takes us into the field to spend time with people in the places they live, work and play. We explain how qualitative data is collected, its possibilities and limits, and the kinds of insights it generates. We provide an extensive case study of a long research project on mobile money in Haiti to illustrate how fieldwork is conducted and the many complex issues and insights that it can generate.

Chapter 6 builds directly on our field exploration. We describe how to use the kinds of insights we glean in the field to innovate for a changing world. We illustrate the importance of understanding people and context when building new solutions. We also share examples from the industry of how such knowledge has been overlooked, leading to higher innovation cost and lesser product success.

We then turn to the important issue of financial inclusion, covering it over the course of Chapters 7 and 8. Chapter 7 is primarily focused on busting some key myths about financial inclusion, and describing the many workarounds ordinary people invent to get unreliable financial systems to work for them. Chapter 8 explores the changes that have taken place in financial inclusion in recent years. We detail the trend towards tailoring financial services to specific marginalized or underserved groups, such as people on low incomes, women and migrants/refugees. We examine the features of these services to build a picture of how designers are targeting customers, what assumptions they are making, how the services may foster inclusion and what the limits are of technical solutions.

In Chapter 9 we go back to the future, discussing a question that we have often been asked when suggesting fieldwork in innovation. How can spending time with customers who may not even know about technology throw light on future innovations? We dive into the changes that have taken place in relation to customer knowledge, customer roles and the interplay between financial service providers and customers – including consumers, small and medium-sized enterprises (SMEs) and corporates. We then describe some examples of the introduction of innovations and new technology – both successes and failures.

In Chapter 10 we provide a practical guide to building a customer-centric organization. We argue that in order to be customer-centric, organizations need to put customer research front-and-centre. We define applied research, explain how it relates to existing user practices and give practical advice on how to start integrating systematic research in innovation. We discuss how valuable customer insights can be part of the company development of future scenarios or 'future preparedness'.

Finally, in the Conclusion, we return to the question of what it means to create a financial world fit for humans and point to ways forward.

References

Broløs, A and Taylor, E (2022) *Female Finance on the Move: Switzerland*, EWPN, Keen Innovation and Unblu. ewpn.eu/research-network/white-papers-reports/female-finance-on-the-move-switzerland (archived at https://perma.cc/V5NY-TFSY)

Graeber, D (2011) *Debt: The first 5,000 years*, Penguin, London

Hart, K (2022) *Money in a Human Economy*, Berghahn Books, London

Hart, K, Laville, J L and Cattani, A D (2010) *The Human Economy*, Polity Press, Cambridge

Holmes, D R (2013) *Economy of Words: Communicative imperatives in central banks*, University of Chicago Press, Chicago

Kahneman, D (2011) *Thinking, Fast and Slow*, Penguin, London

Kusimba, S, Chaggar, H, Gross, E and Kunyu, G (2013) Social networks of mobile money in Kenya, Institute for Money, Technology and Financial Inclusion, Working Paper 1

McFall, L (2014) *Devising Consumption: Cultural economies of insurance, credit and spending*, Routledge, Abingdon

Scott, B (2022) *Cloudmoney: Cash, cards, crypto, and the war for our wallets*, HarperCollins, London

Servon, L (2017) *The Unbanking of America: How the new middle class survives*, Houghton Mifflin Harcourt, New York

Sørensen, K B (2013) Designing for self-leadership, Nordic Design Research Conference 2013, Copenhagen–Malmö

Stoll, D (2012) *El Norte or Bust! How migration fever and microcredit produced a financial crash in a Latin American town*, Rowman & Littlefield Publishers, Washington DC

Truitt, AJ (2013) *Dreaming of Money in Ho Chi Minh City*, University of Washington Press, Seattle

Zelizer, VA (2005) *The Purchase of Intimacy*, Princeton University Press, Princeton

Digital and social transformation in finance

02

What's at stake for customer-driven innovation?

As we saw in the previous chapter, financial service providers (FSPs) play an important role in society. They support spending, savings and risk management for people and companies across time and space, ultimately contributing to building personal lives and society. Across the centuries, this has led to continuous adaptation to changes in needs, power structures and technology.

In this chapter we discuss the current digital transformation and the changes it is bringing to financial services. We relate it to the changes for both society and customers (consumers and businesses). Much is written about the changes that society is undergoing on the path towards a digital environment. Our aim is not to describe these in detail but to make a few general points about how this affects financial services. We first give a view of recent developments that have moved the financial industry from technological evolution to digital transformation. We then discuss how these digital developments affect customer expectations. Finally, given that digital change is ongoing, we take a short look into the future, including up-and-coming phenomena such as the metaverse and decentralized finance.

But since we have experienced changes in technology for a while, let us start with a short comment on why digital transformation is different. Introducing digital technology can begin simply by turning existing processes into digital flows, thus creating faster, more dependable and better-documented solutions. We call this 'digitization'.

Digitalization takes this one step further: it is about (re)creating a business to be prosperous in a digital environment. It means adapting customer services, organization, culture and infrastructure to a digital environment. Digital transformation is a broad agenda optimizing processes, meeting increasingly digital customer expectations, embracing real-time data and taking advantage of new technologies like artificial intelligence, machine learning, virtual reality, tokenization and more. It also means coping with increased competition and changing business models, including the building of partnership in open banking structures.

Most importantly, digital transformation is also a cultural change. This is so for all involved: company management, employees, suppliers, customers and even regulators. Some of the big banks and insurance companies have been used to working with proprietary technology, strong customer relations and a highly regulated space in which safety, continuity and a culture of 'no mistakes' have been important qualities. It is a challenge to manage, let alone prosper, in a fast-changing and agile environment with many new external partners and a need to 'fail fast'. It requires a shift in cultural mindset to encourage innovation, diversity and change – in itself no small development. It requires changes in skills to manage new technologies. And it also requires an understanding of changes in customer behaviour, customer expectations and customers' financial situations.

A NOTE ON SUSTAINABILITY

Digital transformation is not the only major change in progress. There is one major issue that we have not discussed in this book, and that is the effect of climate change and the need for much more sustainable behaviour – and therefore also for more sustainable finance. This is a big and very important subject and deserves a book of its own. There is much going on already including the development of sustainable practices in both products and internal processes of all FSPs. We expect that the development of new and innovative solutions will offer new types of assets, including electricity, water and more. We also expect that some groups of financial customers will be way ahead of others just as we just described above. For one relevant source of issues and examples see Thompson (2023).

Financial services: From implementing technology to digital transformation

FSPs were early adopters of digital technologies, using them to digitize backend processes of transactions, account updates and reporting. Most big banks and insurance companies developed their own systems in the 1960s and 1970s, as computers became affordable for companies. Investing in this technology meant that companies were able to better manage calculations and data. In the Nordics, the smaller players in banking established common data centres in the early 1960s, but standard core banking systems did not become widely available until early 2000. Credit cards became digital from the 1950s onwards, with services launched including:

- Diners (1950)
- VISA (1958)
- Mastercard (1966)

They grew rapidly into the international collaborations and standards that we still rely on today. For cross-border banking, SWIFT was formed in 1973 to develop standards for communication in payments and put their first telex-based solution in place in 1977. Through the 1980s and 1990s, customer services were increasingly provided digitally, initially via floppy disks and CDs, and later via online computer access or, indeed, over the mobile phone.

Over the last 25 years, we have seen an accelerated change in technology and globalization. Digital transformation changed the whole business environment of finance, from customer demands and regulation to infrastructure and value chains to business models and partnerships. The agenda throughout the period has been digital, mobile and global.

Around the millennium expectations of digital development were much higher than the real pace of change. The technology and the potential existed, but infrastructure, standards, regulation and behaviour were taking time to adjust. In the early days, focus was very much on learning about the new digital tools (like big data, artificial intelligence, cloud computing), and how to understand and implement them via the new channels of the internet and mobile devices. Now, twenty-plus years later, we see much more insightful and purposeful use of technology and marked changes in business models as part of the digital transformation. And we see change happening at a much faster pace, perhaps even faster than expectations. In the following paragraphs we go through a few of the major changes in the environment.

First of all, the world turned mobile. A mobile phone today has the capacity to manage most of our daily needs, and across the world most people have access to smartphones even if they do not own a computer. For consumers, most activities like browsing, seeking information, shopping and managing spending or insurance can be handled 'on the go' – and in real time. For business and in finance, this means that customer reach is best obtained through mobile solutions.

Second, the internet has changed access to information, giving FSP customers access not only to knowledge but also to ranking and rating information. This made it theoretically possible for customers to choose services globally. While relatively few still do, this possibility definitely serves the growing group of (younger) freelance development and communication professionals working and travelling across the globe.

The internet prompted a move toward finance as a service. Financial services are information goods that can be built and sold over the internet and they are highly scalable. With solutions developed in modules and available at low investment cost in a highly scalable environment, building financial services requires far less capital investment than before. As a very clever developer and strategist (and a personal friend of one of the authors of this book, Anette) said ten years ago, 'With the development of standards for data models, access and processes as well as the movement towards cloud computing, anyone can build a bank through social media.' Over time, however, it has become clear that while the services themselves are digital goods, the knowledge and systems required to understand and fulfil regulatory requirements are high and costly. It is also still quite national in nature. A great example from the 2010s is a Nordic insurance company that tried to set up in the UK, only to realize that the automatic update of customer identification that they were used to had to be built from scratch, as the UK did not have a national identity card.

Third, the possibility of collecting, managing and analysing very large amounts of data is changing financial processes in areas such as fraud detection and customer service. This is due to a combination of fast growth in computer power and storage, and electronic registration of data, including cloud computing. Higher capacity for data management allows for the collection of real-time data and the ability to combine highly structured data with more unstructured information including pictures, videos and social media – referred to as volume, variety, velocity and veracity. Or, in the often-cited words of Edwards Deming, 'In God we trust. All others must bring data.'

Fourth, the use of artificial intelligence (AI) and machine learning (ML) has been gradually evolving from small test services to broader integration in financial services. Artificial intelligence (AI) and machine learning (ML) are both terms coined in the 1950s and represent a toolbox of smarter ways of managing and understanding data based on the process of the human brain. Early AI models were trained on existing cases and data to mimic processes and decision-making. Machine learning is based on algorithms that are trained on data. The algorithms can detect patterns and learn how to make predictions and recommendations that can serve customers by answering routine questions. The algorithms also adapt in response to new data and experiences to improve over time.

Deep learning uses algorithms based on artificial neural networks. This allows the identification of patterns in large amounts of data of different types, including pictures. Learning can be supervised, meaning that it is based on existing data and decisions. The algorithm 'learns' to mimic these and make predictions. Learning can also be unsupervised, meaning that the algorithms learn without the help of humans and data labels, often through data clustering, etc. In this way, it is possible to identify use patterns in vast datasets, including customer data. This takes customer knowledge way further than the learning obtained through occasional or recurring surveys. We will come back to this in Chapter 3.

The most recent use of AI is known as generative AI, in which models generate content in response to a prompt. The best examples are the open source or proprietary solution of search machines or problem solvers trained on internet data, such as ChatGPT.

Most FSPs are already using artificial intelligence in a variety of ways, such as in fraud detection, regulatory compliance, algorithmic trading, call centres and chatbots that provide customer advice in specialized fields. And a large number of fintech start-ups provide services based on AI. An open finance study from Italy (Grassi et al, 2022) analyses how both traditional banks and fintechs now successfully combine transactional data (demographic data and product usage) with relational data (lifestyle, preferences and habits) and alternative data (from external sources like social media) to build customer-centric services. The study does not look into the customer impact of this work, but it does conclude that fintechs are not guaranteed to succeed in open finance.

In financial services we have already seen the widespread development of automated processes based on robotic process automation (RPA). These tools help organizations bring down the time spent on routine work. They increase productivity, often to the satisfaction of customers who prefer not to spend a long time on the phone waiting for answers. An often-used example is customer onboarding. Once a customer has decided to work with a financial company there are a number of regulatory requirements to fulfil. It is an advantage for all concerned that this can happen as quickly and easily as possible. Another area is fraud management; for example, detecting credit card fraud based on changes in spending patterns. Some of the earliest solutions to be introduced used algorithms for asset trading. Chatbots provide numerous investment solutions for general customer advice and are often used in call centres in different financial areas. They can also be used to serve employees or customers in insurance (examples include Amelia and Lemonade). Automated processes are also being increasingly used in credit assessment. In some countries, with China as a good example (Síthigh and Siems, 2019), such assessment is based on models for habits in spending and collateral; in others they are based on repayment scores. Introducing models that include different types of behavioural data, including social media behaviour, is expected to help companies reach groups of people who were previously excluded from credit.

The transformation to digital does however bring changes in the well-known patterns of risk, in principle at all levels (customers, FSPs and society). The increasing mobility in consumer finance raises a range of issues for consumers, both positive and negative. On the one hand, mobility can expand consumer choice, increase access to product information, assist with financial literacy and improve security. On the other hand, it can increase certain social and economic risks, such as fraud, user errors, learning difficulties, stress and financial mismanagement. Bank robberies change to credit card scams luring money from customers. Digital infrastructure is vulnerable to cyber crime – and even to something as simple as power cuts. And the problem of data protection (ranging from protection against unwanted marketing to abuse of personal data or identity theft) is as yet not solved. AI and ML algorithms still need to be tested for faults, biases and direct manipulation. We will not discuss these here beyond mentioning that they are very much part of the regulatory requirements with the purpose of protecting users. Risks are especially high when products and services are offered across jurisdictions – a scenario that is only set to grow as consumers become accustomed to buying products over the internet.

Changes in competition and business models

Digital transformation has created opportunities for new players in financial services by driving down the capital needed to offer financial services, by opening the possibility for third-party providers to access bank accounts for data or to initiate transactions, and by the introduction of open finance (for more on open innovation, see Chapter 3). In many industries, continuous development through new arrivals, closure and mergers is the rule. In finance this has been quite unusual for decades, where consolidation of smaller companies into bigger ones has been the most usual change. As late as 2012 the idea of new start-ups in *finance* was so striking that when staff of the US not-for-profit organization Startup Weekend were planning a start-up event in finance it had to be approved by the international main office. (One of the authors of this book, Anette, headed the innovation cluster in finance and IT in Denmark that planned the event.) Who are the new entrants to the market, and how are they partnering with each other or with incumbent institutions?

New entrants

The early fintech start-ups began by offering services in payments, money management, peer-to-peer (P2P) lending or crowdfunding. Later they moved into investment solutions as well as cyber security, customer onboarding and compliance. They were offering online services providing easier, cheaper and quicker access for customers, as well as a greater choice of services across locations. The entrance of fintechs to insurance started later due to its higher degree of product complexity (including a need to access data on policy risks and/or reinsurance), and a high degree of regulation of some insurance types, such as life insurance. It is expanding fast through fostering partnerships with incumbents.

Since many fintech start-ups did not aim to start a bank, they often focused on solving specific pain points for customers (like P2P payments), rather than providing the whole range of traditional services.

Their ideas came from their own experiences or from funding partners, but also, in some cases, from extensive customer surveys. The early fintechs were generally not regulated and some would see this as a market advantage, as it allowed them to offer lower prices to their customers. These developments have led to the expansion of the term 'fintech' to paytech, wealthtech, regtech, insure(e)tech, proptech and more.

WHAT IS FINTECH?

The term 'fintech' is interesting:

- It has often been associated with start-ups in finance.
- It has been subdivided into different streams of focus.
- Others have defined it as only the technology that serves financial providers.

Fintech is an umbrella term for innovative technology-enabled financial services and the business models that accompany those services. This is how we use it here.

When fintechs first appeared, industry observers predicted that they would disrupt financial services (primarily banks) by offering a range of cheaper and more convenient services – not least to young, digital customers. This prediction of the unbundling of financial services was often depicted in an infographic showing a bank or an insurance company in the middle and logos of a large number of fintechs around, showing their alternative offerings to different parts of incumbent services.

Fintechs are not the only new entrants to financial services markets, especially in areas such as payments, consumer credit and services for SMEs. Bigtech players like eBay, Google, Apple and Amazon, as well as their Chinese counterparties Baidu, Alibaba and Tencent, rely on their existing knowledge of customer shopping and search histories to offer payment services, and from there move into lending, investment and other related services. For these big players, it makes sense to offer payment services to provide an end-to-end service (loyalty) and to get more economic data on their customers/users – data that can be used for marketing purposes, among other things.

So far, the rise of fintech has, however, not been so straightforward as to completely disrupt existing institutions. This can partly be related to the fact that financial services are among the most highly regulated industries. The regulation of FSPs is of course quite different in countries across the world but at a very high level regulation is concerned with protecting consumers – depositors, investors and users of insurance products. And regulation is still predominantly concerned with types of institutions (payment providers, retail banks, investment banks, insurance companies, etc.).

Fintechs who serve new markets and provide new services often operate in spaces where regulatory guidance is limited. This can sometimes be seen as an advantage (fewer requirements, cheaper services) but can also become a barrier. Less customer protection requires customers to understand the services provided and any risk involved instead of just relying on what is well known. The regulation and the intricate payment practices around credit card payments provide a good example. Customers are used to being well-protected and able to get their money back if their shopping does not arrive as expected. This may not be the case with a new payment service. During Finthropology's work in Brazil we saw that for users of the recent central bank instant payment solution Pix. Pix does not automatically let customers have their money back if they make a wrong payment. But based on their credit card experience most users who experienced such problems were angry with their banks, accusing them of not taking responsibility.

Partnerships

The existing financial services markets have not been disrupted. But competition has changed significantly. Business models for the big incumbents have also changed. In the early days of fintech start-ups many commentators and organizations discussed potential business models, often identifying three ways of developing the traditional all-round banking model based on in-house innovation, product development and customer service. One way would be to include products and services from new players in the portfolio of existing customers and focus on the customer relationship. A second way would be to become a fast and innovative product or solution developer and leave the distribution to partners. The third way would be to develop into a financial platform principally connecting providers and customers. While these options are still valid, the first model has become the most common.

Many have found different ways of offering fintech offerings to their customers through partnerships. Partnerships help existing players (incumbents) become more innovative and reach out to customers in new ways. Fintechs gain access to customers helping them scale (Mention, 2019). Often it also helps them avoid the cumbersome process of becoming a regulated entity. Now in the early 2020s we see less disruption and more partnerships than anticipated. Statista surveyed US banks in 2021 and found an average of 2.5 fintech partnerships per bank (Statista, 2023). Copenhagen Fintech found 280 fintechs in 2020 – and 150 fintech partnerships. And several fintech start-ups have changed their business models to provide 'white label' services to banks, investors or insurance companies, helping them to offer better customer solutions. One example is Dreams, a Swedish fintech helping people save through describing, sharing and fulfilling their dreams (of a holiday, a dog, a home, etc.). Dreams is now partnering with Storebrand, a Nordic bank. Another example is Limitless.app, which is similarly providing white label investment services for millennials. In insurance such partnerships are also common.

Whereas the first partnerships were built from the bottom in each relationship, we now see the development of extensive open banking or open finance ecosystems based on standards for data sharing and reuse of code (application programming interfaces, APIs). We see this process globally either driven through regulatory requirements and in Europe or market-driven (such as in the USA). We will come back to this in Chapter 3.

Interestingly, despite the broad and varied scope of fintechs, and despite the potential of developing value chains that completely cut out incumbent players, such value chains are still not common. One might imagine services like customer onboarding, money management, payments and savings/investments. Or customer onboarding, payments and fraud detection is another possibility. Or a bundle of services targeted at SMEs. Regulation probably plays a major role here as a combination of services might be considered close to a banking solution requiring permits and higher capital.

Other types of partnerships are appearing. Fintechs and retailers, for example, are now providing customers with types of credit that compete with existing credit card solutions. These are the so-called buy now, pay later (BNPL) solutions. Their uptake is driven by changes in customer habits, including their growing desire for seamless solutions in finance (Broløs and Taylor, 2022). The consequence for financial services is a downward pressure on the prices of particular services, such as payments and credit, as well as the integration of financial services in the total shopping experience. This is known as 'embedded finance'. This new wave of consumer credit was originally introduced by Swedish company Klarna in 2005, but gained traction in 2015 when Afterpay launched in Australia to serve the new mobile shopping habits of millennials. With a typical BNPL service, a payment provider such as Klarna or Afterpay provides an app that connects with a number of merchants. Consumers shopping in store, online on the merchant website or in the BNPL provider app will be met with an offer to, for example, 'Pay in 4' using the app. The consumer generally pays the first instalment at the time of shopping and the further three instalments after two, four and six weeks. However, Worldpay (2023) estimates that while BNPL credit represented 5 per cent of global e-commerce spending in 2022, it is only likely to grow to 6 per cent by 2026 as regulation and increasing interest rates are curbing BNPL's development.

Platforms, meanwhile deserve a specific comment. Platforms are markets that connect users on one side with suppliers on the other side. They can be two-sided, connecting just a group of buyers with a group of sellers; for instance, people needing a place to stay with people who want to rent. They can also be multi-sided, connecting several service providers to the platform. Some of the very well known examples are in communication (Facebook), e-commerce (Amazon) or services (Uber and Airbnb). Platforms are neither buyers nor sellers, but facilitators. Their revenue models differ widely, from merchant fees to marketing. Their success depends on scale and network effects; as they become more valuable, the more users are involved. Successful platforms have, over time, added new service to their businesses, moving from two-sided platforms to multi-sided platforms. Scale and lower prices can help them reach previously unserved customer groups, but they also carry the risk of monopolies and lock-in, with users experiencing high switching costs if they change to another service.

There are numerous examples of financial platforms in finance – and particularly in payments, lending and investments. Many mobile payment solutions can be considered platforms connecting, for instance, providers (merchants) and users (card or mobile device holders), or, put simpler, payees and payers. The platform providers are diverse. Some are traditional banks that develop mobile payment solutions, like the Danish Mobile Pay. Some are telecom companies (Ericsson, Orange), some are big techs (Google, Apple), some are merchants (Amazon, Shopify) and some are fintech start-ups (Stripe, PayPal). BNPL solutions can often be characterized as platforms. Similarly, crowdfunding is often organized on platforms connecting borrowers and lenders. This caused many discussions in the early days, as customers did not realize that the platform was not responsible for loan repayments. Currently we see many examples of investment platforms offering non-intermediated solutions – sometimes facilitated by technology algorithms.

Changes in customer experience and expectations

As we discussed in Chapter 1, financial services are shaped by customers' expectations and decisions, just as customer choices in finance are shaped by the services available to them. So, how have customers and financial services changed in response to each other?

FSPs definitely show an increased focus on providing customer-centric solutions, whether this is advanced customized solutions or broader use of financial services by new groups, or via financial inclusion. Customer-centricity is often an important goal of digital transformation. Indeed, according to a recent Harvard Business School survey (Hill et al, 2022) it is the main goal. In Chapter 3 we will come back to how this is affecting innovation processes through new types of customer relationships as well as through new ways of collecting, combining and analysing data.

Globally, consumers have changed their financial practices in response to changes in the availability of mobile devices, availability of new financial services and shopping experiences more broadly. Mobile phones are particularly useful because they give people access to a range of services on the one platform, including domestic and international transfers, merchant payments, savings accounts, insurance and credit. Particularly in the Global South, basic financial services are increasingly offered through microfinance agencies and mobile phone based systems. These services replace or complement a wide array of informal services, speeding up transactions and reducing costs.

With access to mobile phones and new types of services, the number of unbanked people globally has fallen significantly. The latest data (from 2021) shows that worldwide, account ownership (with a bank, microfinance institution or mobile money provider) increased by 50 per cent in the 10 years spanning 2011 to 2021, to reach 76 per cent of the global adult population as compared with 51 per cent in 2011. Globally, about 1.4 billion adults were still unbanked in 2021. This number has declined from 2.5 billion in 2011 and 1.7 billion in 2017.

Although account ownership increased on average in both high-income and developing economies, the average rate of growth in developing economies was steeper. Overall, account ownership in developing economies grew by 30 percentage points, from 42 per cent in 2011 to 71 per cent in 2021 – a more than 70 per cent increase. The increase from 2017 to 2021 was 8 percentage points.

In the Global South, mobile money is especially driving growth in account ownership. From 2014 to 2021 the number of mobile account holders grew from 2 per cent to 10 per cent globally. These numbers were considerably higher in developing economies, particularly in Sub-Saharan Africa, where account ownership grew from

12 per cent to 33 per cent of adults. We describe such countries as 'leapfrogging' over traditional financial intermediation, heading directly to the use of other providers.

The World Bank finds evidence that the use of financial accounts supports the development towards broader use of financial tools including saving, borrowing and insurance (Demirgüç-Kunt et al, 2022). This helps people to increase their financial resilience and counteract issues of not being able to manage issues such as unemployment, medical bills or school fees.

Financial services are increasingly becoming available across borders, and in principle customers can pick and choose from financial solutions across the globe. In practice, however, the majority of people stick to local solutions – and indeed still very often to their traditional bank, or their usual cash payments. This is so in both the Global North and the Global South. A Danish study from 2023 showed that as many as 33 per cent of adult private customers consider changing their bank, but only 13 per cent of those actually do (Voxmeter, 2023). At the global level, a survey of 10,000 people found that 23 per cent were likely or somewhat likely to switch banks within the next year while the number for insurance companies was 27 per cent (Caliber, 2023). A US survey (Mobiquity, 2021) showed similar figures, with an average of 46 per cent indicating that they would change bank. There are a number of reasons for this. Firstly, habits and culture are important, as is a general resistance to change. We will discuss this much more in Chapter 4. Secondly, regulation and consumer protection are different across countries, and there may be trust issues with non-national providers. Thirdly, it takes time and effort just to become aware of international solutions and to continually follow their development. Few people have sufficient interest in finance to follow the market closely enough that they can make informed choices to use these new services.

In payments, where digital change has perhaps been underway for the longest time, we see marked differences in global transaction patterns. Whereas just a few years ago cash was the dominant means of payment at the global level – 27 per cent of point-of-sale (POS) in 2018 according to FIS (Worldpay from FIS, 2023) – it had fallen to 16 per cent in 2022 and was predicted to fall even further. While credit cards are still used for 12 per cent of e-commerce transactions and 26 per cent of POS transactions in 2022, the use of digital wallets is growing, reaching almost half of e-commerce transaction value and almost one-third of the value of POS payments. Also, with the development of open finance, account-to-account payments reached 9 per cent of e-commerce value globally in 2022, mostly using instant payments.

Generally, this development is faster and earlier among young people or younger groups. It is stronger among males than females and higher in urban areas than in rural areas. It also tends to be more pronounced among populations with higher incomes and levels of education (European Central Bank, 2022).

Younger people – millennials (born between 1980 and 1995) and Generation Z (born between 1996 and 2010) – are much more likely to change their financial service providers, and indeed to use several providers (Caliber, 2023). This is particularly true for young people who travel or work internationally. They often feel less well served by traditional FSPs, as traditional cross-border solutions are expensive and cumbersome to use. Similarly, these mobile young workers experience a great deal of difficulty in saving for retirement, as regulations and tax regimes differ across countries. Fintech providers like Revolut, N26 and Wise have made it their mission to provide money management in several currencies across the world, charging relatively low fees. Similarly, some providers specialize in solutions that allow workers to connect savings across borders (like the UK-based fintech Smart and the 2019 cross-European collaboration between Monese and Raisin). Young people are also among the most frequent users of BNPL services, as has been documented in many reports (see for instance Nets, 2023).

As society changes, so does trust, as aptly described by McAuley and Weiner (2015). People used to trust authorities, institutions and face-to-face dialogue. But millennials and later generations who have grown up as digital natives trust in technologies, networks and social causes. Young people may trust internet-based solutions more than anything offered face-to-face. Their networks are more likely to combine personal and social networks, and ratings on media used by these networks. And, finally, it is well documented that these younger generations value brands and brand visions (like sustainability) rather than the institutions themselves. This change affects older generations as well, as habits change and digital solutions become commonly used across age groups. Meeting the needs of this group of customers is important as they are the customers and require changes in communication, organization and company culture – changes that tend to develop slowly.

Most of our examples have come from consumer studies but the principle of understanding customer context is the same for business customers, whether they are corporates or SMEs. Corporate customers have long required digital integration between enterprise resource planning (ERP) systems, payroll solutions and bank accounts to ensure smooth transactions as well as reporting requirements (taxes and accounts). Similarly, they have required the ability to integrate bank accounts in different countries to optimize interest rates and keep down exchange fees. With the development of open banking, these big players can manage larger parts of their operations themselves. SMEs have been an underserved group till recently (Ouass and Reuttner, 2022). Many have the same requirements of integration and smart administration as bigger companies but can ill afford the time and price of dedicated employees and large system solutions. This is a space where fintechs are currently building new solutions (Prove, 2022).

This confirms that digital transformation is creating major changes for both the finance industry and its customers, and particularly that customers' access to new solutions has widened and developed substantially. It also becomes clear that customers' needs and contexts are changing and adding further to the demand for changes in financial services, both incumbent and new players. Growing requirements are likely to become the norms as we look to a future of further change.

Looking to the future: Change continues

While FSPs are still handling digital transformation, change is ongoing, with even more disruptive changes in financial intermediation as we look to the development of Web 3.0 bringing decentralized finance and the metaverse (an interoperable network of 3D virtual worlds).

Decentralized finance and Web 3.0

The internet, or Web 1.0, opened access to information. It was quickly followed by Web 2.0, our current formation, which allows interaction and also the creation of new business models such as platforms. Currently, the centre of attention is Web 3.0, which promises a more decentralized, online experience that allows individuals to take back control of their data and information, monetize the content they create and easily organize with others who share common interests and objectives (Ma, 2023).

Web 3.0 is built on blockchain, or distributed ledger technology (DLT), that supports the decentralized management of ownership, even in untrusted environments. This technology supports so-called smart contracts – computer programs that automatically execute pre-agreed activities. Web 3.0 opens the possibility of decentralized finance (DeFi), a broad term covering, for instance, stablecoins, exchanges, credit, derivatives, insurance and asset management. DeFi services typically operate without centralized intermediaries or institutions. At this point the development of financial companies and solutions is still nascent. Transactions are undertaken through the exchange of tokens – either native tokens like bitcoins or other crypto coins or non-native tokens that represent the value of different types of assets. Fungible tokens represent ownership of an existing asset fully or in part. The asset could, for example, be stablecoins (backed by cryptocurrencies or fiat currencies) or equity. Non-fungible tokens (NFTs) represent ownership of virtual assets like digital art, events and more (Ma, 2023).

A recent working paper from the Bank for International Settlements (Auer et al, 2023) recommends taking the DeFi development very seriously. DeFi definitely holds potential for cheaper, simpler and more accessible financial services. Currently, transactions, savings and loans all go through intermediaries like banks. This comes with a price in the form of interest and fees – but also with protection through government regulation and with trust in the sense of knowing who is the intermediary. Decentralized finance could allow everyone to manage their own payments, savings, investments and loans, interacting directly over the blockchain-based smart contracts systems. The advantage of course lies in the lack of payment to intermediaries. It also lies in the way services are provided through pooling of liquidity, meaning that in contrast to today anyone can gain access to rates and conditions that under existing solutions would only be offered to the larger and 'better' (more profitable) customers.

There are, however, still many uncertainties. For now, there are few standards and several solutions available. Some are based on participant proof of work (like Bitcoin mining) which is very energy-consuming. It is also clear that the overall system relies on several types of services building solutions, helping to set governance rules, verify market transactions, set interest rates and obtain market information – all remunerated through fees and/or governance rights. How cost will evolve and transparency will be secured is not clear yet. Moreover, there are critical questions of customer engagement to consider, given the difficulties people face in keeping up to date in financial developments. As people will not necessarily all want to transact directly, other exchanges or organizations are likely to appear. As the Bank for International Settlements article (Auer et al, 2023) also describes, there are risks associated with the DeFi solutions as they are known today. First of all, regulation for the protection of customers is not (yet) in place. Furthermore, there is currently a risk of manipulation, fraud and disagreements between players.

Virtual worlds: The metaverse

DeFi is well positioned to serve transactions in virtual worlds. Virtual worlds are familiar from the gaming environment, where players or their avatars are already spending large amounts of money or virtual currencies to pay for upgrades – as well as spending many hours in one or more virtual worlds. The metaverse is described as an interoperable network of real-time, 3D virtual worlds with an unlimited number of users. Users can be people with traditional identities, avatars or 'things' like your car.

In early 2023, McKinsey estimated that banking is among the use cases with the highest potential to create value in the metaverse in 2030, whereas insurance and investment hold low potential (Hatami et al, 2023). FSPs are working with their potential in the metaverse in different ways – in 2023 mostly at test level, such as by establishing a presence in virtual environments, developing their brand, or experimenting with payments and investments. It may make sense to look to one of the many overview articles for ideas of what that presence could look like. A 2022 paper from ISG (Wheatley et al, 2022) identifies the following obvious use cases: marketing and communication, loyalty and reward programmes, digital marketplaces or platforms in collaboration with other partners, digital solutions (payments, including micropayments for customer data, investments, lending, forex and wealth management), and digital twins (digital representations of services and relationships that allow both monitoring and exploring) and advisory services.

Central banks' digital transformation

Central banks are working on their version of digital transformation, including extensive ongoing research and experimentation with the introduction of central bank digital currencies (CBDCs) either in addition to existing money or to replace cash. CBDCs are digital currencies issued by central banks either as a wholesale solution similar to cash or as a retail solution issued directly to users.

Money plays a central role in macroeconomic policy, national sovereignty and international payments. There is currently substantial agreement that the discussion of CBDCs is likely to result in different models as countries have different priorities. They are also likely to undergo change over time. Here, we will only discuss some of the perspectives that could affect financial intermediation.

The introduction of a CBDC could simply mean the replacement of physical cash by digital money (or the introduction of digital money alongside cash). If a CBDC is introduced as a digital wholesale service, banks could continue to fulfil their role for consumers and companies as before. A retail CBDC with customer claims (accounts or tokens) directly at the central bank could help reach larger groups of consumers and result in financial inclusion (Narula et al, 2023). It could also diminish bank deposits, as consumers prefer to hold deposits at a state-backed central bank – particularly if CBDC holdings earn interest. Reducing bank deposits will also reduce their ability to offer loans and credit.

Another central issue for FSPs is how CBDCs can be exchanged across borders, despite the differences among them. The BIS Innovation Hub (Bank for International Settlements, 2022) has developed a model (the Icebreaker) where a payment across borders can be handled by any holder of CBDCs of the relevant types (a bank, a large company, etc.). A hub is created at the international level to identify the best rate available for any transaction, potentially driving down the high cost of international transfers.

This means that on top of digital transformation, FSPs (and particularly banks) could see major changes in their fundamental raison d'être. The existing financial intermediation is based on banks transforming short-term deposits into long-term loans and credits. If some of this is handled by central banks – and, indeed, in a decentralized model by customers themselves – this role will change. If central banks change regulation to let new players participate in international payments this will also affect existing models.

So, while still contemplating how best to survive and retain valuable customers who trust their FSPs, it is also necessary to start a long-term discussion of the roles and business models that might be possible in a decentralized environment. Here we might see central banks lead part of the account management issuing remunerated retail CBDCs and taking over part of the deposits. How would this affect banks' revenue model, which was previously based on the interest margins between deposits and loans? We might see quite different models of customer identity develop. Some customers might have several identities in different environments (real world, games and more) and there could be a choice for customers between different types of identity (national, self sovereign or private providers). Changes in identity will change risk management in both banking and insurance. A particular issue is how regulation (protecting depositors, investors and insured) will develop, and how fast it will be able to adapt.

DIGITAL IDENTITY

There is no doubt that mobile phones and internet connections have been major drivers in a more widespread use of both traditional and new financial services. A third element has been the increasingly widespread introduction of digital identity solutions. Where before it would generally be necessary to physically bring a certified document, such as a passport or a driver's licence, to prove your identity, this is replaced by a digital identity, whether issued by a government, a bank or an authorized party. Digital identity is a collection of verified information about an individual or an organization (or potentially a device). The digital identity enables individuals or companies to establish their authenticity when doing business online. Digital identity is by no means limited to technically developed countries in the Global North. Most countries globally have provided government-issued digital identities in different technologies and some countries like Brazil and India very successfully so. Providing a systematic overview of the technology and potential of digital identity is, however, beyond the scope of this book.

Towards an uncertain future

What kind of services could or should be offered in a decentralized money environment? Should they be offered by humans or by automated algorithms? And which competitors might offer to serve them? These are questions for both fintech start-ups and traditional FSPs to consider in the long term.

Today, it is still not clear how future solutions should work. We are used to security in credit card payments with regulation and common standards for refunds. But would this be necessary in a future with wallet-based micropayments? Banks adhere to standards for cross-border payments – but are increasingly being challenged on their fees as cross-border payments become increasingly common for consumers of very different backgrounds, including freelance workers and workers needing to make remittances. It is not yet clear how this will change; for instance, with the introduction of national central bank digital currencies.

In other industries like retail, automation, building and more, organizations have looked to future thinking to come to grips with questions like this. Less so in the financial industry. Future thinking and future studies are very different from traditional customer surveys or even AI-based data collection and analysis. Such longer-term studies are important to understand potential effects of broader trends and to be prepared for making decisions when change happens fast. Some call this 'future preparedness'. Only in recent years do we see FSPs engage in systematic work of this type. Think of discussing scenarios based on considerations of the change from human to digital combined with the change from central to decentral (thanks to Handelbanken for the idea at Finovate Europe 2023). FSPs need to start this wave of change by learning and exploring with customers – just like regulators who are already building sandboxes.

TAKEAWAYS

- Digital transformation is changing the whole concept of finance – but the outcome is not yet clear.
- Despite much talk about customer-centricity and inclusion potential, the focus so far has been on FSPs' adaption to the challenges through new technologies and business models.
- While FSPs are still adjusting to the consequences of digital and mobile solutions, a new wave of change is pointing towards a potential digital and decentralized environment.
- The next wave of change should be met through explorative and learning models with customers to meet their requirements.

References

Auer, R, Haslhofer, B, Kitzler, S, Saggese, P and Victor, F (2023) The technology of decentralized finance (DeFi), BIS Working Papers No 1066

Bank for International Settlements (2020) *Central Bank Digital Currencies: Foundational principles and core features*, Report No 1, Bank for International Settlements, Basel

Bank for International Settlements (2022) Project Icebreaker: Breaking new paths in cross-border retail CBDC payments, BIS Innovation Hub Nordic Centre. www.bis.org/publ/othp61.htm (archived at https://perma.cc/B53W-KE4Y)

Broløs, A and Taylor, E B (2022) *Buy Now, Pay Later: Understanding consumer behavior*, Filene Research Institute No 550. www.filene.org/reports/buy-now-pay-later-understanding-consumer-behavior (archived at https://perma.cc/Y8L2-NJ4S

Buchanan, B G (2019) *Artificial Intelligence in Finance*, The Alan Turing Institute, London

Caliber (2023) Global financial services reputation report 2023, Group Caliber. www.groupcaliber.com/global-financial-services-reputation-report-2023 (archived at https://perma.cc/KXG8-UAGX)

Croxson, K, Frost, J, Gambacorta, L and Valletti, T (2022) Platform-based business models and financial inclusion, BIS Working Papers No 986

Demirgüç-Kunt, A, Klapper, L, Singer, D and Ansar, S (2022) The Global Findex Database 2021: Financial inclusion, digital payments, and resilience in the age of Covid-19, World Bank. www.worldbank.org/en/publication/globalfindex (archived at https://perma.cc/7WSG-G7BG)

European Central Bank (2022) Study on the payment attitudes of consumers in the Euro area (SPACE), European Central Bank. www.ecb.europa.eu/stats/ecb_surveys/space/html/ecb.spacereport202212~783ffdf46e.en.html (archived at https://perma.cc/9SWE-KPAQ)

Grassi, L, Figini, N and Fedeli, L (2022) How does a data strategy enable customer value? The case of fintechs and traditional banks under the open finance framework, *Financial Innovation*, 8, 75

Hatami, H, Hazan, E, Khan, H and Rants, K (2023) A CEO's guide to the metaverse, *McKinsey Quarterly*, January

Hess, T, Matt, C, Benlian, A and Wiesböck, F (2016) Options for formulating a digital transformation strategy, *MIS Quarterly Executive*, 15 (2), 123–39

Hill, LA, Le Cam, A, Menon, S and Tedards, E (2022) Digital transformation: A new roadmap for success, Harvard Business School. hbswk.hbs.edu/item/leading-in-the-digital-era-a-new-roadmap-for-success (archived at https://perma.cc/PWK5-BDC7)

Koderisch, M (ed) (2018) Producers, distributors, aggregators: Strategic options for banks in the post-PSD2 age, Mobey Forum Open Banking Expert Group. mobeyforum.org/producers-distributors-aggregators-mobey-forum-charts-strategic-options-for-banks-in-the-post-psd2-age (archived at https://perma.cc/JE9X-DCPM)

Ma, A (2023) What exactly is Web3 and is it the future of the internet? World Economic Forum, 2 March. www.weforum.org/agenda/2023/03/what-is-web3-and-how-could-it-change-the-internet (archived at https://perma.cc/V8RR-X6DL)

Maixé-Altès, J C (2014) ICT the Nordic way and European retail banking, in C Gram, P Rasmussen and S D Østergaard (eds) *History of Nordic Computing 4: 4th IFIP WG 9.7 Conference, HiNC4 Copenhagen, Denmark, August 13–15, 2014*, Springer, New York, 249–62

McAuley, D and Weiner, S (2015) The millennial generation and the future of finance: A different kind of trust, Innotribe. www.swift.com/swift-resource/14231/download?language=en (archived at https://perma.cc/25CV-V8D6)

Mention, A L (2019) The future of fintech, *Research-Technology Management*, 62 (4), 59–63

Mobiquity (2021) Mobiquity survey reveals potential for digital tools to drive loyalty, especially among younger generations, Cision, 17 February. www.prweb.com/releases/mobiquity-survey-reveals-potential-for-digital-tools-to-drive-loyalty-especially-among-younger-generations-801721270.html (archived at https://perma.cc/SY2Q-9WFQ)

Murray, A, Kim, D and Combs, J (2022) The promise of a decentralized internet: What is Web 3.0 and how can firms prepare? *Business Horizons*, May

Nadkarni, S and Prügl, R (2021) Digital transformation: A review, synthesis and opportunities for future research, *Management Review Quarterly*, 71, 233–341

Narula, N, Swartz, L and Frizzo-Barker, J (2023) *Expanding Financial Inclusion or Deepening the Divide? Exploring design choices that could make a difference*, MIT Digital Currency Initiative/Maiden Lab, Cambridge, MA

Nets (2023) Why European banks can benefit by adding BNPL services to enhance customer experience and profitability, Nets. www.nets.eu/solutions/mobileservices/Pages/Why-European-banks-can-benefit-by-adding-BNPL-services-to-enhance-customer-experience-and-profitability.aspx (archived at https://perma.cc/9R4C-PQQ6)

OECD (2021) Artificial intelligence, machine learning and big data in finance: Opportunities, challenges, and implications for policy makers, OECD. www.oecd.org/finance/artificial-intelligence-machine-learning-big-data-in-finance.htm (archived at https://perma.cc/ECC8-NGZE)

Ouass, M and Reuttner, N (2022) A digital approach to SME banking, McKinsey, 25 October. www.mckinsey.com/industries/financial-services/our-insights/a-digital-approach-to-sme-banking (archived at https://perma.cc/G835-W3AK)

PFA (2018) Think Tank releases its recommendations for a prospective good life as a senior, PFA, 2 February. english.pfa.dk/news-archive/2018/02/02/08/03/think-thank-releases-its-recommendations (archived at https://perma.cc/XN8Y-MBQG)

Prove (2022) Top 15 SME-focused fintech startups, Prove, 21 January. www.prove.com/blog/top-15-sme-focused-fintech-startups (archived at https://perma.cc/E2SK-KEFP)

Ringland, J (2011) In safe hands? The future of financial services, Qatar Financial Centre. www.longfinance.net/documents/110/In_Safe_Hands.pdf (archived at https://perma.cc/92DJ-PPNG)

Schueffel, P (2016) Taming the beast: A scientific definition of fintech, *Journal of Innovation Management*, 4 (4), 32–54

Shapiro, C and Varian, H (1999) *Information Rules: A strategic guide to the network economy*, Harvard Business School Press, Boston

Síthigh, D M and Siems, M (2019) The Chinese social credit system: A model for other countries? *Modern Law Review*, 4 September. cadmus.eui.eu/bitstream/handle/1814/60424/LAW_2019_01.pdf (archived at https://perma.cc/86ZC-BM5M)

Statista (2023) Average number of fintech and bank partnerships in the United States from 2019 to 2021, Statista. www.statista.com/statistics/1315142/us-number-of-bank-fintech-partnerships (archived at https://perma.cc/5P9L-GDRF)

Taylor, E B (2017) Consumer finance in a mobile age: Methods for researching changing user behaviour, EPIC2017 Conference Proceedings, Perspectives, Montreal, 22–25 October

Thompson, S (2023) *Green and Sustainable Finance: Principles and practice in banking, investment and insurance*, Kogan Chartered Banker Series, Kogan Page, London

Voxmeter (2023) Flere privat- og erhvervskunder vil skifte bank, Voxmeter, 29 March. voxmeter.dk/bankbranchen-flere-privat-og-erhvervskunder-vil-skifte-bank (archived at https://perma.cc/7F7Y-746H)

Wharton Blockchain and Digital Asset Project in collaboration with the World Economic Forum (2021) DeFi beyond the hype: The emerging world of decentralized finance, Wharton. wifpr.wharton.upenn.edu/wp-content/uploads/2021/05/DeFi-Beyond-the-Hype.pdf (archived at https://perma.cc/V66V-N6PP)

Wheatley, O, von Geyr, J and Bakthavatchalam, S (2022) What does the metaverse mean for the banking and financial services industry? ISG. isg-one.com/articles/what-does-the-metaverse-mean-for-the-banking-and-financial-services-industry (archived at https://perma.cc/Z9AU-ZBLA)

World Economic Forum (2020) Forging new pathways: The next evolution of financial services, Future of Financial Services Series, World Economic Forum. www.weforum.org/publications/forging-new-pathways-the-next-evolution-of-innovation-in-financial-services (archived at https://perma.cc/2JDJ-JZPJ)

Worldpay from FIS (2023) Global payments report 2023, FIS Global. www.fisglobal.com/en/global-payments-report (archived at https://perma.cc/5ALB-4WHV)

Technology and data-driven innovation in finance 03

Where do people fit in?

As we have shown in Chapter 2, digital transformation puts financial development under pressure. Technology is changing fast, competition is strong, and customer expectations push innovation. Digital transformation is also changing the innovation potential and the innovation process. We start this chapter with an overview of different perspectives on innovation. We then look into the development of innovation practices in finance, focusing first on incumbents and later on fintechs. We finally compare these insights with what we know about customer preferences in finance. We will look deeper into this in Chapter 4.

Perspectives on innovation

Innovation has been categorized in many ways. The most usual is according to the degree of change. Incremental innovation refers to smaller innovations, often associated with daily routines, while radical innovation refers to the introduction of new or different products or processes. This distinction can also be made at the organizational level, referring to either change in parts of company processes (incremental), or 'business concept innovation' (radical), which is 'the capacity to reconceive existing business models in ways that create new value for customers, rude surprises for competitors and new wealth for investors' (Hamel, 2000). An innovation can occur in internal processes, organizational structure or business models as well as in products or services for customers.

Defining innovation as commercialized or realized success renders it a relative term. Innovation need not be new to the world or even to the market, as long as it represents a more attractive solution to customers. This could be a higher-quality solution, or faster and cheaper transactions. This means that technological change can lead to innovations for customers in different companies across an industry, which is often called 'diffusion of innovation' (Rogers, 2003).

No matter the type of innovation, there is no doubt that innovation is most often based on systematic explorations and development in organizations – or, as Pasteur is often cited, 'Fortune favours the prepared mind' (Mønsted, 2003).

The Austrian economist Joseph Schumpeter (1934) defined innovation as 'an effort of one or more individuals to create economic profit through a qualitative change', stressing market success as opposed to creativity or inventions. His focus was very much on the entrepreneur and creative destruction as the basis for new developments.

In the traditional sense of 'disruptive innovation' as defined by Clayton Christensen (Christensen et al, 2015), this represents new providers offering simple services to either non-consumers (unbanked) or underserved consumers (underbanked) and moving later to provide also for high-quality customers as served by traditional providers. This quality is exactly what causes incumbents to overlook new entrants until it is too late. There are several areas in finance where this may well prove to be the case; international remittances, mobile money and financial solutions for SMEs are good examples.

There has been some discussion about innovation in service industries as being distinct from product innovation (Engen et al, 2021). This is because services are often developed and delivered in close relation with customers (for instance, advisory services), which means that the customer plays an important part in the service production and that the service may differ from delivery to delivery.

When this happens in an analogue situation, the customer preference and possibilities to develop the service may be picked up by the individual adviser but never be shared across the organization. This is one area where the introduction of robotic process automation and digital advisory services can help collect and share knowledge. Such service innovations generally cannot be patented. This means that there is a high risk that some companies may copy others – or, to put it in a more positive light, we could say that it provides the possibility for a company to learn from others.

As discussed in Chapter 2, digital transformation has changed innovation processes. From the start of the new millennium we have seen the development of new ways of engaging customers in innovation: user-driven innovation. We come back to this in the next section.

Currently, data-driven innovation is an important driver of new customer-centric services in finance (Bigliardi et al, 2021; Das et al, 2023). New technologies allow more advanced data analytics, including pattern recognition and combination with data from the customer context. This takes customer knowledge way further than the learning obtained through occasional or recurring surveys.

Open innovation

The potential of open innovation or co-creation can be explored in different aspects of innovation. One aspect is the direct involvement of customers (whether consumers or companies) in innovation through different ways of collecting customer feedback, ideas and complaints – customer-driven innovation. This can begin before innovation, such as through basing ideas on customer input (positive or negative). It can occur during the innovation process as co-creation, or it can be part of the testing process of early versions, such as beta-testing (Rocheska et al, 2014).

Co-creation can occur either in open fora or with particular frameworks for engaging with lead users – that is, users with particular interest and skills in the service area. This could be customers able to detect bugs or malfunctions and suggest changes to fix them. There are also examples of such users functioning as super-users, helping others to overcome problems.

The introduction of digital tools including AI and ML is changing the focus of this type of process from customer driven innovation to data-driven innovation because it is easier, cheaper and probably also more complete to collect customer input digitally and put it to use in the innovation process. The process is still customer-centric but does not involve customer co-creation.

However, digital tools offer more ways of engaging customers in innovation. Some examples of collaboration with corporate customers in connection with open banking. In some sense this builds on older examples of connecting digital banking solutions with corporate ERP systems to save administration cost.

Another possibility is to take a next step from analysing digital user patterns to establish user communities or learning communities where customers can discuss and learn from each other. We have seen examples like this in Afterpay's Facebook group where users are primarily positive and focused on bringing more merchants to contract with Afterpay. In the USA, users of Klarna established a user group to help people get started with BNPL. It has since changed name to 'Beautiful Girls Thrifting' and become a discussion forum for BNPL users. The majority of users are women, and they discuss both Klarna and other BNPL solutions, sharing tips and tricks about how to use the different solutions. Frequent complaints are about lack of transparency in credit ratings and difficulties when returning products bought.

A different user group solution comes from our studies of financial solutions for females. A good example is the Facebook group Miss Moneypenny, which connects female investors with like-minded people to discuss and learn from. Taking part in such groups could be a great help in building more customer-based solutions.

Social media has a place in this type of collaboration because it is an obvious place to identify input and lead users, as well as to maintain open dialogues with users (Bhimani et al, 2019).

Another aspect of open innovation is Chesborough's (2003) well-known definition related to identifying ideas that can become a sort of company capital. Ideas generated within a company can be put to use there or sold off, just as new ideas can be bought from external sources and be integrated into the innovation process. In 2014,

Chesborough expanded the concept from management of product innovation to combining internal and external innovation to suit strategic business model innovation.

From a third perspective, von Hippel (2005, 2007) developed open source innovation and a framework for user-driven innovation based on innovation networks. He points out that such an approach could lead to a more democratic process of innovation that could thrive when users/contributors find the motivation (money, profit or recognition) to develop solutions and share their insights. We have particularly seen this type of innovation network in open science and open source development, exhibiting the following overarching characteristics:

- free access to the result (the software)
- broad participation – meaning broad access to idea generation
- meritocracy, meaning that participants build their credibility and influence through their contributions
- a central version management

Although you could argue that open source development might not be relevant for core bank systems (whether developed by FSPs in-house or by IT providers), two points are worth making as we pass into the age of Web 3.0. One is that DeFi based on contributions in decentralized autonomous organizations (DAOs) has some similarities to open source and can learn from experiences. The other is that open source development provides free access to use results. In a world of proprietary innovation solutions and competition from big tech, keeping this an option (like ChatGPT) is important in the ecosystem.

The last aspect of open innovation is related to open finance (open ecosystems). Basically, open finance means the introduction of 'connections' – which will hopefully at some point be standardized – between different financial institutions to allow customers to share data and conduct actions like payments through third-party providers. But these connections are generally provided in the form of APIs that are accessible only under certain conditions. This creates new potential to collaborate with customers and partners as users of such

APIs. Such collaboration could lead to innovation as ideas start flowing. Cases are becoming common in big banks like ABN Amro, sharing APIs with corporate customers and, to an increasing degree, also with SMEs. Another example is Züricher Kantonalbank, which participates in a broad open wealth network in Switzerland providing a first step data access to different users through APIs (Züricher Kantonalbank, 2021: 59).

Following this perspective, the introduction of digital solutions has led to more systematic use of digital crowdsourcing of ideas. The collaboration between incumbent FSPs and fintechs is rich with experiences of idea creation, sometimes with open idea sharing in digital networks. One specific example is the Living Lab of a Nordic insurance company sharing a platform for ideas, which is simply called 'the platform for ideas'.

The whole idea of open innovation and innovation networks can be nicely summed up like this:

> The innovation benefits of networking include: (1) risk sharing (2) obtaining access to new markets and technologies (3) speeding products to market (4) pooling complementary skills (5) safeguarding property rights when complete or contingent contracts are not possible and (6) acting as a key vehicle for obtaining access to external knowledge.
>
> (Pittaway et al, 2004: 145)

While the idea of open innovation may sound logical, research on open service innovation largely bypassed the financial sector. A literature review (Schueffel and Vadana, 2015) found only 17 articles related to financial services. The authors cite two major reasons for this. One is that small financial institutions find the integration of clients in the innovation process to be a complex and time-consuming undertaking. The second reason is that branches of international financial institutions prefer to use the knowledge and experience possessed by affiliates belonging to the same corporate group.

At the end of this short recap of financial innovation, it is relevant to stress that digital transformation is changing the way innovation develops. It is shifting the focus from customer-driven innovation to data-driven innovation based on new data sources, new data channels like social media, and new tools for data analysis. It is also creating new network opportunities through open finance and crowdsourcing ideas.

Financial innovation practices

We know surprisingly little about innovation in finance from academic studies. Fortunately, consultancies have reported continuously on developments, trends and cases.

Incumbents

When we look at the general development of financial services, the industry has adapted continually to new trade patterns, technologies, new ways of communicating and new services. Yet we have often heard that traditional FSPs are slow adapters and innovators (Alaassar et al, 2023; Glyptis, 2023), that they are reliant on legacy systems and therefore less agile, and that they support a culture that avoids mistakes and is therefore not conducive to innovation.

Why does this stereotype of FSPs exist? One reason could be that banks and insurance companies have innovated more in the backend of business than in business models and customer services, as customer service has for a long time been based on the trusted relationship between customers and advisers. These kinds of innovations would be less visible to observers.

These innovations might go unnoticed – particularly if they are incremental. Continuous, small technological innovations in back office processes may make a lot of difference to the organization's competitiveness and potential for partnerships – but will not, of course, change infrastructure from legacy systems to a modern cloud platform. The CEO of a Nordic pension service company once said that he felt that the company was very innovative and digital in back-end processes, but that their customer interaction still had some way to go before reaching digital transformation.

Another reason for appearing less innovative could be that FSPs actually need to understand and test technology to be sure that solutions adhere to regulation. This may sound counterintuitive, but when introducing new technology it may make more sense to introduce simple solutions to customers to fit their position on the learning curve rather than to go all the way to develop the optimal solutions and risk it arriving too late and with too little uptake.

Two examples can help illustrate this. One of the authors (Anette) took part in the banking implementation of mobile payments. To offer the best security, two solutions were developed in parallel. One was based on the download of security certificates and the other based on the SSL security that later became the market standard. The expectation was that risk-aware customers would go for security and choose the certificate solution. But almost no one did, preferring instead the solution that was easier and more convenient. The easier solutions could probably have been offered earlier, if customers had been involved in the development and, for instance, in reviewing mock-up solutions.

Another example relates to the Danish introduction of mobile P2P payments. Two competing solutions were developed by a major bank and a group of smaller players in parallel. The bank implemented Mobile Pay, which was based on card payments and was downloadable for account holders at all banks. The group of other banks opted for an account-to-account based solution that would only work for participants in this particular banking infrastructure solution. You could call Mobile Pay a simple solution (built on the card infrastructure that people were already using) that was easy to use and easy to introduce to consumers. The alternative account-to-account solution might have been faster and more direct (as well as future-proof) but represented a change in customer behaviour and a restriction to only some banks.

So, summing up from company descriptions, consultant reports and cases, we see incumbents innovate in at least three different ways. The first is through experimenting with new technology and the ways it can serve customers; the second is data-driven customer innovation; and the third is through collaboration and partnerships with fintech start-ups. And, of course, sometimes in different combinations between the three.

As described above, most FSPs continually follow the development of new technology with a view to streamlining internal processes (credit assessment and management, call centres) as well as providing new customer solutions (mobile payments and investment tools). Studies of this type of innovation have often been focused on customers' willingness to adopt new technologies, like mobile phones or other wearables. As young male customers have been one of the most tech savvy customer groups, this type of innovation has in some instances overlooked other customer groups – as we have seen in our studies of financial services for women (Broløs and Taylor, 2020, 2022; Taylor and Broløs, 2021).

THE TECHNOLOGY ACCEPTANCE MODEL

Technology adoption is often based on the Technology Acceptance Model (TAM) (Davis, 1989; Venkatesh and Davis, 2000) developed to predict use and acceptance of information systems and technology by individual users. TAM has been widely studied and many further developments made but the core of the model is the following. In TAM, two factors are key to the adoption of technology. These are perceived usefulness and perceived ease of use. Davis defines perceived usefulness as the prospective user's subjective probability that using a specific application system will enhance his or her job or life performance. Perceived ease of use can be defined as the degree to which the prospective user expects the target system to be free of effort. These two factors are influenced by external variables such as social factors (language, skills), cultural factors and political factors.

The study of human behaviour in innovation has led to a critique of the thinking behind these models with a focus on two central elements (Glover et al, 2019). The first is that technology or innovation tend to be represented as 'a black box'. The second is that the model represents a dichotomic view of either adoption or non-adoption. Based on the understanding of agency, networks, institutions and affordances, a framework appropriation of innovation can be developed. This allows a broader understanding of how new technology can be adopted by different users. The theory includes four aspects of interaction: propositions (how new technology of different types is encountered), encounters (how communities become aware of technologies), dispositions (how affordances and potential are considered) and responses (the way users engage with and start to use technology). This idea of appropriation in a community and context where technology may also be changed is interesting and close to similar findings of human bridges by Finthropology. It also relates to the idea of co-creation as described above.

Currently, the focus of FSPs is very much on understanding customer needs through collection and analysis of more and more granular data, resulting in data-driven innovation. The data power to analyse large and real-time data can reveal patterns in customer use of services over time and inspire innovations.

Collaborative innovation with fintech serves several purposes. First, the process of connecting with start-ups and listening to their ideas can help drive the first two processes through alternative views of services needed. Second, connecting fintech start-ups with people responsible for product innovation in the existing organizations can support a broader understanding of driving innovation. Third, and perhaps most frequently, collaboration is based on adding fintech products to the incumbent's portfolio. This is a quicker and more direct way of providing new offers to customers – and to test whether customers like them. For fintech start-ups, such collaboration provides customer access, scalability and compliance. The process is not without risk – neither for incumbents nor for start-ups. Most FSPs have experienced potential partnerships that went wrong somewhere along the way. Banks and fintechs most often have very different cultures, different decision structures, different development and implementation processes, and, in the end, very different timelines. Many studies have discussed potential and risk for incumbents under the heading of 'build, buy or partner'.

As mentioned above, there are also examples where FSPs have not been so active and where disruption might occur. One is the area of payments that allow immigrants and overseas workers to send money home. Providers of remittances across the world may not be cheap, but they are still more accessible and cheaper than traditional bank transfers.

Another potential area is business solutions for SMEs. A report from EY (Kærhøg and Jensen, 2019) cites the EU for evidence that 99 per cent of European businesses representing 100 million employees are SMEs. Yet SMEs have often been overlooked. Small, and in some instances unprofitable to serve – even though the SMEs will generally feel that they pay expensive fees – many of these businesses are managed by people who do their administrative work at night or on weekends 'as it is not core business'. These business owners or entrepreneurs may be passionate about their work, but may lack administrative capacity and feel that their bank really ought to manage such tasks. And, indeed, such tasks can cover a wide variety of areas, including payments and liquidity management, investments, tax reporting and a host of other reporting requirements.

Recently, however, a number of nimble fintechs have been building solutions for these companies and hold the potential to actually disrupt innovation. Fintech solutions include digital banking (payments, loans and investments), but also broader services like customer onboarding, cybersecurity, employee management, salaries and pension. Ernst & Young (2019) has shown that 25 per cent of SMEs globally have adopted fintech solutions for their businesses. In developed markets these mostly include online solutions for bookkeeping and payroll management, billing and payments. In emerging markets, the most-used fintech services are billing and invoice management, payment processors and mobile point of sale (mPOS). This illustrates how fintechs offer services in broader areas.

The last example is mobile money – here understood to cover payments via phone service that do not require a bank account. Such services are usually offered by mobile network operators (MNOs). Particularly in Eastern Africa, South of Sahara Telecommunications Solutions, combined with a host of local agents, have over the last decade or so offered mobile money services to previously unbanked Africans. The World Bank (Demirgüç-Kunt et al, 2022) reveals that 11 countries in Sub-Saharan Africa have more adults with only a mobile money account than adults with a financial institution account. Several economies in this area have even seen the growth in access to mobile money increase in parallel with stagnant (Ghana) or falling (Benin) use of financial accounts.

Fintechs

There is no doubt that the host of new FSPs have contributed to the innovation agenda in financial services through new ways of engaging with customers, new and agile infrastructures, and through new ideas for products and services to help customers overcome pain points and to reach customer groups that were previously unserved or underserved. But how do these companies work with innovation themselves? We have found very little evidence on this, and we expect that there are many differences across the wide variety of companies from new start-ups, to well-established challenger companies, to big tech players. The examples illustrate that fintech innovations are built on new and agile technologies offering simple and easy-to-use solutions to customers. Since many of the fintechs start small, their focus is generally on solving a specific customer pain point like expensive remittances, cumbersome onboarding, or a need for P2P payments.

SOME EXAMPLES OF FINTECH INNOVATION PRACTICES

One study by Alaassar et al (2023) focuses on three types of facilitators: regulators with sandboxes, existing FSPs with development challenges and incubators, and numerous fintech ecosystems like Level 39 in London offering start-ups office spaces as well as access to mentors and investors. These types of organizations help start-ups build knowledge, brand and customer access and traction, and raise capital. But there is little written about the fintech innovation process. From the companies that we have worked with and interviewed in previous projects, we do, however, have examples of innovators being in close contact with their customers.

Starling Bank

As Starling Bank, a well-known and successful bank started in 2019, tells us on their website:

> Starling was created to deliver a banking app designed around the real needs of customers. That's why, when a customer tells us about a feature they'd like to see in the app, we take that feedback on board and, often, build it and release it. It's something that we've always done. And something we'll always do.

Similarly, a recent blog by Starling Bank identifies a number of savings and budgeting solutions as the result of this process including 'spaces', virtual cards that allow you to set money aside for use on particular spending (like groceries or holiday), rounding off spending to send the remaining few pennies in the pound to a savings account, and automatic transfers to a special children's pocket money solution (Team Starling, 2023).

While much of this customer input could be derived from digital tools, a recent case study from PWC describes the development of Starling's services for SMEs through the use of interviews and focus groups (PWC, 2020).

Dreams

Dreams, a Swedish company, providing savings for private customers (now predominantly as a white label service for big financial institutions) builds on neuroscience to understand customer behaviour and build solutions that cater to their needs. Customers are encouraged to save for a dream, setting not only a purpose with a visualization (such as a picture of a boat), but also an amount, method and timeframe for the saving process. The process can also be undertaken in a group or in competition with other friends and family members.

Hiveonline

Hiveonline provides blockchain-based software for consumers and cooperatives in Sub-Saharan Africa. They do extensive research with customer groups and stakeholders to build technology that reflects existing analogue processes.

Together, these kinds of companies provide an interesting insight into an innovation process that is not only built on the implementation of technology based on digital insights, but also on introducing digital problem solving solutions by taking the time to understand customer needs. This throws an interesting light on our understanding of how to build customer-centric organizations – which, as we have shown, is an important vision within the digital transformation process.

Customer-centricity and customer needs

We have discussed how digital transformation puts pressure on competition and focus on customer-centricity. We have considered how digital transformation affects innovation with new possibilities of networks and digital interaction. We also know that the measure for innovation is market success; that is, customer acceptance and adoption of solutions. And we use the words 'acceptance' and 'adoption' on purpose instead of customer praise or excitement – because these are measurable.

In the following sections, we first illustrate changes in customer behaviour and preferences with observations from the areas of investment and insurance to add to the changes we have already described in the areas of payments and savings. We follow this up with findings that describe customer preferences at a more general level, focused on economic control, convenience and value.

Changes in investment behaviour

AI and big data in combination with mobile apps have made it possible for far more people to follow markets closely and consider the consequences of investment decisions in real time. Previously, this possibility was only available to professional dealers in big organizations. So, what are some of the customer behaviours that you need to understand to build the next generation of investment solutions?

We are already seeing very diverse market activities. Some people feel secure in understanding the markets and are sufficiently wealthy to set up as 'day traders', making a living out of continued transactions in different assets to make money out of margins. Yet, as we found in our Swiss study, many people don't feel comfortable making investment decisions in individual stocks and bonds and feel they would need to learn more about it first.

As described in our report *Female Finance: Digital, mobile, networked* (Broløs and Taylor, 2020), there are many networks and investment organizations setting up to help people (in our case, women) learn about investing (like Female Invest) – or just to meet fellow investors (like Miss Moneypenny). There are solutions taking a broader look at investments over time and focusing on sustainability, community and gender (like Ellevest). And there are solutions integrating investments and savings to help the young or low-income groups set money aside by offering continued small savings to be invested with the chance to earn a reasonable revenue (like Limitless).

A different way of learning is the increasingly widespread idea of copying investments made by other successful investors who allow their decisions to be shared. eToro is a good example of this business set-up. Along similar lines, we have seen widespread growth in financial influencers who offer their investment profiles with the promise of high gains. In some of these cases, the business model has been for the influencers to be paid by the number of members who follow them and set up accounts with (non-regulated) investment platforms.

It is not only learning and investing opportunities, but also the investment assets themselves. We have long been used to digital stocks and bonds. With the development of tokens (as described in Chapter 2), we increasingly see new investment opportunities such as dividing property or art into many small portions, making such investments a possibility for larger groups of people (Zunino, 2023). From our study of women in Switzerland, we know that people may consider virtual investments to be different from traditional investments (Broløs and Taylor, 2022). Some of the women we interviewed considered investing in virtual assets like cryptocurrencies even if they did not feel ready to invest in stocks or bonds. But they considered cryptocurrencies to be a little like a lottery ticket, investing only amounts they would feel comfortable losing.

We have long known that (wealthy) people will invest in physical goods like furniture, art, jewellery and more, whether as collections, for portfolio diversification, or indeed sometimes for tax purposes. With the development of virtual worlds in the metaverse, we will see new investment opportunities appearing, opening opportunities for investment, investment advice, insurance and more. Some examples are already appearing. For instance, gamers develop valuable profiles and gaming assets that can act as investment objects. Similar developments are likely to follow with regards to both virtual business assets (a metaverse property or business) and digital brands. An interesting question is how to handle personal or virtual identity as trading changes.

To this mix we can add the potential of DeFi. This is an area where more people may feel familiar with managing assets or investments themselves (gaming) than they might be with daytrading. What happens if people add their own chatbot solutions to the mix?

The point is that (as we discuss in Chapter 4) people's investment behaviour will rarely be rational, and they may consider different assets in different ways. The best way to build successful solutions is to observe behaviours in different environments among included and excluded customers, as well as in both virtual and real environments.

Changing behaviour and insurance

Non-life insurance is traditionally a way to protect personal or communal assets against probable but random incidents (such as fire, theft, breakage, floods), all based on ownership of the assets. But digital transformation and changes in assets and asset ownerships is changing in response to different developments. Technology, including data management, AI and ML, is creating the potential to include many new and often individual factors in the calculation of potential risk. And a movement from asset ownership to sharing or renting of assets (cars, houses and even clothes) is changing the field of insurance.

Micro-insurance refers to the unbundling of insurance coverage of limited assets, risks and time periods. A well-known example is buying car insurance for a rented car, for only the time of renting. The insurance policy may be held by the individual user or by the car fleet owner. In the latter case, micro-insurance is an embedded service in which insurance is part of a rental package. Along similar lines, we see a trend from general insurers of personal possessions to offers of specific insurance policies for (typically) individual electronic assets.

The capacity to collect, share and analyse large amounts of data is changing business models towards more precise offers. Hippo Insurance, for instance, offers home insurance and provides a reduced premium package based on the collection of data from water, smoke and intrusion sensors. Interestingly, in their model, customer data collected is not shared with the insurance company; rather, any sensor alerts go to the homeowner's phone. Along similar lines, computers can share driving data (speed, acceleration, braking, etc.) or personal health data (exercise, eating and sleeping habits, weight, etc.). The ethical perspective of this has not yet been addressed.

Digital transformation is opening windows of opportunities for insurance that we seldom talk about, such as protection against cyber fraud in all its forms. Another market opening relates to insurance of virtual assets such as gaming profiles, brands and so on. These could also include assets that are virtual but similar to real world assets like property. An interesting perspective comes from the development of risk analysis. In the real world we have ample statistics on risks in different forms and locations. In the virtual universe these might be very different. Added to this is the difficulty of identity persons who take different and several identities and with no register of personal ID.

These examples make it clear that the combination of changing customer behaviour and data technology is creating new services and new partnerships. The development of insurance based on extensive micro data is also changing the ways that risk can be calculated and priced, potentially leading to new inequalities or exclusion issues. So far, we have not touched upon life insurance, but parallels might develop for digital personas as well.

Customer preferences at a general level

For an FSP to build a vision or a future strategy in uncertain times, it is much more important to understand impact; that is, why financial solutions are adopted or not, and how solutions fit into people's (or companies') lives to assist with money management over time. From previous studies, we can start by drawing attention to a few important points (illustrated in Figure 3.1).

First of all, money management is social in several ways. Money management represents a relationship between user and provider, even if there is no physical contact. The creation of user groups around the BNPL solution Afterpay is a good example of this. Money management is also social in the sense that most decisions on money affect more people than just the account holder. Many women manage daily spending and budgets for their whole family but discuss larger decisions with their partner. And money management is social in the sense that it is context dependent – and differs from culture to culture. A good example could be this: Why did high-income countries not implement the mobile money solutions like M-Pesa that became a great success in East Africa? Well, in many high-income countries, the majority of people already had well-functioning payment solutions in place. But for M-Pesa users, the possibility of depositing and withdrawing cash with the mobile through a trusted agent was a game changer.

Second, money management is about trust. Trust in banks and insurance companies has long been a question of trusting your personal adviser or insurance agent. For quite some time it seemed like this could continue indefinitely, even though people in general felt that these institutions were too expensive and did not have their customers' interest at heart. This has, however, changed with digital transformation as branches are closed and employees don't stay in the same organization for long. Building a relationship with a bank through digital media, with changing personnel and even chatbots, is not good for building trusting relationships. What is left is often a trust in traditional players with regard to the basic securing of their money, which in part is related to regulation. We have seen that though people still trust banks with the safekeeping of savings, they often place more trust in friends and family for personal advice.

Figure 3.1 Three basic needs in financial choice

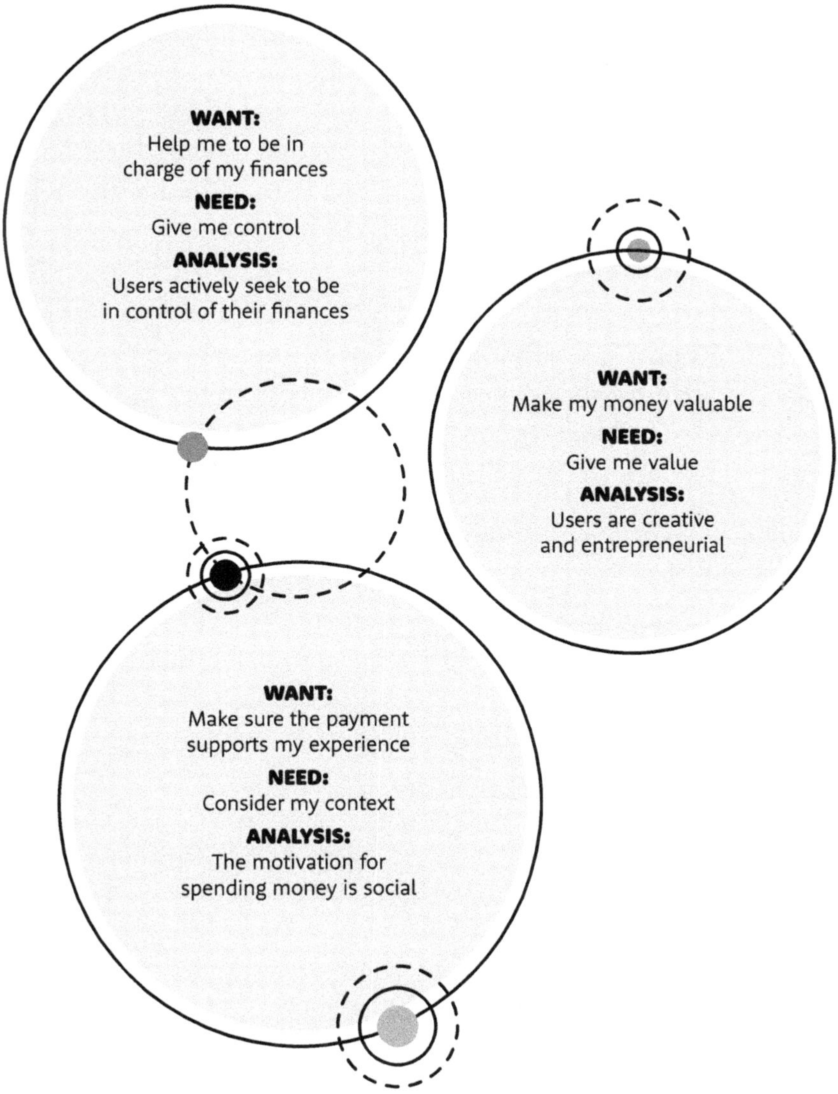

SOURCE Broløs, 2016

Of course, as we described in Chapter 2, as society changes so does trust. People used to trust authorities, institutions and face-to-face dialogue. But digital natives trust in technologies, networks and social visions. This may change financial relationships altogether. As trust is cultural, this change may take some time. In our study of Swiss women, we found that even well-educated women were reluctant to talk to their bank adviser. They felt that they should first do better with their budgets – and, as we mentioned earlier, that they should know much more about stocks and bonds before asking their advisers questions. Unfortunately, they did not seem to question this situation. This expectation is so ingrained that it is not actually visible, neither to the companies providing the services, nor to the women using them.

Third, though context matters, the few studies that we know of looking into people's actual use of money highlight three core elements that services should keep in mind. These appear across different settings in both high-income countries and the Global South, and we will come back to them throughout the rest of the book:

- Financial solutions should enable and support users to be in control of their finances, both daily and long term.
- Financial solutions should be convenient, integrating seamlessly into users' everyday lives and routines, to make their lives easier and more manageable.
- Financial solutions should provide value for users in the context, including potential partner discounts.

Furthermore, a gradual introduction of new technologies will help build user trust, as this will allow users to embrace the technology at their own speed. But to do that you need to know where your different customer groups are. A great example is the assumption that elderly people would not be able to manage mobile payments but would rather use cash. Yet some users of Mobile Pay are over 100 years old – and feel that this technological solution is much more appealing than running the risk of keeping cash at home, not to mention the difficulty in counting out cash with poor eyesight.

This clearly illustrates that customers' financial decisions are complex and dependent on context, communities and culture.

Innovation is changing

With broader digital access to information and tools, and changing business models, the process of innovation itself is changing. Financial intermediation is moving from direct FSP–customer relationships to platforms that connect multiple providers and customers. In the case of open finance, customers and partners innovate internal processes based on access to their financial data. In the near future, there will be more open spaces where customer exchanges can inspire new innovation – and contribute to it. This is something that we will come back to in later chapters. Customer behaviour and expectations are changing as possibilities widen. Yet some underlying key parameters of decision-making are still in place like convenience, economic control and value for money. We go deeper into this in Chapter 4.

TAKEAWAYS

- Innovation is the key to successful digital transformation.
- Digital transformation is changing the understanding of innovation and introducing new ways of working, including open innovation, co-creation and networked innovation.
- FSPs should work more closely with customers to understand how change is affecting their needs for financial services, what pain points they experience with existing solutions and how these can be overcome.
- Customers look for control, convenience and value.
- Access is still an issue among some customer groups in most countries – but predominantly in the Global South.
- FSPs should realize that though customers have the same types of preferences it is necessary to study many different customer groups.

References

Alaassar, A, Mention, A L and Aas, T H (2023) Facilitating innovation in FinTech: A review and research agenda, *Review of Managerial Science*, 17, 33–66

Beukenhout, M (2021) Digital transformation: Customer centricity starts with data assets, Ernest and Young, 11 August. www.ey.com/en_be/big-data-analytics/customer-centricity-starts-with-data-assets (archived at https://perma.cc/K6KZ-FRSE)

Bhimani, H, Mention, A L and Barlatier, J P (2019) Social media and innovation: A systematic literature review and future research directions, *Technological Forecasting and Social Change*, 144, July, 251–69

Bigliardi, B, Ferraro, G, Filippelli, S and Galati, F (2021) The past, present and future of open innovation, *European Journal of Innovation Management*, 24 (4), 1130–61

Broløs, A (2016) The future of money, in B Bátiz-Lazo and L Efthymiou (eds) *The Book of Payments: Historical and contemporary views on the cashless economy*, Palgrave, London, 367–78

Broløs, A and Taylor, E B (2020) *Female Finance: Digital, mobile, networked*, EWPN and Keen Innovation. ewpn.eu/female-finance-digital-mobile-networked (archived at https://perma.cc/7BZQ-BB9S)

Broløs, A and Taylor, E (2022) *Female Finance on the Move: Switzerland*, EWPN, Keen Innovation and Unblu. ewpn.eu/research-network/white-papers-reports/female-finance-on-the-move-switzerland (archived at https://perma.cc/JU3P-VAVZ)

Chesbrough, H W (2003) *Open Innovation: The new imperative for creating and profiting from technology*, Harvard Business School Press, Boston, MA

Chesbrough, H W (2006) *Open Innovation Models: How to thrive in the new innovation landscape*, Harvard Business School Press, Boston, MA

Christensen, C M, Raynor, M E and McDonald, R (2015) What is disruptive innovation? *HBR Magazine*, December. hbr.org/2015/12/what-is-disruptive-innovation (archived at https://perma.cc/V5KH-2UWG)

Das, A C, Phalin, G, Patidar, I L, Gomes, M, Sawhney, M and Thomas, R (2023) The next frontier of customer engagement: AI-enabled customer service, McKinsey. www.mckinsey.com/~/media/mckinsey/business%20functions/operations/our%20insights/the%20next%20frontier%20of%20customer%20engagement%20ai%20enabled%20customer%20service/the-next-frontier-of-customer-engagement-ai-enabled-customer-service.pdf (archived at https://perma.cc/LEY2-EKCP)

Davis, F D (1989) Perceived usefulness, perceived ease of use, and user acceptance of information technology, *MIS Quarterly*, 13 (3), 319–40

Demirgüç-Kunt, A, Klapper, L, Singer, D and Ansar, S (2022) The Global Findex Database 2021: Financial inclusion, digital payments, and resilience in the age of Covid-19, World Bank. www.worldbank.org/en/publication/globalfindex (archived at https://perma.cc/MYF9-UJP9)

Engen, M, Fuglsang, L, Tuominen, T, Sundbo, J, Møller, J K, Scupola, A and Sørensen, F (2021) Conceptualising employee involvement in service innovation: An integrative review, *Journal of Service Management*, 32 (5), 702–51

Ernst & Young (2019) Global Fintech Adoption Index 2019, Ernst & Young. assets.ey.com/content/dam/ey-sites/ey-com/en_gl/topics/banking-and-capital-markets/ey-global-fintech-adoption-index.pdf (archived at https://perma.cc/D82D-Y6YK)

Glover, D, Sumberg, J, Ton, G, Andersson, J and Badstue, L (2019) Rethinking technological change in smallholder agriculture, *Outlook on Agriculture*, 48 (3), September, 169–80

Glyptis, L (2023) *Bankers Like US: Dispatches from an industry in transition*, Taylor & Francis, Abingdon

Grassi, L, Figini, N and Fedeli, L (2022) How does a data strategy enable customer value? The case of fintechs and traditional banks under the open finance framework, *Financial Innovation*, 8, 75

Hamel, G (2000) *Leading the Revolution*, Harvard Business School Press, Boston, MA

Hill, L A, Le Cam, A, Menon, S and Tedards, E (2021) *Digital Transformation: A new roadmap for success*, Harvard Business School, Boston, MA

Hornuf, L, Milan, F K, Lohwasser, T S and Schwienbacher, A (2021) How do banks interact with fintech startups? *Small Business Economics*, 57, 1505–26

Kærhøg, H and Jensen, T K (2019) The untapped potential for fintech companies to serve small and medium-sized enterprises, EY and Copenhagen Fintech. www.ey.com/en_dk/financial-services/the-untapped-potential-for-fintech-companies (archived at https://perma.cc/M7C8-2HTD)

McAuley, D and Weiner, S (2015) The millennial generation and the future of finance: A different kind of trust, Innotribe. www.swift.com/swift-resource/14231/download?language=en (archived at https://perma.cc/5P4G-GMYV)

Mønsted, M (2003) *Strategic Networking in Small High Tech Firms*, Samfundslitteratur

Pittaway, L, Robertson, M, Munir, K, Denyer, D and Neely, A (2004) Networking and innovation: A systematic review of the evidence, *International Journal of Management Reviews*, 5–6 (3/4), 137–68

PwC (2020) Side by side with Starling Bank to reinvent banking, PwC. www.pwc.co.uk/issues/transformation/case-studies-and-insights/starling-bank.html (archived at https://perma.cc/2WXS-YW9M)

Rocheska, S, Kostoska, O, Angeleski, M, Mancheski, G (2014) User-driven innovation: Towards a new innovation paradigm, *Economic Review – Journal of Economics and Business*, XII (1), May, 31–41

Rogers, E M (2003) *Diffusion of Innovations*, 5th edn, Free Press, New York

Schueffel, P and Vadana, J (2015) Open innovation in the financial services sector: A global literature review, *Journal of Innovation Management*, 3 (1), 25–48

Schumpeter, J A (1996) *The Theory of Economic Development: An inquiry into profits, capital, credit, Interest, and the business cycle*, Transaction Publishers, New Brunswick

Servon, L (2017) *The Unbanking of America: How the new middle class survives*, Houghton Mifflin Harcourt, Boston, New York

Taylor, E B and Broløs, A (2021) *Female Finance in Figures*, EWPN, Keen Innovation and Bank Cler. ewpn.eu/research-network/white-papers-reports/female-finance-in-figures (archived at https://perma.cc/PPB4-H3NW)

Team Starling (2023) Bright ideas: App features inspired by Starling customers, Starling Bank, 11 January. www.starlingbank.com/blog/banking-app-features-inspired-by-starling-customers (archived at https://perma.cc/25GT-HV9U)

Tillisch, M and Pedersen, N O (2019) Winning the future through fintech partnerships: How incumbent financial institutions and fintechs can forge successful partnerships, PA Consulting. www.paconsulting.com/industries/financial-services/fintech-partnerships (archived at https://perma.cc/RX64-HGKN)

Venkatesh, V and Davis, F D (2000) A theoretical extension of the technology acceptance model: Four longitudinal field studies, *Management Science*, 46 (2), 186–204
Von Hippel, E (2005) *Democratizing Innovation*, MIT Press, Cambridge, MA
Von Hippel, E (2007) Horizontal innovation networks – by and for users, *Industrial and Corporate Change*, 16 (2), 293–315
Zunino, A (2023) The future of real estate: Tokenization and its impact on the industry, Forbes, 22 May. www.forbes.com/sites/forbestechcouncil/2023/05/22/the-future-of-real-estate-tokenization-and-its-impact-on-the-industry (archived at https://perma.cc/CS5U-RKHF)
Züricher Kantonalbank (2021) *Annual Report*, Züricher Kantonalbank

04 Using behavioural science for decision-making and product development in financial services

Given all the changes taking place in financial services, how do people make decisions? With so many different products and providers, how can customers possibly figure out which ones are right for them? How do they assess risk and build trust? And, most importantly, how do they incorporate all these new services to build financial management practices that make sense in the context of their everyday lives?

Understanding the present behaviour of customers is tricky – let alone trying to figure out what they might do in the future. People simply do not behave like the 'economic man' described using economics. We make rash decisions, do things that are against our interests, and change our minds often. We ignore information we don't like.

One of this book's authors (Erin) remembers having a conversation once with a professor of finance. He told her that he regularly receives letters reminding him how much money he has lost in the stock market. To avoid the pain of thinking of his losses, he puts these letters in a drawer as quickly as possible and tries to forget that they are there. If finance professors can't face their financial realities, what hope is there for the rest of us?

Over the past few decades, there have been significant advances in our understanding of human behaviour. While there are still many gaps in our knowledge, researchers in the behavioural sciences have made great strides in developing methods to understand consumer behaviour and build realistic models that can be used for innovation. Economists, psychologists, anthropologists, sociologists and other specialists have radically transformed the ways in which we understand people's needs and preferences, and how they make choices. Indeed, it is essential that we have a solid understanding not only of how people shape finance, but also how finance shapes people.

This chapter presents a short tour through approaches to financial behaviour in the behavioural sciences. We examine how they have challenged our assumptions about financial behaviour over the past half a century. We explain why it's difficult to build models of human behaviour that reflect real life, walk you through some great research that offers better ways of understanding people and touch on some of the implications for innovation in finance (we will come back to these in more depth in later chapters).

WHAT IS BEHAVIOURAL SCIENCE?

Behavioural science is the study of human behaviour. A behavioural scientist uses scientific methods to learn about why people do the things they do and how they react to different treatments. It is possible to use behavioural science to predict future behaviour.

Behavioural science includes several disciplines. Psychology, behavioural economics and neuroscience are usually the first disciplines that come to mind when people think of behavioural science.

These disciplines rely heavily (but not exclusively) on quantitative techniques, especially doing experiments in a lab or in the field. Indeed, while psychology researchers often do experiments, they also use qualitative methods such as interviews and case studies.

Sociologists also often take a mixed method approach, using both quantitative data (such as surveys) and qualitative data (such as interviews). Anthropologists depend more heavily on qualitative techniques, spending extensive time in the field conducting observations of real-life behaviour. They often also do interviews, run focus groups, and record life histories. Indeed, anthropology has the distinction of being both a social science and a behavioural science. It's social in the sense that, like sociology, it focuses on human society and social relationships. But it's also a behavioural science because anthropologists spend a great deal of time observing people's behaviour.

Behavioural finance theory takes psychological considerations as an essential feature of the security markets. It attempts to explain and increase understanding of how the emotions and mental mistakes of investors influence the decision-making process. It focuses on four key themes: 1) overconfidence, which is the tendency to overestimate one's own skills and failing to learn from errors; 2) financial cognitive dissonance, or the wish to reduce conflict between for instance beliefs and choice by rationalizing contradictory behaviours; 3) regret, which may cause investors to hold on to stock bought earlier despite its fall in the market; 4) prospect theory, which states that decisions tend to over-weight small probabilities and under-weight high probabilities.

What's wrong with economic man, anyway?

Before the 1970s, there were vast differences in how the behavioural sciences understood people's behaviour (financial or otherwise). While sociology and anthropology tended to focus on the social and cultural contexts of decision-making, economics saw people as individuals making rational decisions. According to microeconomic models, people dispassionately assess the options available to them and make decisions that maximize their 'utility'. In other words, they calculate how to get the most value for their money. These models assume that people do this not only at the moment of purchase (or investment), but they also calculate how much they will earn over their lifetime and devise ways to smooth consumption over the course of their lives.

A more realistic model of human behaviour is represented in modern game theory, or the study of strategic decision-making, developed by John von Neumann and Oskar Morgenstern in the 1930s. Game theory lent itself more readily to experimentation than theoretical microeconomics or macroeconomics because it was concerned with how people make choices under specific scenarios.

However, the turn to realism began in earnest not among economists but among psychologists who began to carry out experiments that questioned economic models of rationality. Two of the earliest (and still the most famous) psychologists working on this problem were Daniel Kahneman and Amos Tversky, who were interested in documenting how people make decisions under realistic conditions. Their groundbreaking papers on decision-making under conditions of uncertainty influenced young economists such as Richard Thaler, who became one of the founders of behavioural economics. Behavioural economics studies the differences between what people 'should' do and what they actually do (albeit usually in a lab experiment), including limited rationality, social preferences, nudging and lack of self-control. Kahneman went on to publish the well-known book *Thinking, Fast and Slow* (2011), while Thaler authored books such as *Nudge: Improving decisions about health, wealth, and happiness* (2008) and *Misbehaving: The making of behavioural economics* (2015).

Indeed, Thaler did much more than simply write about behaviour: he worked with companies and the UK government to incorporate nudging techniques into their practices. In *Misbehaving*, Thaler discusses a scheme he developed called Save More Tomorrow to help American employees save for retirement. At first glance, the name of the scheme is surprising: shouldn't people start saving today? The problem, Thaler explains, is that many people simply cannot imagine saving more now because their budgets are already stretched. But they can imagine that, if they get a pay rise in the future, they will be able to put more money aside. The scheme Thaler developed nudges employees to sign up to voluntary savings schemes and opt to increase their savings in the future. Thaler reports that the scheme was highly successful.

Nudging techniques such as these have gained widespread popularity in many fields, not just economics. Today, it is common for companies and governments to use such techniques in their service design, marketing and policies. For example, governments experiment with best ways to phrase letters and emails to get people to pay their taxes. Financial management apps use various means to encourage people to save more, including reminding them of why they are saving by encouraging them to use photographs that represent their goals. Pension schemes sometimes prompt people to think about their retirement by showing graphs of how an individual's savings level compares with that of their peers. These are just a few of many techniques applied in financial services.

Another important application of behavioural techniques is in field experiments carried out by economists, psychologists and other behavioural researchers. For example, a field experiment in Malawi conducted by Xavier Giné and Dean Yang tested whether the provision of insurance induces farmers to take out loans (Giné and Yang, 2009). The researchers selected a sample of 800 farmers and offered them credit to buy high-yielding seed. Half of the farmers were required to purchase insurance to receive this credit. They found that farmers were less likely to take up credit if they were offered insurance with their loan. These kinds of experiments are valuable because they involve people making real-life decisions.

There are limitations, however, to experiment-based approaches precisely because their strength lies in testing specific questions. Much of people's financial behaviour is complex. If you doubt this, think about the last time you had to decide how to spend a limited amount of money. Perhaps you had $100 left in your monthly budget and you were unsure how much of it to save, spend on going out for drinks and dinners, or put towards a household item. It is unlikely that you seriously weighed up the costs and benefits of each option. Most likely you were influenced by subjective considerations such as how guilty you felt about the state of your savings, your enthusiasm about spending time with your friends, and the pleasure you would feel about finally getting that dinner set you've wanted for some time (and the relief at being able to cross it off your list). Perhaps you actually made your final decision on the spur of the moment when a friend called you and pressured you to join them for dinner.

Behavioural economics understands these complexities well but struggles to model them. And human financial life gets much more complex than this. People do not usually think about one aspect of their finances in isolation: while you are considering how to spend your last $100 you may also be contemplating next month's budget, reflecting on past decisions, remembering bills you need to pay and making a mental note to save more in the future. People also often make decisions collectively, actively consulting with other household or family members, or at the very least keeping other people's preferences in mind. On top of this, financial behaviour is influenced by social and cultural values, habits and practices.

Another issue that models can be misleading. As Nicholas Nassim Taleb points out in his book *Fooled by Randomness* (2001), few people understand the limits of the statistical models that they create. When people place unwarranted faith in their models, they can end up making worse decisions than if they had used no model at all. According to Taleb, many models do not factor in unlikely events, preferring to generate averages and trends that exclude the real-world effects of anomalous or outlying events. When these 'black swans' do eventually occur, financial predictions fail and people lose money that they are not prepared to lose.

For example, many Dutch pensioners saw their expected retirement funds plummet as a result of the global financial crisis of 2008. This created a public outcry, since consumers had been led to believe that their funds were stable and reliable. Since then, Dutch pension legislation requires companies to be much more open with customers about investment risks. However, because the pension providers themselves seem not to have understood or accounted for this risk, the problem cannot be solved through disclosure to consumers alone. After all, it caught financial professionals and economists around the world by surprise.

When it comes to modelling, the road to crisis is paved by good intentions as well as bad ones. No matter how sound and complete your data, you cannot turn it into sound evidence unless you understand how reliability, risk, biases and other contingencies (even unknown ones) affect a model's accuracy.

However, several disciplines are getting very good at dealing with complexity. Computer science, mathematics and social science have all developed sophisticated ways of understanding networks, whether mathematically or qualitatively. Anthropology is another discipline that is brave (or foolish) enough to try to understand this level of complexity without reducing it to models. Since at least the 1880s, anthropologists have been travelling to fieldsites around the world to study people in context. Like researchers who do field experiments, anthropologists study people in their real-life contexts. But anthropologists often spend much longer in the field, staying months or even years while they build up a body of data. This research process is known as 'ethnography', which literally means 'writing about people', but in practice means collecting data through extensive observations, interviews and a range of other methods. While behavioural economists focus on what people actually do, anthropologists go a step further: they analyse the difference between what people think they should do or say they do, and what they *actually* do (this is sometimes referred to as 'ideal norms' and 'actual norms'). Rather than trying to simplify behaviour into testable models, they embrace this complexity, developing what Clifford Geertz (1973) called 'thick descriptions' of behaviour.

In his book *Anthropology, Economics, and Choice* (2011), Michael Chibnik explains how anthropology differs from economics in understanding people's economic behaviour. As well as arguing that economic methods are insufficient for understanding complexity, he notes that economics tends to assume that humans everywhere have similar motivations, and that their choices are reducible to a limited number of factors. Chibnik argues that they are wrong: humans are diverse and should be treated as such. We agree with Chibnik, and push his point further in arguing that if we do not take complexity and diversity into account then we cannot hope to design appropriate products, policies and programmes for real humans.

Organizations that need to understand people's real-life contexts work with anthropologists to help develop successful programmes. Over the past few decades, the business world has embraced anthropologists: they work in all kinds of companies, from Intel to Nissan to ING to Varo Money. Anthropologists also work in governments, where they shape programmes and policies. We will talk more about applications of anthropology in the next chapter. For now, we will turn our attention to two critical questions for this book: What do people want? And how do they make choices in real life?

What do people want?

In order to understand how people make decisions and how they use financial tools it's important to first understand what they want. This is not necessarily as straightforward as it may seem. Microeconomic theory assumes that people know what they want and that their preferences are consistent. But Thaler and others have shown clearly that this is not the case. People change their minds often, sometimes in response to new information, but often also on gut instinct. This is true not only for the things people want to buy, but also for the risks they are willing to take (their risk preferences). We will discuss risk preferences later in this chapter.

Preferences are not the same as choices. People can prefer one thing but choose another. Erin might prefer to eat Greek food for lunch, but Anette really wants Thai, and Erin gives in to Anette's preference to make her happy. Or you, the reader, might prefer to leave all your money in a savings account so you can spend it on a nice holiday, but you (reluctantly) decide to put it in a fixed term account so you can't spend it. Economists assume our actions match our preferences, but they clearly do not. People make decisions all the time that go against their preferences.

There is one more 'elephant in the room' to discuss when it comes to preferences. Economists tend to discuss preferences as though they are innate. They don't come from anywhere in particular; they just exist. But, clearly, while we were born with our own sense of taste (some people have a lifelong hate of coriander, for example), we were not born desiring consumer goods and services. We did not begin life preferring Google Wallet over Apple Pay. Where, then, do preferences come from?

Most work on the origin of preferences comes from non-economic disciplines, such as philosophy, sociology and anthropology (for an exception, see Dietrich and List, 2013). Perhaps one of the most famous attempts to understand how preferences are formed comes from the sociologist Pierre Bourdieu. His book *Distinction: A social critique of the judgement of taste* (1984) argues that to a large extent we inherit our preferences from others. People with large amounts of cultural capital (education, intellect, style of speech, style of dress) decide what is tasteful and what is not. Those of us with less cultural capital (the majority of us) largely accept their decisions, and this forms our preferences. This does not mean that all people aspire to conform to dominant notions of good taste. However, those of us who aspire to join a higher social class, or get a better job, will probably find that we need to conform to these notions of taste in order to be accepted in the higher echelons of society. To put it simply, while our 'natural' taste may not be for high-end watches and handbags, or minimalist outfits, we find our preferences trending towards an elite aesthetic. We may secretly admire gaudy outfits, or wish we could dress in tracksuits every day, but our shopping lists will probably not contain these items.

Marketers understand very well that people's aspirations shape their preferences. If you have ever leafed through a duty-free catalogue on an aeroplane you will have noticed that the products for sale are noticeably aspirational: jewellery, watches, perfume, high-end luggage and upscale tourism are all featured prominently. These advertisements try to catch us at a moment where we may feel that improving our life status is possible (note that this is also an attempt to belong to a different social group).

Financial services also play on our aspirations: just think of platinum or black credit cards, which allow us to flash our status when we pay for drinks for our colleagues or our date. A person may use the latest payment technology partially because it is a way of showing their peers that they are up to date and competent enough to be included in the contemporary globalized world.

We should not see aspiration as just a human folly. When people aspire to belong to a more powerful social group they are not just being shallow. For much of the world's population, successfully 'passing' as belonging to a higher group can mean the difference between staying poor or gaining stable employment.

However, it is critically important to acknowledge that we do not always fall victim to aspirations: realism also shapes preferences. If Erin prefers tea, and Anette prefers expensive champagne, why might that be the case? It is possible that Erin has not developed a taste for champagne because she does not feel she can afford it. While aspirations undoubtedly shape preferences, in the main, people are quite realistic about what they can afford. This has clear implications for how people budget, save and invest. People who are driven by aspirations may get into more debt due to unnecessary consumption than people who are realistic. And while there are many people in such a position, there are many more who are not. People – especially those with low incomes – are generally financially practical, as we have shown in our research on money and payments in Brazil (Taylor and Broløs, 2022).

Beyond aspirations, cultural context is immensely important. Humans are the most prosocial animal on the planet, meaning that we rely heavily on the other members of our species and form strong social bonds. We put a lot of effort into fitting into groups, and we use material things to demonstrate our group belonging. Our group affiliations therefore shape our preferences.

An intriguing example of this comes from a study by the anthropologist Daniel Miller. In 1994, Miller published a book called *Modernity: An ethnographic approach*, based on his ethnographic research in Trinidad. Miller explains how he observed culture shaping purchasing decisions in Trinidad. He was surprised to find that, at the time, Trinidad boasted two kinds of shops to decorate cars: one shop sold things to decorate the inside of cars, and the other sold things to decorate the outside of cars. He was intrigued that people often preferred to decorate either the inside of their car or the outside, but not both. Miller notes that Trinidadian stereotypes viewed Indo-Trinidadians as preferring the 'flash' look of car upholstery, while Afro-Trinidadians were thought to prefer the 'cool' look of window tinting and stripes.

Financial preferences can also have cultural roots. For example, whether we pay our tax happily and on time, or try to avoid paying it at all, can be determined not only by our personal characteristics, but also by differences in tax culture. These have been described in many different branches of research, including psychology, economics and sociology. In the early days, this work focused less on the behaviours of people, and more on why tax systems varied from place to place. In the late 1950s there was a shift towards trying to understand 'tax mentality', which the economist Nerré (2008) describes as the unique relationship between the tax authorities and the taxpayers. People's preferences for paying their tax (or not) may well align with dominant ideas about how much paying tax matters. In a society with high levels of corruption people may have low preferences for paying tax if they think the government will not spend it wisely. In a society with high levels of tax payment, it is likely that there is a collective belief that paying tax is the right thing to do as an individual and is good for society. Far from being innate, our preferences are very much shaped by the sociocultural context in which we live.

COMMON ISSUES IN CUSTOMER-CENTRIC FINANCE RESEARCH

- Consumer finance markets are changing fast globally, and our methods need to be adaptable to shifting consumer practices.
- Due to the global connectivity of financial systems, collaboration between different kinds of organizations (universities, industry, NGOs) is becoming increasingly helpful to understand and reach consumers in different places.
- Financial practices often include both qualitative and quantitative elements, making it important for researchers to have a good basic knowledge of methods outside their own area of expertise.

- Getting good data while protecting research participants' privacy is a major challenge where issues of money and technology are concerned.
- There are competing theories about how people make financial decisions, and being familiar with a range of different methods can help us understand why researchers' explanations differ.

How do people make decisions? Some key factors

This short introduction to behavioural science illustrates that there is still much to understand about how people make decisions, taking into account the complex roots of preferences and the many sociocultural factors that shape choices. It also illustrates the importance of studying the customer's context when developing new financial tools in a fast-changing environment, and why relying on data patterns drawn from existing behaviour can be deceptive. In the remainder of this chapter we introduce the major factors we need to consider to move forward. We will come back to these in later chapters. For simplicity we collate these into six groups: value, convenience, control, trust, risk and emotions. In the remainder of this section we outline these factors. We cover sociocultural context and complexity in the following chapter. In the next section we will attempt to complicate the picture by providing examples of how different groups of people make decisions taking into account multiple variables and in complex sociocultural environments.

Value

Value is one of the first things we consider when making a decision to buy something or not. 'Do I want it?' is often followed quickly by the question, 'Is it worth it?' When weighing up value, we tend to consider both price and what economists call opportunity cost –

what else we could do with the money. In terms of price, we might really want to buy a milkshake but feel that $10 is far too expensive (even if we can afford it, as was the case for John Travolta's character in the film *Pulp Fiction*). Alternatively, we might decide that $10 is reasonable, but we might prefer to spend that $10 on an item of clothing instead.

We value our financial services in the same way that we value anything else. For example, we interviewed 14 women in Switzerland about how they learn to manage their finances, how they gain confidence, issues of financial control, who they trust or don't, their pain points with respect to financial tools, and more (Broløs and Taylor, 2022), our interviewees reported being motivated by price and value for money. They were aware that credit card fees are higher than the cost of debit cards. The women also considered points schemes to be valuable. Some consistently used their credit card for shopping to earn points – for instance, using the Cumulus Card, which is available as a credit card. Our interviewees were also careful to take advantage of loyalty cards and offers that span from getting their 'eleventh coffee for free' to collecting points in supermarket shopping, to travel points, and so on. We found similar practices in our study of people on low incomes in Brazil (Taylor and Broløs, 2022). People were highly aware of the price of transactions and would use several bank accounts to lower their overall costs (we will discuss this further in Chapter 7).

Convenience

Convenience (or 'transaction costs') is a strong driver of decision-making processes and will deter people from choosing an option that is otherwise the best. In the course of developing his Save More Tomorrow scheme, Thaler discovered that many employees were failing to sign up for the savings programme even if they wanted to because the forms they had to fill out were too long. In this epoch of digital financial services many of these problems are reduced, as online forms and authentication processes are becoming easier to achieve.

For women in our Switzerland study, 'convenience' also meant that the ability to carry a card in their phone case, or to pay with their phone, meant that they could go out without a handbag. Several of the women also told us that they started using a digital wallet because they had forgotten their card or it wasn't accepted in a particular store. But these digital processes are often buggy, and many people still need access to brick-and-mortar services such as banks and ATMs. One female entrepreneur in Switzerland switched banks to one that had a branch within a few hundred metres of her home because her clients still paid her in cash and she needed to deposit the money easily.

Convenience is especially an issue in countries where infrastructure is underdeveloped. For example, in countries such as Haiti mobile money services were developed with the idea that they would be far more convenient than banks, which were few in number and located in urban centres. However, although mobile money allowed people to transfer money and make payments using their phone, they still needed to deposit and withdraw money at an agent. The development of agent networks was plagued by a 'chicken and egg' problem that customers wouldn't sign up for mobile money unless there was an agent near their home or work, but businesses were reluctant to become agents unless there were already plenty of customers. Creating convenience in areas of low infrastructure can be challenging.

Control

Unsurprisingly, people prefer to have control over the choices they make, and they also make choices that give them greater control. In order to have control over choices, people need to feel they are voluntarily choosing financial services rather than having a choice made for them. This is one reason why Australia passed a law in 2005 permitting employees to choose their own pension scheme. However, in order to feel they have control, people first need to feel confident that they can make the best decision. This issue arose in our study of women's payments choices in Switzerland. Several women felt that they did not have enough knowledge to make investment decisions – even if they had plenty of experience already. Besides investments, they all actively managed their finances in ways that made them feel they knew their financial position and were confident about their budget. They found banking apps especially helpful because they show transactions instantly and so provide transparency.

Control is especially important for people with low incomes. In her book *The Unbanking of America*, Lisa Servon describes why ordinary Americans are turning away from banks in favour of payday lenders. She explains that many banks have rules that result in unmanageable uncertainty for people on low incomes who live from paycheque to paycheque. For example, a person may write a cheque thinking they have enough money in the bank to cover it, only to find they had insufficient funds and have been charged a hefty overdraft fee. Then, if another cheque they have written is cashed, they receive yet another overdraft fee, and end up in a cycle that is difficult to escape. Payday lenders, while expensive to use, are more predictable.

Indeed, everywhere people on low incomes exist we find problems managing financial services and payments. They are less likely to sign up for direct debit services or automatic top-up for travel cards as this may mean the difference between having enough money to eat and get to work until the next payday or having to take a loan from a friend or payday service (or simply stay at home and not eat). People who are poor make what the sociologist Pierre Bourdieu (1984) called the 'choice of the necessary'.

For people on low incomes, control is about making ends meet, caring for one's family and reducing the stress of poverty. For wealthier people, control is often about having the ability to make real decisions and build a nest-egg.

Trust

In order to feel secure depositing, transferring and spending our money we need to trust the financial intermediaries who are managing our transactions. In countries with long histories of a stable banking sector, trusting banks is usually a given.

Governments guarantee our deposits up to a certain value and we rarely worry about whether a financial crisis will undermine our savings, or whether there will be a run on the bank meaning that we cannot access our funds. But in countries with less stable financial histories or experiences with banking, trust in the formal financial sector may be a major issue. People who have lived through periods of hyperinflation, for example, may be more wary about keeping all their money in one place.

People also exhibit different levels of trust in digital financial services. Sometimes a lack of trust exists because people have encountered problems transferring money. This was the case in our study of payments in Brazil, where we interviewed several people who had encountered problems when using Pix, the interoperable payments platform developed by the central bank. Customers access the service through their usual bank account and can transfer money for free to anyone in Brazil. Some people accidentally transferred money to the wrong person, and others encountered bugs that meant their transactions failed. The newness of the system did not help, but neither did the fact that Pix did not include a system for dispute resolution.

Given how important trust is, we know surprisingly little about how it functions. We need a far more granular understanding of trust. Many surveys measure things like how much people trust the government versus banks or other institutions. These can be helpful. When Erin was doing research in Haiti she and her colleagues found that people held an incredibly high degree of trust in the telecommunications company Digicel, while they had low levels of trust in the government or banks. This augured well for their acceptance of Digicel's new mobile money service – but there was still no guarantee that they would use the service. It is also unclear what it means to trust the government. In some countries, such as Cambodia, people may trust some government ministries but not others, or they may trust certain public servants. This has obvious implications for the development of central bank digital currency (CBDC). If people don't trust the government, does this mean that they also distrust central banks? Not necessarily. Trust matters immensely to people's choices, but we still have only the vaguest picture of how trust guides decisions.

Risk

Risk is possibly one of the most-researched topics in decision-making, particularly by psychologists and behavioural economists. A great deal of research has been carried out on people's risk preferences (what risks people are willing to take and under what circumstances), whether these risks are stable and whether some people take risks more than others. In relation to financial services, the lion's share of the work has been done in relation to investment decisions and insurance. This body of literature is immense, and we don't have the space to do it justice here. Instead we will focus on a few examples of risk to show just how broad the topic is.

An important topic in risk is the question of who is willing to take risk on, and under what circumstances. Rational choice theory assumes that when making financial decisions, say, to invest money or buy insurance, we weigh up the risks and possible payoffs involved before making a rational decision. However, thanks to Kahneman and Tversky, we have known for some decades now that people simply do not have a good enough understanding of statistics to undertake these calculations. Kahneman (2011) points out that even statisticians' intuitive understanding of statistics is poor. Instead, we use heuristics (rules of thumb) to guesstimate risk, based on factors like past experiences, trust, the opinions of others, the appeal of marketing and gut decisions. What's worse, we often pay far more attention to things that are visible in our everyday lives, but are low risk, than we do to things that are unlikely to happen but could be disastrous (Taleb, 2001, 2007).

People's inability to calculate risk may seem alarming, but there is one saving grace: we tend to be loss averse. Loss aversion is problematic because it can prevent us from taking risks that are actually a reasonably good bet (especially over the longer term). But it does also stop us from making too many bad decisions that may wipe us out.

An interesting question is whether some people are more loss averse than others. From our research it seems likely that people with low incomes who are struggling to meet their basic needs take fewer financial risks than people with more money. People with families tend also to take fewer financial risks: they are less likely to engage in risky entrepreneurial activities or investments if they lack another source of income. There is a widespread belief that women are more risk averse than men. This may be partly true, especially considering that women are often the main family caregivers. However, it has been challenged in recent times. Women are certainly more risk averse when it comes to physical activities (especially among younger people). When it comes to finances, some research on women and investments finds that women are more risk averse than men (Charness and Gneezy, 2012; Deo and Sundar, 2015). However, other research contests this. Marinelli et al (2017), in a study of clients of an Italian bank, found that men and women made investment decisions differently, but that the quality of their portfolios was the same. Taking this a step further, some commentators argue that it is better to view women as being risk aware rather than risk averse, meaning that they will take more time to assess risks before making a decision, but will ultimately take on the same level of risk as men (Rach, 2022).

Like trust, risk has many social dimensions. Our research in Brazil made it clear that when people choose how to pay for a purchase in public they take social risk into account. We carried out a questionnaire in several markets in São Paulo and the countryside near Rio de Janeiro to find out how people choose a payment method when shopping. The results were not what we expected. Customers were highly individual in how they chose between cash, debit card, credit card and Pix. Some people preferred to pay in cash because they were worried that their card would get cloned. Others preferred to pay by card because they feared they would get robbed if they carried cash. Yet other people preferred to pay with Pix because they trusted it more than cash or cards. The results varied somewhat from place to place: people were most reluctant to pay in cash in the most 'dangerous' areas of the city. But otherwise people's choices seemed to depend highly on how they weighed up different variables.

Emotions

As we saw in the beginning of this chapter with our fearful finance professor, all people have emotional relationships with their money. These emotions play a critical role in our financial decisions, mental health and general well-being. But most advice regarding money is practical and urges people to focus on making rational decisions. Not only do financial advice, financial tools and financial literacy training tend to ignore emotions; advisers often counsel people to put their emotions aside completely when dealing with their finances.

This advice ignores a large body of behavioural research that shows that putting our emotions aside is actually impossible. In reality, people do not act like 'rational economic man' at all. People make all kinds of decisions that go against their best interest, even when it isn't necessary. They forgo things they want to buy because they think they can't afford it, when the truth may be that they just don't think they deserve it. They may be terrified of facing the realities of their finances, even when they are actually in good shape. Or they close their eyes to bills and account statements and end up in bad economic shape, even though this was completely avoidable.

Many people don't recognize the role emotions play in their finances. As a result, they may go through their lives completely ill-equipped to deal with their finances and make them work for the well-being of themselves and their families. Attempting to ignore emotions only contributes to stress (American Psychological Association, 2015) and puts people at risk of developing mental health issues. People commonly cite money concerns as one of the primary factors that impact their mental health. Unfortunately, there is little professional guidance available to learn how to better manage emotional states regarding finances.

It is critical that we take feelings into account when designing financial services. If people are afraid of a service, they will be reluctant to use it, no matter how high their financial literacy is. On the upside, it is possible to design financial services that are fun and help people feel positive about their financial practices. A simple example is a payment request service called Tikkie that was launched in the

Netherlands in 2016. Anyone, no matter who they banked with, could download the app and use it to send other people a payment request. Due to its simple and friendly design, people found the app fun to use. It was far more convenient than trying to get the right amount of cash together, especially given that many people no longer carried cash. Any service that reduces stress and complexity, such as by making payments easier or sending reminders that help people avoid late payment fees, also provides a psychological benefit to its users. Indeed, doing research on which financial activities stress people the most would be likely to result in many ideas for new products or features.

Bringing in complexity

As we have seen in this chapter, customers cannot be expected to make rational, dispassionate decisions by calmly calculating the value of their options. Certainly, people consider factors such as price, value and convenience when making decisions, and are generally quite adept at identifying value for money. It is surely rational to want control over one's finances, and it is sensible to consider how much we trust a service before using it. It is also arguable that taking one's feelings into account is, indeed, rational, so long as those decisions do not harm us in the long run. Behavioural scientists know this well, so perhaps it is time to declare that 'economic man' has been replaced by 'socioeconomic humans'.

But there is more to the story. So far we have only considered decision-making factors in isolation. However, as we flagged at the beginning of this chapter, people do not consider just one thing at a time when making decisions and taking action. First, individual differences shape decision-making. Second, people rarely make decisions or take actions entirely as individuals: they consult with (or keep in mind) their families, friends and peers. Third, culture influences individual and collective financial practices. Fourth, people's use of financial services depends on what other financial services they are using or that are available to them (their 'financial portfolios'). How can we begin to understand such complex behaviour?

Our research in Brazil provides a good example of how individualized decision-making can be (Taylor and Broløs, 2022). People would pay in different ways depending on the context, available infrastructure and personal preferences. It seems that no one type of payment is an obvious choice but that they all have pros and cons, resulting in substantial variation in how people choose between them.

And yet, while people's decision-making was clearly highly individualistic, it was also very much influenced by their sociocultural context. Sometimes people made decisions in response to the context of the particular place where they were buying and selling. At other times people drew upon their broader experiences to make decisions. Often they did both. For example, we found many people who would not carry cash to street markets they considered to be dangerous, but would happily carry cash when visiting other areas of the city. People who were afraid of card fraud were often not influenced by their own experiences but by stories they had heard through friends or via the media. People's use of Pix was also dependent upon how comfortable they felt with the technology, and some had been taught to use it by friends. And so, while on the surface people made individual decisions, we do not have to dig very deep to find an abundance of social and contextual influences.

If you are not convinced, try this exercise: think about all the decisions you made today and what influenced them. Chances are that you made your own decision about what to eat for breakfast (more or less). But you may have also decided what groceries to buy based on your family's preferences. You may have made work decisions based on your understanding of what your colleagues would prefer. And you may have bought a new outfit to attend a social event – in which case you were certainly influenced not only by your own preferences, but also by your knowledge of what would be appropriate to wear and what people would think of your outfit.

How can we understand such complexity – and why should we try? Surely we need to simplify our understanding of people if we are to design appropriate financial services, programmes and policies for them? Well, yes and no. Clearly, we need to be able to identify patterns of behaviour among the groups we are interested in. But this doesn't mean it's necessary to throw out complexity altogether. In this chapter we attempted to show how complex financial behaviours can be understood without reducing them to simplified understandings. In the next chapter we move away from decision-making to discuss how we can generate insights about people's practices in the round.

TAKEAWAYS

- In the past few decades, social and behavioural scientists have made great strides in understanding people's financial behaviour.
- People's preferences are rooted in their culture, social upbringing, personal experiences and relationships with others.
- Key factors in decision-making include value, convenience, control, trust, risk and emotions
- People rarely make decisions as true individuals; instead, they take into account other people's preferences, needs and behaviours.

References

Ambroz, A, Shotland, M and Hira, S (2021) Randomised controlled trial, Better Evaluation. www.betterevaluation.org/methods-approaches/approaches/randomised-controlled-trial (archived at https://perma.cc/A5MQ-YNWH)

American Psychological Association (2015) Speaking of psychology: The stress of money, with Linda Gallo, PhD, Episode 22, APA. www.apa.org/news/podcasts/speaking-of-psychology/financial-stress (archived at https://perma.cc/P4JU-GBJ3)

Bourdieu, P (1984) *Distinction: A social critique of the judgement of taste*, Harvard University Press, Cambridge, MA

Broløs, A and Taylor, E (2022) *Female Finance on the Move: Switzerland*, EWPN, Keen Innovation and Unblu. ewpn.eu/research-network/white-papers-reports/female-finance-on-the-move-switzerland (archived at https://perma.cc/46DS-XBE5)

Carpena, F, Cole, S, Shapiro, J and Zia, B (2013) Liability structure in small-scale finance: Evidence from a natural experiment, *The World Bank Economic Review*, 27 (3), 437–69

Charness, G and Gneezy, U (2012) Strong evidence for gender differences in risk taking, *Journal of Economic Behavior and Organization*, 83 (1), 50–58

Chibnik, M (2011) *Anthropology, Economics, and Choice*, University of Texas Press, Austin, TX

Deo, M and Sundar, V (2015) Gender difference: Investment behavior and risk taking, *SCMS Journal of Indian Management*, 12 (3), 74–81

Dietrich, F and List, C (2013) Where do preferences come from? *International Journal of Game Theory*, 42 (3), 613–37

Geertz, C (1973) *The Interpretation of Cultures*, Basic Books, New York

Giné, X and Yang, D (2009) Insurance, credit, and technology adoption: Field experimental evidence from Malawi, *Journal of Development Economics*, 89 (1), 1–11

Innovations for Poverty Action (IPA) (2015) Evaluating financial products and services in the US: A toolkit for running randomized controlled trials, IPA. poverty-action.org/sites/default/files/publications/Evaluating%20Financial%20Products%20and%20Services%20in%20the%20US%20-%20A%20Toolkit%20for%20Running%20RCTs%20(1).pdf (archived at https://perma.cc/H4H8-9KVQ)

Kahneman, D (2011) *Thinking, Fast and Slow*, Penguin, London

Marinelli, N, Mazzoli, C and Palmucci, F (2017) How does gender really affect investment behavior? *Economics Letters*, 151, 58–61

Miller, D (1994) *Modernity: An ethnographic approach: dualism and mass consumption in Trinidad*, Routledge, Abingdon

Nerré, B (2008) Tax culture: A basic concept for tax politics, *Economic Analysis and Policy*, 38 (1), 153–67

Rach, S (2022) 'Women are not more risk-averse; they are risk-aware', FT Adviser, 20 May. www.ftadviser.com/investments/2022/05/20/women-are-not-more-risk-averse-they-are-risk-aware (archived at https://perma.cc/Z7EE-UPB2)

Servon, L (2017) *The Unbanking of America: How the new middle class survives*, Houghton Mifflin Harcourt, New York

Taleb, N (2001) *Fooled by Randomness: The hidden role of chance in life and in the markets* (vol 1), Random House, New York

Taleb, N (2007) *The Black Swan: The impact of the highly improbable*, Random House, New York

Taylor, E B and Broløs, A (2022) *Money and Payments in Low Income Brazil*, Finthropology/SICPA

Thaler, R H and Sunstein, C R (2008) *Nudge: Improving decisions about health, wealth, and happiness*, Yale University Press, New Haven, CT

Thaler, R H (2015) *Misbehaving: The making of behavioural economics*, WW Norton & Company, London

Into the field 05

Understanding financial behaviour in context

So far in this book we have argued that in order to undertake customer-centric innovation we need to retain some sense of the complexity of people's lives, and that qualitative research is especially helpful here. In this chapter we spend some time explaining how qualitative data is collected, its possibilities and limits, and the kinds of insights it generates. Since this is a book about insights, not about research methods per se, we describe this process in the form of stories, building what anthropologists call 'thick description'.

We are often asked how qualitative researchers actually work. People are especially curious about anthropologists, who often spend considerable time in their fieldsites. What could we possibly be doing for weeks or months at a time? How do we get to talk to people? To answer these questions, we present a substantial account of a research project we undertook on mobile phones and money in Haiti. This project is a little unusual, since it was undertaken when Erin was an academic researcher, and the researchers spent months at a time in the field over the whole three years of the project. But the general approach and methods are also relevant to smaller, commercial projects: in 2021, when we spent a month doing research on payments in Brazil, we used a very similar approach. Indeed, once you have done ethnography it is difficult to switch ethnographic thinking off: even if we are conducting interviews over video, it's normal for us to be making observations and trying to get a sense of the context of someone's life.

After describing the fieldwork in Haiti, we dig deeper into methods. People familiar with quantitative methods often ask us about the validity of qualitative research. Since we use small sample sizes, our insights are not statistically significant. But this doesn't mean that they are not useful. Indeed, a relatively small dataset can tell us a great deal about broader trends as well as providing micro level insights into people's everyday behaviour. We also assess the pros and cons of qualitative research. For more on research methods, see Chapter 10 of this book.

Mobile money in Haiti

On 12 January 2010 a 7.0 magnitude earthquake hit the Caribbean nation of Haiti. It flattened a large part of the capital, Port-au-Prince, and killed more than 300,000 people. The humanitarian community responded quickly, rushing to Haiti by plane, by land from the Dominican Republic, and even by boat. Coordinating the relief effort was difficult as the infrastructure had been seriously damaged. Among other things, the banking system did not function in the aftermath of the earthquake, and aid agencies found it difficult to move money around to pay for the relief effort.

As well as being a terrible tragedy, the earthquake highlighted the inadequacies of Haiti's infrastructure, both in a time of crisis and generally. At the time, there were few banks outside of Haiti's urban centres, and the rate of access to formal financial services was very low. According to GSMA's Mobile Money Deployment Tracker, formal banks had just 15 per cent penetration in Haiti (this data is no longer available). Even people with bank accounts struggled to use them, since lines outside banks were often several hours long and their systems were frequently not working. How could the infrastructure be improved to cope better with such events in the future? And could an improved infrastructure help Haitians in the course of their ordinary lives?

A USAID organization in Haiti, HIFIVE, teamed up with the Bill and Melinda Gates Foundation to run a competition that aimed to improve Haiti's financial infrastructure. The competition challenged Haiti's mobile network operators, Digicel and Voilá, to develop mobile money services that would allow Haitians to send money to each other via ordinary analogue handsets. In the past three years, M-PESA had taken off in Kenya, and the sponsors hoped that it would also be successful in Haiti.

Just a few days before the earthquake, Erin and an academic collaborator, Dr Heather Horst, had received a small grant from the Institute for Money, Technology and Financial Inclusion (IMTFI) at the University of California Irvine, to carry out a research project on the southernmost point of the border of Haiti and the Dominican Republic. This project was designed to study the use of money and mobile phones to manage economic and social activities in the two towns on either side of the border, Pedernales and Anse-à-Pitres (Ansapit in Haitian Kreyol). We were meant to spend just three months in the field. But soon we received an email from the director of the IMTFI, Bill Maurer: could we extend our project into a larger, three-year project covering several regions of the country? Of course, we said yes.

This was the beginning of a collaboration between Erin, Heather and a third academic researcher, Dr Espelencia Baptiste. Over the next three years we carried out qualitative research in three different locations in Haiti: the original border location, Port-au-Prince, and a town called Jacmel in the south of Haiti. In 2010, before mobile money was launched, we focused on understanding how people were sending money around the country and using mobile phones in all three locations. Not long after mobile money was launched in 2011, we returned to spend three months looking into how people were using the new service. At the time, mobile money was only available in Port-au-Prince and nearby towns, so we did not do research in the other two locations Finally, in 2012, we spent three months on the border, with Espelencia carrying out several weeks of further research in Port-au-Prince and Jacmel. We published several reports and articles on the topic (see, for example, Baptiste et al, 2010; Taylor et al, 2011).

For the research that took place on the national border, we carried out interviews with 25 low-income Haitians. With a subset of ten interviewees we carried out a 'portable kit' study, a type of interview that involves asking interviewees to talk about the objects in their bags, wallets and pockets. We held informal conversations with hundreds of people and carried out extensive observations, all of which we wrote up into field notes.

Why was qualitative research useful to understand money and mobiles in Haiti? Surely quantitative data would better to understand cash circulation and mobile phone usage?

First, there simply wasn't any quantitative data on the things we needed to know. There were no figures on how people sent money around the country or what services they used. Even if such data had been available for digital services, most people still used cash, and there were no studies tracking cash circulation. Such a study would have been expensive and time-consuming to undertake.

Second, while there was data on how many SIM cards and mobile phones were in use, poor infrastructure meant that people struggled to charge their phone or pick up a signal, meaning that they were often not usable. A survey may have been able to gather data on

Figure 5.1 Map of cash circulation routes in south-eastern Haiti

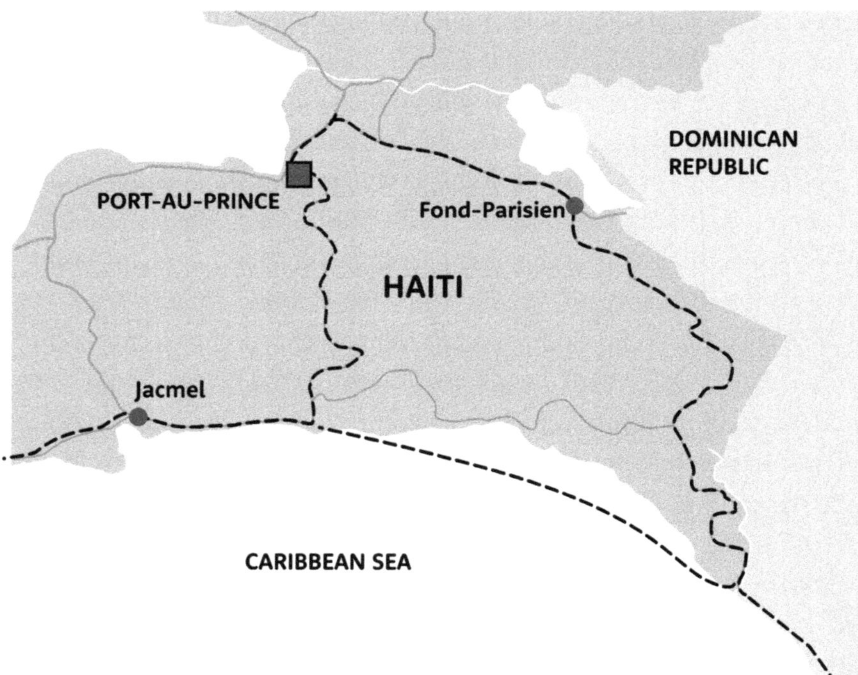

SOURCE Erin B Taylor

usage issues, but would struggle to go into depth about the ways in which people dealt with these problems on a daily basis.

Third, spending time in the field allowed us to understand the context in which people used money and phones. Practices differed from place to place, and from people to people, depending on a large range of factors.

Fourth, doing fieldwork allows researchers to discover the unexpected. Fieldworkers always discover behaviours and practices that they could not have guessed existed. By definition, it is not possible to survey things you don't know exist.

We will now use 'thick description' to describe two insights in relation to Haiti: moving cash and adoption of mobile money.

Moving cash

How people move money around was one of the first things we investigated when we arrived in Haiti in 2010. At the time, Espelencia carried out research in Port-au-Prince, while Erin worked on the border of Haiti and the Dominican Republic. Both researchers carried out semi-structured interviews, but, more importantly, we spent a great deal of time in the field carrying out observations and having informal conversations with residents. By spending time in public places such as markets and the town square, we got to talk to many people and became quickly recognized. The possibility of being immersed in local life allowed us to witness people's financial practices with our own eyes, rather than relying on what they told us. It also made us more sure that the insights we gained from interviews were accurate. Indeed, while we have published many articles and book chapters based on the results of our interviews, this section is mostly drawn more from our informal fieldwork.

Sending money is critically important in Haiti. Many Haitians, especially those living in the countryside, depend on relatives who live in Port-au-Prince for financial support. For some, sending money was as simple as depositing the money into the recipient's bank account and for them to withdraw it at their local branch. The unbanked and those who do not live close to a bank depended on transfer services such as CAM, SogeXpress, Unitransfer, Western Union and MoneyGram. But for people who reside in places where these services are not available, sending and receiving money could be an expensive and time-consuming undertaking. This is a major reason why USAID and the Gates Foundation were motivated to develop mobile money services in Haiti.

One of our interviewees in Port-au-Prince told us a story to illustrate how complicated and costly sending money could be. David needed to send money to his cousin in his hometown, Le Borge, because he still owed some money for his brother's funeral. In order to reach the office in Port-de-Paix, his cousin had to walk one and a half hours from his house to the town of Anse a Foleur. Once in Anse a Foleur, he spent two hours and paid 300 gourdes for the tap-tap (bus) that took him to Port-de-Paix, then 30 gourdes for a taxi to take him to the money transfer office. In sum, David and his cousin spent 760 gourdes and 7 hours to send 1,250 gourdes from one part of Haiti to another. As well as the time and cost associated with the money transfer services, some Haitians do not trust them. Many Haitians preferred to wait until a friend or relative was going to their village to send money to their family. They relied heavily on trusted relationships to make remittances work. We will discuss such 'workarounds' further in Chapter 7.

In our Anse-à-Pitres research site, access to formal financial services was scarce in comparison to Port-au-Prince. Based on our interviews and conversations, we estimated that less than 1 per cent of residents of Anse-à-Pitres had a bank account, and 40–50 per cent owned a mobile phone. These are not exact statistics, because we did not use a representative sample. Rather, we tallied results from our quantitative sources: interviews and conversations recorded in field notes. While we would have liked to have access to more accurate data (or carry out a survey ourselves) this was not possible within the scope of our work. Nor did we consider it necessary to answer our research questions, since we were engaging in 'discovery'-style research about a new service that was bound to show a range of emerging practices.

Although formal financial services were scarce, sending money was common. Most people living in the border area had family members living in other towns, and Anse-à-Pitres's location on the Dominican border renders it a strategic point of trade. At the time, residents depended upon alternative formal and informal transfer services, including the Western Union office in Anse-à-Pitres, the Western Union and Caribe Express offices in Pedernales in the Dominican Republic, and a range of transport systems, especially the boats that travel twice per week to Marigot in the south of Haiti. These were simple open fishing boats with outboard motors. They anchored just off the narrow beach in Anse-à-Pitres. There was no wharf; instead, local men were hired to carry all the goods from the market (primarily flour, coconuts and plantains), customers' baggage and the customers themselves (up to 60 people) onto the boats. Loading the boats began at around midday and finished at eight in the evening when the boats departed all together. The fleet took around seven hours to arrive in Marigot (using 70 gallons of gasoline), where tap-taps (small open vehicles) waited to take clients to their next destination (primarily Belle Anse, Peredo and Jacmel). Each boat had one owner, a captain, and a crew of two to three men.

The captains ran a regular, free money transfer service. The boats were the fastest method of non-electronic transfer because there was not a single paved road connecting Anse-à-Pitres with any other part of Haiti. To use the service, people simply gave a boat captain the cash they wanted to send and the phone number of the recipient. When the boats arrived at the other end of the route, the captains would send the recipient a text message to tell them to come down to the beach to collect their cash. Money sometimes transfers to second destinations, especially Jacmel and Port-au-Prince, after it arrives in Marigot. From Marigot, produce and money goes to the north into the rural areas overland. Boats also leave from Marigot to Jacmel to the west. From Jacmel, goods and money move overland to the west and overland via a paved road north to Port-au-Prince.

It was clear from our research that Haitians had found ingenious ways to complete critical financial transactions, either by travelling themselves or by sending money with trusted parties. However, these informal solutions had significant limitations. While the boat service was widely used and is considered to be relatively trustworthy, the boats only travel as far as Marigot. Sending money beyond Marigot was difficult due to issues of time, social capital and logistics. Indeed, the boats have been known to sink, with two reported incidents in the preceding year. Travelling was also an issue due to safety issues and its time-intensiveness. Women in particular worked long days, waking up at dawn to cook their family's food for the day before heading out to work, returning home only after dark. It was simple enough to conclude that a mobile money service could greatly benefit Haitians, especially those who were on low incomes and living in remote parts of the country.

The launch of mobile money

In November 2010 Digicel and Voilá both made mobile money services publicly available in Haiti. Building upon our previous research on domestic remittances and financial practices, we returned to Haiti from December to April in 2011 to identify mobile money's potentials and challenges, given the specific characteristics of the mobile money services offered and the needs of the Haitian population. We investigated how the new mobile money services were fitting into Haiti's existing socioeconomic environment, and how customers were adapting and using the services. Our Year 2 research differed from Year 1 in that we spent far more time talking with mobile money agents. We spent time in sites with a mobile money agent nearby, including the Marche en Fer and various agents around Port-au-Prince, looking for people using the services but also talking with people who weren't. This involved very few formal interviews due to the difficulties of talking to people at length while they are out and about doing business. Instead, we depended heavily on informal conversations and observations.

At the time, the HIFIVE competition was still running, and the two MNOs, Digicel and Voilá, were contending for the various money prizes. While, technically, mobile money could already be used around the country, agents were only present in Port-au-Prince and nearby towns. This essentially limited mobile money's use to areas with agents, since people needed agents to cash in and cash out. HIFIVE and the MNOs had mobilized various organizations to help introduce people to mobile money. For example, Mercy Corps was delivering cash grants through mobile money in the town of Saint Marc. As yet there was no mobile money agent in Saint Marc but several grocery stores were accepting mobile money. Cash grant recipients spent their money there.

In Port-au-Prince, mobile money agents were distributed around the city, including a prominent one in the capital's famous market, Marche en Fer. But many agents were not fully operational. On numerous occasions, we were unable to make transactions at agencies around Port-au-Prince. Occasionally agents were shut. The most common problem was that there was no staff member present who knew how to do a transaction. Sometimes he or she was close by and was called to come and help us; at other times we were told to return later in the day. There was one occasion when a café employee called the person who knew how to do the transaction and was talked through the steps over the phone, essentially being trained on the spot. The deposit was successful, though the customer was not asked to show her identification or sign the paperwork.

On another occasion, we visited a high-end clothing store with prominently displayed mobile money signs. However, none of the employees had been trained how to do a mobile money transaction. They called the store owner, who told them that the paperwork and the phone needed to do our transaction was locked in his desk and could not be accessed until after 5pm when he arrived from his day job. We left the store without doing the transaction because none of the employees present could help us.

Such failures in process, either due to lack of staff training or disinterest in observing legal procedures, are quite common with respect to mobile money deployments in different countries. There is certainly a gap between how mobile money is supposed to work and how people actually use it (or are able to use it),... and this needs to be taken into account when designing new financial services.

Despite these teething problems, we found that people were beginning to benefit from mobile money and use it for different purposes. One of our research participants, Bruno, the owner of an electronic workshop in downtown Port-au-Prince, told us that although he had a bank account, he preferred to use his TchoTcho account because he could access his money almost anytime. As he told us:

> If I run out of money on Friday night, I have to wait until Monday morning before I can get my money out of the bank, but with TchoTcho mobile, it does not matter if it is 5pm on a Sunday. I know that my agent will be there and I can get my money.

Several research participants also explained that an advantage of using mobile money outlets over existing ways of transferring money is privacy. With mobile money, customers can transfer money to anyone from the privacy of their home or wherever they find themselves. Other transfer services are not private. Using traditional modes of transfer such as bus drivers and boat captains means that others will know who sent money to whom, how much and when. In transfer houses, not only will people be observed going in and coming out of the transfer house, but other customers can often hear the agent checking the customer's ostensibly private information, including name, phone number and amount of money being transacted.

We also discovered people undertaking what we called 'Me2Me' transactions: depositing money to store temporarily. These Me2Me transactions serve three main purposes:

- First, storing money in a mobile money account is more secure than hiding it in your house or carrying it around town in your pockets. Bianca, a vendor who sold vegetables on Route Delmas and a TchoTcho customer, told us that an advantage of mobile money is that she could deposit her day's wages at an agent near her stall and withdraw at an agent in her neighbourhood. Bianca thereby avoided the stress of travelling with money and the possibility of being robbed as she travelled home. She told us that she would rather pay the cost of withdrawing money than risk losing everything. Indeed, this topic of safety appeared in an early Digicel advertisement for mobile money. The advertisement depicted an elderly woman hiding money in various places in her house – in her couch, behind paintings, in a jar. She then decided that she would move it to her mobile money account to keep it safe from thieving relatives.

- Second, people left a balance in their mobile money account so they could top up their phone credit after hours. When shops are shut and mobile Pap Padap vendors have gone home for the day, mobile money customers can still top up their airtime when it runs out by transferring money from their mobile money account onto their phone accounts. While online top-up is available, it is not an option for many people because it requires internet access and a credit card, two luxuries that are not readily available in Haiti.
- Third, people used Me2Me transactions to save money. Haitian common wisdom tells us that if you have money in your hand, it will not remain there for long. As Josué, an artist, explained to us: 'If I have money in my pocket, I will use it on beer, cigarettes and women, but if it is not there I cannot spend it as fast. After all, money is the devil, it makes you do crazy things.'

No story could illustrate the significance of mobile money for topping up your phone as well as this scenario presented by Samuel, a 19-year-old university student. He told us:

> Have you ever been talking to a girl late at night and just when the conversation gets interesting you run out of money on your phone? At this hour there is not a store open or an available Pap Padap vendor. Even if there were, you would be too scared to go out at that time. With mobile money you can continue the conversation without losing momentum because, once lost, you cannot recapture that moment.

Despite the many creative ways of using mobile money, when we returned to the field a year later we found that its use had not achieved 'scale' around the country. While usage was relatively common in Port-au-Prince, few people living in our border field site knew much about it, and just a handful of people used it. The previous year, in 2011, we had the honour of helping HIFIVE host a visit by Safaricom CEO, Michael Joseph, who explained to us the importance of marketing mobile money and developing a solid agent network. Mobile money may hold incredible potential to benefit people, but if they don't know what it is then they won't use it. Shortly after our 2012 visit, Digicel rebranded their mobile money service with the name MonCash and relaunched it. Nearly a decade later, when we carried out research in Brazil, we found that the central bank had got marketing right: they carried out a campaign over radio and television to market Pix, the new payments platform. It gained rapid uptake. The lesson is clear: demand is necessary, but it is not enough. Nor is design, in fact. Companies also need to think about how they are going to reach their customers. We discuss this further in the following chapter.

The above story provides a 'thick description' of our research in Haiti. Indeed, it only represents a small part of all the insights we collected over the three years in which we were doing fieldwork. Besides cash and financial tools, we have published book chapters and journal articles on financial literacy, mobile money and privacy, the movement of goods, people and money across the Haiti–Dominican Republic border and the role mobile money plays as a development tool. In 2010 we were even able to exhibit some of the money-related items we collected in Haiti in the newly refurbished Citi Money Gallery in the British Museum. Some of our insights were taken up by the funders and used in the relaunch of mobile money, especially our observations about the need for agent visibility and marketing to raise awareness of mobile money. We also suspect – but will never know for sure – that Digicel's advertisement showing the elderly woman hiding her cash in her mobile money account was inspired by our findings.

Generating quality qualitative research

Chapter 6 will focus specifically on how insights from qualitative research can feed into innovation. In the remainder of this chapter we want to focus on how qualitative research results in insights in the first place. The Haiti research provided a host of insights into issues relating to mobile money and its adoption and use, including people's need for privacy and security, the potential of mobile money to relieve people from the hard work and inefficiencies of sending money in cash form, issues with mobile money agents, and the ways in which people cooperate to complete transactions. It highlighted the importance to mobile money's success of having adequate infrastructure and a well-developed agent network, and the need to ensure customers understand how the system works.

But how do fieldworkers – and qualitative researchers generally – actually get these insights? How do they frame research questions, collect data, and analyse it to get the best data possible? What kinds of biases can creep in during the research process, and how can we avoid them? If qualitative research isn't statistically significant, how do we know that we can rely on it? In the remainder of this chapter we talk through these issues.

Framing a research problem

Finding out what customers and clients are doing, or what they want, generally involves carrying out some kind of research. Perhaps you are a company planning to enter a new market, or an non-governmental organization (NGO) considering implementing a new programme. You realize that you don't know enough about your customers or participants to be sure that your new product or project will be a success. What do you do? The first step is to clarify what your problem is so that you can formulate a solid research question (and often sub-questions).

There are various ways of formulating research questions. Quantitative researchers in academia tend to come up with both a key question and a hypothesis – what they think the answer will be. They do this so they can generate a clear answer. For example, an academic economics researcher might hypothesize that mobile money use increases savings. They will collect and analyse data on these two factors and generate a clear answer. In other cases, questions might be posed without suggesting hypotheses. When designing a long survey, it may not make sense to generate hypotheses for all the questions it includes.

Quantitative researchers in companies or not-for-profit organizations are less likely to formulate a hypothesis. For example, market researchers draw on statistical studies and other sources to find facts that give insights into market characteristics, such as market size, competitors, customer spending patterns, and so on. Similarly, data analysts working with large sets of customer data often have specific questions they want to answer, or they search in the data for unexpected patterns.

Qualitative researchers, whether working in universities, companies or not-for-profits, do not usually formulate hypotheses, since the nature of qualitative data means that hypotheses cannot be rigorously tested. This is particularly true when the research is highly exploratory, since narrowing the topic too soon can inhibit discoveries from being made. To prepare for research, qualitative researchers often develop lists of primary research questions and sub-questions. These list the things they want to know – not just about individual behaviour, but also how people cooperate. Based on these lists of research questions, qualitative researchers devise questions for interviewees to get the data needed to answer the research questions. However, they are often flexible to change, and may refine the research questions based on early findings.

Additionally, anthropologists usually write field notes, which are generally descriptions of our daily conversations and observations. While anthropologists generally write field notes that concentrate on our main topic and questions, they also use them to record interesting observations that are not central topics of investigation, but which may prove useful down the track. Often these observations concern how people interact with each other. In this way we ensure that our work is focused enough to collect relevant data, but also leave open space for exploration and new discoveries.

UX researchers and service design researchers working in companies, not-for-profits and government use a mixture of qualitative and quantitative methods. Some UX research problems are highly specific; for example, do users prefer the green interface or the blue one? In this case, UX researchers might set up an A/B test, showing half of their customers the green interface, and showing the other half of their customers the blue one. In many cases, UX and service design researchers will bring customers into the lab to understand how they use products and services. This is generally a qualitative research process in which they make observations and ask the participants questions about their experience, and so their framing of the problem will reflect this. They are unlikely to generate a hypothesis, but rather a list of questions and sub-questions that are of interest. Service design researchers particularly need to understand customer journeys, so they often find themselves framing problems quite broadly.

Sampling and confidence

Quantitative and qualitative studies can work well in combination. Qualitative studies can help prepare a larger quantitative study by assisting in getting the questions right, whereas qualitative studies may help researchers to dive deeper into unexplained issues from a quantitative study. But the ways in which qualitative and quantitative researchers choose samples of participants is very different.

Simply put, it is virtually impossible to do qualitative research with a representative sample today. In the early days of anthropology, it was possible to speak to everyone living in a village, or choose every second house to be part of a survey (quantitative methods were used more often in the early days of anthropology). This is not the case today, when people live in large-scale societies. No funding body would allocate the enormous amount of funds needed to do qualitative research with thousands of people. Nor, we believe, is it necessary. Qualitative research doesn't need to generate statistically significant data for us to be reasonably confident in the results. We generally don't require absolute answers in order to generate meaningful and relevant insights, or make recommendations to organizations on how they should act on the basis of the data.

The best way to explain this is by providing an example. In our research in Brazil, we interviewed 63 people across two sites (one rural, one urban). This is actually quite a large number of interviews for a short (five-week) qualitative study. Almost all interviewees were on a low income; we interviewed a handful of professionals in order to make a comparison and get a sense of alternative viewpoints. Interviewees were a mixture of men and women with different occupations. Once we were about a third of the way through the interviews we began seeing clear patterns in what people told us, and the number of new things we were discovering started to decrease. By the time we were two-thirds through the interviews, there were very few new insights emerging on our chosen topic. (Of course, we were hearing new things about people's personal experiences, as everyone is different.)

Afterwards, when we analysed the data, we noticed that it aligned quite nicely with the data we had seen when preparing for fieldwork. Our preparation included desk research in which we mapped out the main features of the financial system and collected statistics on things like people's use of financial services and literacy rates. We noticed that our findings were more or less in agreement with these statistics, but that they added 'thick description' to complement and personalize such statistics. The ability to compare our findings with statistics was particularly useful given that Brazil is a large and diverse country with many different ethnicities and local contexts that could have affected the results. It meant we could be more or less certain that our results would apply to most people on low incomes living in Brazil, not just in the locations we studied.

It is important to note that the question of what a 'sample' is depends on what you think your unit of observation is. Quantitative studies tend to define one unit as an individual or a household. Qualitative researchers tend to describe their sample in terms of number of individual interviewees. However, interviewing individuals always means collecting data about a wider number of people. No interviewee will exclusively talk about themselves: they also mention friends, family, colleagues, neighbours and more. These people are not strictly part of our sample since we did not talk with them directly. However, they appear as characters in our analysis because we describe how individuals perceive their social and familial lives.

Moreover, it is relatively common for anthropologists to talk with people who know each other. This is especially useful for us to build pictures of practices within families and communities. For example, in our Brazil study we spoke with a mother and daughter about their use of the new payments platform, Pix. We learned that although the daughter was already an adult living with her family in a home of her own, there was quite a lot of financial cooperation between the households. Various family members would get loans to help out other family members, teach each other how to use Pix, and in some cases use each other's Pix account or bank account. Talking to both the mother and daughter gave us a much richer sense of cooperative financial management than talking to one person alone.

It isn't just qualitative researchers who look to other types of research to gain certainty in their data. Quantitative researchers also look to qualitative research to cross-check their results. Let's take the example of a large, mixed method project we are working on. The project, dubbed Digital Finance and Farming, includes a team of anthropologists, economists and human geographers from four universities in Australia, Cambodia and Laos. As part of this project, agricultural economists Dr Peralta and her team are conducting a household survey in Cambodia and experiments in Laos. In order to design the survey and experiments they are drawing upon both secondary data and insights from the qualitative research being done by the project. Why? Because in order to design quantitative research, it's necessary to have a solid understanding of the context in which you will implement it. If you do not have a sense of people's ways of thinking and their practices, it is impossible to write appropriate questions, or design experiments that will make sense to participants. Indeed, all quantitative research rests on qualitative insights.

Bias and error

In the previous chapter we explained how behavioural researchers have made great strides in identifying people's irrationalities and biases. Researchers are by no means exempt from having biases themselves. The scientific method has been developed to limit bias and error as much as possible, but they can creep in at any stage, and researchers must remain vigilant to try to keep them at bay. This holds for both qualitative and quantitative research.

Bias can first creep in when choosing a research topic. Researchers (understandably) tend to choose research topics that they are interested in, or which will be acceptable to the scientific community and funding bodies. Bias and error in data analysis are also major issues, since there is a risk that researchers' interpretation of the data will reflect their own demographic characteristics, not those of the interviewees. To limit bias and error, qualitative researchers tend to take a number of steps. First, we cross-check our findings with the work of other researchers to look for signs of disagreement. Second, we often run our findings by other researchers and local experts to sanity check it. For example, during our Haiti project we were in regular conversation with researchers, regulators, technology companies, NGOs and others to discuss our research results. In preparation for our Brazil research we held conversations with sociologists and anthropologists working in Brazil to ensure we framed research questions relevant to the context, and so limiting our outsider bias. We ran the results past experts, including a representative from the Banco Central do Brasil (Brazil's central bank) to confirm that they made sense.

Recruitment of research participants is also a potential early source of bias. This is well-understood: much has been written about the tendency for research to be conducted with WEIRD (white, educated, industrialized, rich and democratic) research subjects, particularly in Western countries. The bias towards interviewing certain demographics more than others is partly due to recruitment issues. Most people have little time to talk to researchers, and so many studies use students: this is the source of the WEIRD problem. Researchers attempt to solve this problem by being explicit about who they want to talk to. Professional recruiting companies can be particularly helpful in supplying appropriate research participants.

In the field, anthropologists may use professional recruiters, but they are more likely to find participants themselves by a variety of methods. When working in a small village or town, recruitment is relatively straightforward, as interviewees are likely to recommend others. This method of recruitment is known as 'snowballing'. In urban centres recruitment can be more difficult as it is simply harder to become recognized by the community. Many years ago, when Erin did her PhD fieldwork in the Dominican Republic, she found it easy to recruit research participants even though she worked in the capital city, because she lived in a small community within the city. Conversely, one of her fellow PhD students was doing research in Bangkok, where she lived in a small high-rise apartment by herself, and was struggling to make connections.

In Brazil we resolved the problem of recruitment in three ways. First, we did a short questionnaire in public markets that took five minutes for people to answer. At the end we gave them an information sheet with our contact details on it, explaining that the questionnaire was part of a larger study and that we were looking for interviewees. Second, we did the interviews in a public workspace right near a busy market where many of our potential research subjects hung out, making it easy for them to find us. Third, we offered a small cash incentive to interviewees. This worked perfectly, because we wanted to interview people on low incomes and it was right before Christmas, a time when people had a higher need for the extra cash. Note, however, that incentives won't always work. Our middle-class interviewees were not interested in the incentive, but rather in our topic. In other projects it might be better to give people gift cards as incentives if they would be embarrassed to receive cash. The efficacy and appropriateness of incentives always depends on the context.

Getting the right stories

So far, we have covered issues of framing research questions, sampling, representativeness, bias and appropriateness of analysis. But assuming we have got all these right, how do we ensure that we get the stories we need? For our purposes, this boils down to one critical question: how do we get our research participants to talk about money and finances? How do we need to adapt our methods to achieve this? As it turns out, there are different types of methods and approaches that can be put in place to encourage people to talk about money.

Conducting research into people's financial behaviours can be difficult due to a range of money taboos, ethical issues and practical matters. People can be very private about money and may be ashamed of their financial position. Being wealthy can be as embarrassing as being poor, so asking people to talk about their financial position is fraught with obstacles. Asking people to tell you their bank balance or how much debt they're in strikes at the heart of people's fears that they are using money incorrectly.

When we started our research in Haiti, a number of people (including other researchers) told us that our project was doomed to fail: Haitians are wary of talking with foreigners at the best of times, and certainly wouldn't be willing to talk about their finances with us.

A major obstacle we faced initially in Port-au-Prince was that people thought we were representatives of the companies that offered mobile money services, Digicel and Voilá, and would only tell us about how much they loved mobile money. We had some work to do to explain who we were and what the research was about.

Once this problem was resolved, we learned that asking people about what matters in their lives, and how money works for them as a social tool, is far more effective than asking people for numbers. Our participants were more than willing to tell us how they sent money by boat to their children studying in other towns, complain about how long they spent standing in bank lines, demonstrate how they used the new mobile money service via their phone, show us the 'symbolic money' they carried (such as foreign banknotes), and so on.

As well as doing standard, semi-structured interviews, we used a special interview technique called the Portable Kit Study (Taylor et al, forthcoming 2024). This involved asking people to take all their possessions out of their pockets and bags, display them on a table, and talk about each object in turn. Coins, notes, bank cards, receipts and identification cards were among the money-related objects we were shown. Asking about these objects allowed us to develop a picture of people's financial behaviours without having to confront people directly. The method is also useful to get a sense of the range of financial services people use. People never use just one way of managing money: they combine cash, cards, digital wallets, credit services, insurance and more to make ends meet. This was particularly evident in Brazil, where many people have an account at a traditional bank and a neobank as they charge fees for different things. People transfer money between accounts depending on what they want to accomplish and what fees are charged by each bank.

We are not alone among researchers who have discovered ways of generating insights about money in complex and changing situations. Researchers are successfully adapting classic methodologies to new settings and research demands (Taylor and Lynch, 2020). Joseph Kaye (2014) used a financial tour method in the USA to build up a picture of households' finances. They used innovative techniques including home tours to see where people kept finance-related objects (such as bills stuck on the fridge), asked people to draw maps of where their financial transactions took place, and looked at people's financial spreadsheets (taking care to hide private information by placing sticky notes on screens).

Researchers are responding to how people use online and offline financial tools simultaneously. Tom Boellstorff's (2013) collaborative ethnography in Indonesia shows how people use online and offline money management tools in combination. Combining face-to-face interviews with analysis of the online purchasing and payments environments, they discovered that devices were central to online shopping behaviour in Indonesia, but that people did not always use their electronic devices to complete payment. Why might people choose to deposit a payment via an ATM or cash instead of paying online? The answer was mixed: even when paying online was possible, sometimes it was not preferable due to cost of transactions, security fears, familiarity with technology, or a preference to undertake transactions face-to-face.

In another high-tech context, Alexandra Mack (Taylor and Lynch, 2020) used an online financial diary method as part of a study of financial communications management in the United States. The entire study took place online, with participants using a programme called Revelation to fill out their financial diaries in their own time. Yet Mack maintained a personal connection with her participants, making sure she was available to answer questions and emailing the group daily to stimulate participants' motivation. She made sure she thanked participants for each diary submission and answered questions quickly. She notes:

> This lets them know that they aren't communicating into a black hole. Also, the follow-up questions help to get more details and clarify and encourage more engagement and longer answers.

Mack's study is a good example of how even an online study – a medium often conceptualized as socially distant – can be adapted to ethnographic techniques. A personal approach to researching money does not necessarily require the co-presence of researchers and participants.

There are many ways to do research on money. As we discuss in the following chapter, digital ethnography is also a great method for finding out about financial practices. As new kinds of financial services come onto the market, and new financial systems emerge (e.g. DeFi), researchers will surely come up with new ways to reach customers and find out about their practices. While these changes present a challenge to research, they are also an opportunity, and this is as true of money as any other topic of inquiry.

Socioeconomic humans

Over the previous two chapters we attempted to provide an overview of research writ large. We explained how behavioural research has changed the way we view people, replacing 'economic man' with 'socioeconomic humans'. In this chapter we endeavoured to provide readers with a sense of how qualitative research can help us to get closer to real people and develop deep insights – 'thick description' – of how people behave, not only as individuals, but also as collectives. People's feelings, thoughts, decisions and actions never take place in a vacuum: they are always influenced by other people, and by the broader context in which they live. The point is not to map out every single factor that influences a person or a group: this would be impossible. Rather, the idea is to begin with the customer or research participant – which could be defined as an individual, family, community or even a company – and formulate a research problem that puts them at the centre, then draw in as much contextual information as necessary to understand their behaviour and practices. This, as we have seen, can generate a host of fascinating insights. In the following chapter we describe how these insights can be applied to innovation and design.

TAKEAWAYS

- Qualitative data can help researchers discover the unexpected, understand people in context, fill gaps in understanding due to lack of quantitative data and help design further research (both qualitative and quantitative).

- Ethnographic fieldwork in particular helps us to understand people's financial behaviours in context, especially when the financial ecosystem has recently changed, such as due to the introduction of a new service.
- Techniques for framing, sampling, bias and error, and collecting relevant data, differ from discipline to discipline.
- To capture differences, begin with the customer – which could be defined as an individual, family, community, or even a company – and formulate a research problem that puts them at the centre.

References

Baptiste, E, Horst, H A and Taylor, E B (2010) *Haitian Monetary Ecologies and Repertoires: A qualitative snapshot of money transfer and savings*, IMTFI, University of California Irvine, Irvine, CA

Boellstorff, T (2013) *Landscaping Mobile Social Media and Payments in Indonesia*, IMTFI, University of California Irvine, Irvine, CA

Kaye, J (2014) The financial tour: Method for studying sensitive financial questions, in K Tejinder and C Neustaedter (eds) *Studying and Designing Technology for Domestic Life: Lessons from home*, Morgan Kaufmann, Cambridge, MA

Taylor, E B and Broløs, A (2022) *Money and Payments in Low Income Brazil*, Finthropology/SICPA

Taylor, E B and Lynch, G (2020) *Consumer Finance Research Methods Toolkit*, IMTFI, University of California Irvine, Irvine, CA

Taylor, E B, Baptiste, E and Horst, H A (2011) *Mobile Money in Haiti: Potentials and challenges*, IMTFI, University of California Irvine, Irvine, CA

Taylor, E B, Broløs, A and Horst, H A forthcoming 2024 How to talk about money: The portable kit as a research approach, in N Rangaswamy and S Venkatraman (eds), *Digital Qualitative Methods: Studies from the Global South*, Springer, New York

06 Innovating for a changing world

Using behavioural insights and qualitative data to develop new financial services

The aim of this book is to highlight the importance of human insights, even in a highly digital society. We have discussed how digital transformation changes financial solutions, financial business models and people's money management. We have also discussed that these changes affect both the need to innovate quickly and the way that innovation happens. Essentially, this focus is on how new technologies can help data-driven innovation. In Chapter 5 we emphasized the importance of adding qualitative data to this spectrum. We stressed how observations of behaviour (in a location or in an app) as well as methods adapted to understading financial behaviour (such as financial diaries and interviews about the content of a bag), can support an open discussion about money – even in situations where money is taboo or difficult to share.

In this chapter we build on this insight by illustrating the importance of understanding people and context when building new solutions. We share a series of stories from the field of innovation to show how insights from qualitative research and thick descriptions of complexity can point to innovation potential. We also share examples from the industry on how such knowledge has been overlooked, leading to higher innovation cost and lesser product success. We finally discuss examples of how digital insights can be developed and put to innovative use based on behavioural knowledge. We end the chapter by discussing how these insights can help in designing useful processes for radical innovation, either by drawing upon continued customer dialogue or by designing more systematic research. We will elaborate on this further in Chapter 9, where we discuss innovating for the future, and Chapter 10, where we provide tips on organizing for innovation.

Stories

> And suddenly the memory revealed itself. The taste was that of the little piece of madeleine which on Sunday mornings at Combray (because on those mornings I did not go out before mass), when I went to say good morning to her in her bedroom, my aunt Léonie used to give me, dipping it first in her own cup of tea or tisane.
>
> Marcel Proust, *À la recherche du temps perdu* (1913)

This quote will forever remind many of us of Proust's famous novel – or of the struggle to learn French. It is a great example of how a story, a drawing, a melody, a photo, a smell or even a taste can vividly remind us of a situation in our life, whether good or bad.

This power of description – to make things vivid – is the reason why we start this chapter by sharing stories about human insights in finance innovation. While less sensory than Proust's prose, some of the stories are small insights that could be quickly mediated in practice; some are longer research projects that build concepts over time.

Convenience, convenience, convenience

Our first story is an example from our own research on payments (Broløs and Taylor, 2022a). It is recent but reflects a topic that has shown up in most discussions on new payment tools for the last decade. When you ask people directly, and particularly if you give them a number of survey choices, they will stress security or perhaps a personal principle of 'never carrying cash'. But in real life convenience somehow takes precedence, which is also the case in this story.

We interviewed 14 Swiss women about their payment habits, asking them to show us everything they carried with them on a daily basis (the Portable Kit Method discussed in Chapter 5). As this was during the Covid-19 pandemic, all carried disinfectant and masks. They also carried keys and their phone. In their wallets, most carried a variety of cards (credit cards, debit cards and loyalty cards), personal ID and a little cash.

We next asked them what would be absolutely necessary when, say, they take the dog for a walk or take exercise. Most mentioned their phone and keys. They explained that they had different payment solutions like Twint or Google Pay on their phone alongside payment apps with loyalty points from the most well-known supermarkets. This would indicate that innovations in payments should definitely be mobile – which is basically also what the women said, when asked what they preferred.

There is, however, more to the story. When we asked these women about their shopping habits, they explained how they would use debit cards for day-to-day shopping and credit cards for larger purchases or late in the month when money was running low. They also told us that they generally used physical retail payment cards for shopping – even when they also had the shop app on their phone. Some of the women explained that, while they would like to use their phone to pay at the checkout, it was impractical for two reasons. First, there were too many things to carry and manage at the same time. Second, the internet connection would not always be sufficient, leading to uncomfortable delays and queues. The women further explained that they have to carry coins for parking, shopping trolleys and freeway toll payments.

So, how does this tie together? Why is it that what women say they prefer doesn't exactly match what they do? Well, in the end it was a question of convenience. Whatever was the most convenient in a given situation would be the choice – no matter their general preferences. The women we talked to might use their mobile app when shopping for only a few items, or if they went to a store on the way home from a run when carrying only their phone.

For innovative purposes, this insight could be used to develop solutions that can work offline, or to work with mobile solutions that require fewer clicks while remaining secure. It could be used to discuss with merchant partners how internet connection could be better, and to initiate wider use of mobile apps in areas like parking or freeways – as is, indeed, increasingly happening.

Figure 6.1 What's in a bag?

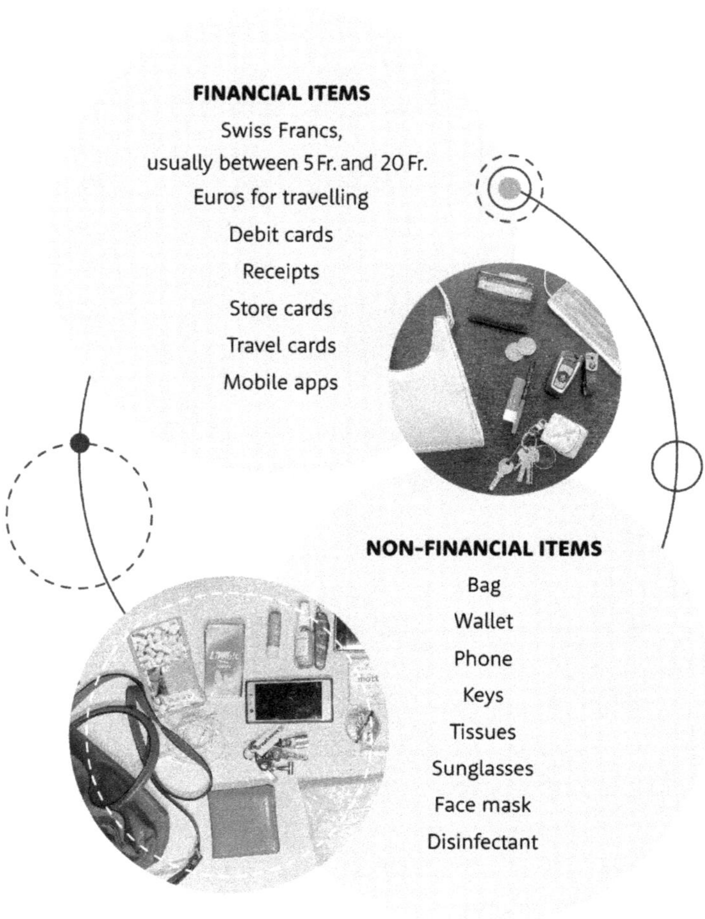

SOURCE Broløs and Taylor, 2022a

Do people use services the way they were intended?

Whether for convenience, to save fees or to access bonuses or other benefits, we have seen a number of examples of people who use accounts or payment solutions in very creative ways that were probably not intended by the FSPs. The authors of this book participated in the analysis of field studies in several low-income countries. The purpose was to understand how CBDCs could be designed to support financial inclusion (Narula et al, 2023). Indonesia's urban areas in particular offer a number of digital wallets. We saw that many taxi drivers and market merchants might be asked by their employer to use a particular wallet. If a customer was not able to pay in that wallet, they would perhaps offer to make the payment and be reimbursed with another wallet. This could also happen to avoid fee payments. Understanding the reason why people might use a financial service in a creative way could offer great ideas for innovation.

Overlooking the obvious

This next example is quite old, but it is illustrative of how easy it is to overlook obvious sources of information – like your own employees. In the 1990s, one of this book's authors (Anette) worked in a Danish regional bank. At that time, banks all over the country were trying to move traditional bill payments from bank branches to digital solutions (internet bank or mobile bank). To drive the transition, pricing encouraged customers to make payments digitally (which was free) instead of standing in line in the branch, which was both expensive and slow. As fewer and fewer people wanted to pay bills in the branch, it was decided to perform the service from just one location. Customers handed in their bills in their local branch, and these were sent on to the employees at the central location where a small group of people would enter the necessary information to perform the payment for the customer. This group of employees quickly realized why customers kept coming to their branch, despite the price. It was all about convenience. They found out that because employees in the local branches knew the customers well, they could automatically add names, account numbers, dates, and so on when making a payment for a customer. When the payments were centralized, the responsible group of employees found themselves without the necessary information to do their job, and spending too many hours calling branches and customers for data. Had we bothered to interview a few employees in some of the local branches that managed the most bill payments, we would have realized that a faster way of ending the old method of payments would probably have been to let the branch employees help the remaining customers learn to do transactions digitally.

Taylor and Uy (2021) also include the potential of learning from employees in their paper on company user research. We will come back to the learning from this work in Chapter 10, but a particular insight regards the possibility to draw on employees to scale up knowledge and technical expertise, for instance through workshops. They cite a seasoned service designer in a software company, who commented:

> More often than not, the problem has already been identified. People have already discussed things. I heavily rely on workshops. Like what has happened and what are the gaps that I can fulfil by reaching out.

Just like in the example above, front line employees very often know of customers' pain points. Often their knowledge does not find the way to company innovation.

What you see and what you don't

In 2022, the authors of this book carried out a short digital ethnography study for Filene Research Institute on the development of buy now, pay later (BNPL) in the USA (Broløs and Taylor, 2022b). We analysed data to identify trends and challenges as well as implications for credit unions in the US. To understand the new type of products, we first looked into a number of reports and articles on the development of the phenomenon. We learned that these solutions were developed to create easy shopping experiences for younger customers, including a low-cost credit option that did not require users to have a credit card or a traditional credit score. We also noticed that BNPL services were often described as a win–win–win solution, bringing benefits to the customers ('free' credit), the provider (more lending business) and the merchant (higher sales and greater customer loyalty).

To understand how users see the benefits of BNPL, we carried out digital ethnography of several user groups of different kinds – some of them started by the providers and some run entirely by users. One of the first things we observed was that the vast majority of the groups' members were women. The groups provide mutual support for women who are trying to meet shopping goals and smooth consumption, or when self-indulging to buy a new dress or cosmetics. The women were of different ages, not only young people.

The next thing we observed was that people would use the groups when running into pain points such as a lack of customer service. Members would turn to each other for help, often successfully. Members' posts almost invariably attract several comments from other members, who would present solutions or alternatives.

Our analysis of these discussions made it clear that customers view BNPL services as being quite distinctive, and combine multiple ones to achieve their shopping and financial goals. Rather than simply choose a BNPL service based on whether a merchant offers it, their choice of BNPL providers is dictated by a wide range of push and pull factors. A customer might use one BNPL service over another because it gives them a higher credit limit, lets them buy a specific item like a gift card, or because they have technological issues with another BNPL service. From the consumer's perspective, BNPL services are not at all homogenous; they form a varied and complex landscape. This indicates that consumers strive to get the most out of available offers. Our findings also indicate that consumers fear running up debt and prefer inexpensive and transparent credit. We were particularly surprised by the clash between our findings and the descriptions from experts and providers of customer free credit and merchant loyalty. We had the opportunity to speak to one expert who expected that customers would be loyal to one BNPL provider, rather than combining several of them.

We expect that providers and merchants are already taking advantage of the wealth of information available in the different user groups to provide ideas for innovation. Our digital ethnography describes several easy insights to draw out. First of all, many users complained that the process for returning goods (and obtaining refunds) was far from seamless, as people were often guided from the merchant to the provider and back again without any solution. Offering an easy process would add greatly to the value of the solution. Users also felt that their credit limits changed without explanation, and felt that they were not transparent enough: another issue to be solved quickly. Finally, there were signs of users looking to use BNPL to build a credit score for future use as they were very aware of the risk of getting into debt. On another note, the consumers' use of several BNPL services underlines the point that competition is increasing as many players are entering the field of BNPL.

Do we speak the same language?

For years it has been suggested that women invest less than men because they are more risk averse, and possibly less knowledgeable (Sent and van Stavern, 2019). But what if this is not the relevant discussion? Barbara Stewart used to work as an investment banker but quit because she saw a need to challenge outdated financial industry stereotypes and share positive messages about women and money. She started interviewing women about their lives and experiences with investment in a broad sense, and today has conducted close to a thousand interviews and told their stories in annual publications and in many talks around the world.

There is a lot to be learned from her work. It includes a confirmation that women's wealth and interest in investments is definitely growing. It also finds that women are probably risk aware rather than risk averse, meaning that many women are ready to take a large risk to start their own company if necessary but may not want to take large market risks to target higher profit. However, the main finding in her work relates to the concept of investment. Most people tend to consider investment in the context of stocks and bonds and related to a trade-off between risk and profit. But what if we considered investment as a much broader term? And we don't just mean investing in crypto assets. What if investment is really about making the big decisions in life on work, savings, children's education, entrepreneurship and more?

Barbara Stewart's stories about women illustrate how investment can be seen in a completely different light. Some women start a

Facebook group to meet other women with an interest in stocks and bonds (for example, Miss Moneypenny). Some women find themselves getting over a difficult divorce and having to start their investment journey by creating a crisis fund or investing in their own education. Some women choose to invest in building a start-up because they need to be able to work from home to be able to care for a disabled child. And yet other women decide to invest in sustainable community services. If this is the customer-centric way of considering investments, then the specialized investment advisers need to reconsider their ways of working to best help their customers.

This ties in nicely with the finding of our Swiss research (Broløs and Taylor, 2022a). We talked to women, and some very accomplished and professional women, about investments. They all – even well-educated women with a professional career – explained that investment was difficult to start, that they needed to learn a lot about stocks and bonds before trying and that they did not like to consult their bank adviser because they felt they were being condescended to. This led them to postpone investments such as pension savings even if there was a tax incentive to save. And it persuaded them to buy property or invest in crypto currencies instead, as these were not associated with the difficult language of market risk. This insight is not linked to a concrete innovation, but the lesson is clear. You can develop easy mobile investment solutions including educational content in understanding risk and markets. This will help many customers but some will consider that spending time learning about finances to be out of their reach or a waste of time as they are preoccupied with life's big questions. Despite the existence of helpful apps, they might greatly prefer help to take the next steps in managing their money.

Are you overlooking customer groups?

We have discussed the potential of massive data collection analysed through ML to support customer-centric innovation. We mentioned one element: that the detailed analysis of customer transaction patterns will not bring you information about non-customer behaviour. This is okay, as long as new customers have a profile similar to existing customers. But if new customers are to be found in new customer groups, the information from existing customer transactions can be misleading.

We already discussed Lisa Servon's (2017) work on payday lending in the USA. As we described, she decided to dive into the alternative finance market to understand why low-income groups would not use the financial services from incumbent banks but instead tended to turn to payday lenders and savings circles. Some expected that this was due to a lack of understanding of the solutions and fee structures. But she discovered that incumbent banks just did not offer relevant services for these people. With very slim or non-existent savings, the fees on an ordinary savings account were too expensive. And with no credit history or credit score they were not able to get a credit card or to obtain other short-term credit. In this situation, a payday lender would be the only choice. To make small, regular savings and have the possibility of getting a loan in case of an emergency (hospital treatment or a car repair), some would use savings circles (community groups saving together and using some of the savings to give loans to participants in turn). We will dig deeper into this issue in Chapter 8. Servon sets her hope on fintechs to provide low-cost digital services for these customers as existing services do not seem geared to create a viable business model.

In Chapter 3 we also described how SMEs are often underserved by banks and are looking to fintechs for more relevant and low-cost alternatives. The problem here is similar. Looking only at the transaction patterns of larger businesses, FSPs are not likely to understand how attractive services for SMEs should be developed.

Another risk in relying on innovation based on the behaviour of existing customers is missing out on identifying behavioural changes. In several studies, we have found that people very quickly adopt new financial services that offer solutions to a problem relating to everyday life. When the Danish Mobile Pay solution was introduced in 2013, the adoption rate was faster than ever seen. Introduced in May that year, Mobile Pay was downloaded 877,000 times (in a total population of 5.5 million) by the end of the year as it was accessible for all banking customers (which is almost all citizens) and allowed P2P mobile payments based on phone numbers. This illustrates that demand and habits can change very fast. At the end of 2022, adoption reached 4.4 million Danes – the eldest over 100 years of age.

One group of customers that is likely to adopt new – and different – solutions is young people. Children may listen to their parents, but even very young people find their role models in digital media and are likely to adopt solutions used by them. The small business volumes that these groups offer may not be attractive to the large incumbents but we have seen very inventive solutions developed by fintechs. In 2023, three fintechs(GoHenry, Pixpay and Acorns) targeting different age groups in different parts of the world decided to merge to serve the whole group of 6- to 18-year-olds.

GoHenry was launched in 2012 in the UK with the aim to make kids (aged 6–18) smart with money. GoHenry offers a prepaid debit card and a financial learning app. Through the app, parents and children can help kids learn about money by earning, saving, spending and donating responsibly. The In-app Money Missions learning tools offers a gamified, financial education experience with rewards for kids.

Pixpay was started in Paris, France, in 2019 and expanded to Spain in 2021. Pixpay offers a solution for teens (10–18) including a MasterCard payment card and a mobile app allowing them to pay, get paid and save – without the need to change banks. Pixpay includes agreements with merchants, allowing for discounts on shopping as well as education on money management and more. For parents, Pixpay offers a solution to monitor and support their children.

Acorns was started in Irvine, California, in 2012, offering micro-investments worldwide. Acorns allows customers to connect a debit card, credit card or checking account and to round up spare change from everyday purchases to be placed in professionally managed funds. To parents, Acorns offers the possibility of opening a savings and investment account for each of their children with as little as $5. Acorns also offers education for children and parents to learn about money and investments.

The point here is perhaps not so much what these companies offer, but rather that they are able to build business from customer groups that have traditionally been well within the grasp of incumbents through the contact with their parents.

Don't underestimate customers

As discussed in Chapters 2 and 3, there is a tendency to consider technology the main driver of financial innovation and to discuss what the best process might be to secure the adoption of technology among different customer groups. As described in Chapter 3, drivers of adoption are mainly considered to be perceived ease of use, perceived usefulness as well as demographic characteristics and environment, including people's understanding of technology and potential education. A common attitude among both FSP professionals and technology developers is that people need help and education to develop an understanding of new financial tools before really taking advantage of them. In Chapters 7 and 8 we will dive deeper into different views of financial literacy that indicate how we might be mistaken.

The authors of this book undertook a study of financial behaviour among people on low incomes in Brazil (Taylor and Broløs, 2022). We expected that low-income groups in a country with low financial literacy levels would find it challenging to work with new digital tools. Instead we found that more than 40 per cent of interviewees had three bank accounts or more – and were quite smart at using them to reduce fees paid. As we will come back to in Chapter 7, this may illustrate a need to change the definition of financial literacy. It also indicates that we should not underestimate customers' ability to manage or overcome challenges.

Understanding what you know

So far in this chapter, we have mostly discussed innovation for consumers. The principles of human insights are, however, relevant for consumers, SMEs and corporate customers as well as for innovation in the internal and strategic processes of FSPs.

In 2022, the authors of this book had the opportunity to interview a number of small US-based credit unions about their values, community base and customers, and their experiences of building partnerships to overcome the challenges of digital transformation and the need to scale (Broløs and Taylor, 2023). These credit unions are small – and sometimes very small. Many are constrained from growing because their charter is to serve local communities, defined either in terms of geography or as employees of a specific company. They were all very much aware of the advantages stemming from being close to the community they serve: by knowing most members personally, by understanding challenges brought by crises, such as inflation or the Covid-19 pandemic, and by being an important contributor to community development, such as through making donations. They did, however, speak of economic pressures to keep branches open and struggling with developing a digital platform to serve young customer groups and future customers. They also found it difficult to attract and employ well-educated and experienced employees, particularly in specialized fields like compliance, loan management and leadership. They had difficulties finding leaders willing to build future strategies as they were not able to pay competitive wages. They also found it difficult to find the time and the knowledge to discuss future strategies centred on working with community-based board members. And most felt pressured by experts and authorities to merge for scale.

Through our work with the credit unions we were able to gain many interesting insights on the development of partnerships to overcome the issues of scale and digital transformation. In the context of learning for innovation two examples stand out.

The first example relates to loan business in small organizations. Most small credit unions explained that they had difficulties expanding their loan business and realized lower revenues than possible. Many explained that they were struggling with traditional credit scoring models that would rate many members with very low scores, thereby making them eligible only for small loans. Many credit union employees were very close to their customers, and felt that they could accept slightly higher risk and ask slightly higher rates. They felt that the higher risk would be acceptable as they knew their customers were willing and able to pay the loans back. They also explained that such loans would be an advantage for customers as they would otherwise have to resort to payday lenders or loan sharks. Some interviewees explained that they had been able to put systems in place to achieve a profitable business along these lines. Towards the end of our work we were introduced to QCash, a fintech providing white label credit to 84 credit unions across the USA. The origin of QCash is actually in itself an interesting story. As Denise Wymore (at that time Market Manager at QCash) told us:

> QCash began with a simple question. Why were so many nonmembers of WSECU (then Washington State Employees Credit Union) cashing credit union member checks? When WSECU's CEO investigated, he found that many members were not only using check cashers but were also taking out payday loans and getting locked into a cycle of debt, taking on additional loans to pay for previous ones.
>
> (Broløs and Taylor, 2023)

This is a very good example of how important it is to bring your customer knowledge and understanding into services that help customers – and create profit. Here the fintech QCash helps build alternative credit scoring models that rely on an understanding of a combination of customer transactions and community knowledge.

The second example is more general in nature. So far, we have given examples of innovation springing from deep customer or community knowledge. We have also illustrated that customer understanding can manifest itself through employee insights. There are, however, other stakeholders that can be leveraged to gain a deeper knowledge of customer needs. In the case of the credit union study it was their competitors – the other small credit unions who experienced much the same challenges. In the course of our study we conducted interviews with a number of credit union executives. We also gained insights from organizations who had hosted roundtables and workshops with credit union representatives. The stories told were quite similar.

Figure 6.2 QCash – affordable loans for credit union members

"We don't turn credit unions down because they can't afford our product. If they're mission-driven and they truly want to make a difference in their community, we will figure out a way to help them."

Seth Brickman, CEO, QCash

WHAT

QCash is a Credit Union Service Organization that provides a small-dollar lending systems to credit unions. It is owned by Washington State Employees.

WHEN 2003

WHY Washington State Employees Credit Union customers were using payday loans extensively. The credit union wanted to provide members with access to more affordable loans.

BENEFITS

- Members get fast access to lower cost loans
- Members can improve their standing with their credit unions to get larger loans in the future
- Credit unions have a simple and reliable way to provide members with a much-needed service
- Access to loans encourages members to stay with their credit union

CHALLENGES

- How to enable credit unions to provide loans to non-members
- Integration with digital banking services

WHERE TO NEXT

- QCash will continue to work closely with credit unions to develop ways to meet members' needs and give them a better experience.
- They will also explore ways that credit unions can offer QCash loans in the process of acquiring new members.

SOURCE Broløs and Taylor, 2023

Leaders of small credit unions often feel that their organizations are overlooked and underestimated, not only by supervisory authorities and larger bank competitors but also by the wider credit union community, including sometimes their own trade organizations. Although they may be stable or even flourishing financially, small credit unions are met by peers and regulators with assumptions that they are underperforming and not innovative. These organizations may also lack the arguments and power to express their potential and particular strengths (Broløs and Taylor, 2023).

Sharing stories and challenges led to a sharing of ideas and, in some cases, also to collaborations in order to realize common benefits. We mentioned the example of QCash. Similarly, another group of credit unions explained how they came to collaborate to exchange their IT infrastructure. As Thomas O'Shea, former CEO of Aspire (one of the credit unions involved), told us:

> We were all in a position where we needed a new core. We wanted to leave the legacy systems that we were on and find something newer and more modern. And we felt that by collaborating, we'd have a [level of] scale where we could negotiate better with the vendors and also afford a level of technology that we individually couldn't on our own.
>
> (Broløs and Taylor, 2023: 31–32)

The main takeaway from our study of credit unions is that sharing challenges with competitors can provide an organization with a 'mirror' to understand its own strengths and potential. In the case of the small credit unions the mirror revealed similar small credit unions experiencing the same issue. This helped them realized that there is a strength and potential strategy in simply building on the credit union background of serving communities. The strategy would be to build new partnerships and collaborations for success.

Innovating with partners: Adopting customer knowledge from others

As already described in Chapter 3, we increasingly see partnerships in finance and particularly partnerships between fintech start-ups and incumbent FSPs. In many cases such collaboration takes advantage of the fact that fintech start-ups are building their business models on solutions that solve specific customer problems or pain points.

By adding a fintech product to the customer offer it is often possible to provide better, cheaper or more relevant solutions to both existing customer groups and to new customers. We already mentioned Dreams and their savings white label offer in Chapter 3. Another solution is Limitless, a company that helps young people manage their finances and identify potential savings for investment. This is actually done through data analytics of customers' economic status through the data in their bank accounts (connecting all bank accounts). Limitless also provides a white label solution allowing FSPs to provide this micro savings service to their customers. In this way they can make use of Limitless' understanding of young people's finances and wishes for saving. Whether this results in customer retention or customer acquisition for the banks will depend on how well the savings solution is connected to the broader customer services.

There are other ways of innovating in collaboration with partners. One is used by most big players in the market through the establishment of hubs or labs where company innovation employees can work with start-ups. This can help start-ups develop their business models and it can of course lead to new partnerships. However, here we are concerned with the effect on FSP customer knowledge. Allowing employee specialists to work in the innovative environment of enthusiastic start-ups can affect both their understanding of innovation and potential development of customer services in the FSP. One of the authors of this book (Anette) had the opportunity to interview the leaders of an early hub in a major Nordic bank. He stressed that one of the major results was actually the creation of more innovative and customer-centric employees.

Some FSPs have created future learning partnerships sharing ideas and potential with many different types of partners. One example out of a growing number is the insurance company AXA with its initiative called 'Next' (AXA, no date). AXA Next is an ecosystem comprising six units to accelerate innovation under the heading of the AXA Group purpose 'to act for human progress by protecting what matters'. The units are Business Innovation Centre, AXA Climate,

Maestro Health, AXA Ventures Partners, AXA Partners and Global Enterprise Management. AXA Next focuses on business-to-business (B2B) initiatives in collaboration with AXA insurance entities, third-party partners, ventures, affinity communities and public authorities. The work is undertaken through projects, services, partnerships, technologies and investments all intended to:

- tackle emerging global risks
- replicate and scale innovative solutions for populations and communities
- radically improve and simplify customers' experiences

City Ventures Studio develops new products and services that drive economic vitality for people and communities. The approach is based on understanding, collaborating and building for the future. Understanding is created through the analysis of technological, behavioural and societal trends to drive change. Collaboration includes partners across the innovation ecosystem and universities and within a city's own organization to develop shared expertise and creative solutions. Finally, building involves the incubation of new products to drive economic vitality and change the lives of people and communities. This part also involves the creation of a free data-driven platform that provides investors with tools and information about local demographics, social needs and investment funds for impact.

Ways of learning

In Chapter 3 we shared examples of how learning from customer observation and interviews can be integrated into innovation and the development of new offers. Hiveonline, Dreams and Starling Bank were the examples. As we saw, Dreams based their development of the savings app on the combination of basic customer knowledge from the company and expert knowledge on behavioural science. Starling Bank is using open customer communication to obtain ideas for adjustments to their account solutions. They analyse customer complaints and customer suggestions to identify potential new offerings.

Hiveonline has a different story. The company develops financial blockchain-based software. The founder and employees are also involved in the United Nations' work on financial inclusion. A great example of their work can be found in a paper on the work that went into the development of a savings and loan app for low-income groups in Niger (Amars and Blakstad, 2018). Instead of introducing new technology and following its adoption among different groups, they turned the process on its head and worked with community groups to develop digital software to support existing village savings and loan associations (VSLAs). In Niger the VSLAs were introduced as community development aids by an international NGO, CARE, during the 1990. VSLAs are groups formed by members who meet regularly with a commitment to save money. As savings grow members can take turns to have a loan either in case of a crisis situation or for investments. Logs of savings and loans are usually kept on paper by a trusted member. This way of working limits the scaling potential and also the size of the loans possible. Hiveonline's app allows this whole process to happen digitally. It was built based on interviews and observations using onsite employees who spoke the local language.

The fact that developers took the time to stay in the community to observe practices and pain points allowed the development of a solution that fitted community needs. The solution works on a blockchain backbone that works both online and offline work and allows automatic systems updates. The front end is shaped to support local conditions including support for local Nigerian languages. It supports the use of feature phones predominant at the time of development and features a user interface that keeps data charges low. It was adjusted with a special font size that is satisfactory to local users. The app updates savings after each transaction just like the pen and paper example would. In extension, however, it offers the opportunity to build an alternative credit score for the participating members based on transaction patterns, which is a good example of how digital quantitative data can be put efficiently to use in the right context. Working on the same digital platform further allows several VSLA groups to join together, providing members with broader possibilities for loans while still keeping transactions within the trusted system of the community.

The importance of understanding the context

Through the stories we have gained insights into situations where qualitative studies are likely to contribute the most:

- When several factors are driving customer satisfaction with a solution, observations are key to understanding what is most important – and why. If you do a survey to measure preferences, customers may answer the way they think is most correct (that safety is all-important or that they are careful spenders). However, as we saw in the Swiss study, convenience may win in real life.
- When developers are keen to introduce new technologies in broader settings, they may set their hopes on introducing the most advanced model in combination with education. Sometimes this will fail because they are not aware of customer pain points or customer workarounds.
- Customers are likely to combine solutions and change their patterns of use over time.
- Similarly, the introduction of a new digital solution (like a trading app) may have all the advantages of easy evaluation and learning about stock markets. It may, however, still miss customers who consider investment in a broader context. Here, qualitative studies can be extremely useful to gain insights into underlying drivers.
- As mentioned, data-driven innovation based on insights from customer spending and transaction patterns can be extremely useful as long as customers in the target groups are the same customers or have similar profiles. When you innovate to target new markets or to develop more inclusive solutions, qualitative research will provide a great help in understanding the behaviour and needs of the new groups.
- Our examples illustrate the potential of combining quantitative insights with qualitative understanding. We included the example of new insights gained from BNPL customer groups and customer conversations. We also included the examples of QCash and

Hiveonline, who build innovative solutions based on deep customer knowledge and field immersion.

- Even more importantly, qualitative studies will help understand changing patterns in behaviour. If competitors introduce alternative solutions (like, for instance, a retailer offering a loyalty programme based on a retail payment solution that can connect spending and savings habits with the shopping experience), it may very quickly change customer behaviours – and customer expectations. When this happens, existing measurements may become obsolete. We mentioned young people as an important customer group – alongside SMEs on the business side.
- Qualitative studies will further be important when a change in business model or strategy requires new perspectives. In this case there is much to be learned not only from customers but also from partners and competitors. This could be done with one-off initiatives or be part of a continued development of 'future preparedness' through scenario thinking.

Designing financial services

At a broader level, this learning is useful for the design of financial services. In Chapter 3 we introduced user-driven innovation as a way of creating solutions based on customer needs and input, and in some cases also on customer participation. The stories above show how important it is to understand customers (both consumers and businesses). One way of doing this is through design thinking.

Design thinking is a human-centred approach to problem solving drawing from the designer's toolkit to integrate the needs of people, the possibilities of technology and the requirements for business success. The concept builds theories of user-centred design and participatory design and is often related to Tim Brown's 'Design thinking' article from 2008.

As an innovation practice, design thinking is focused on the end user of services. This is based on trying to better understand customer needs and behaviours as seen from their perspective – essentially an empathy exercise. This allows learning from customers to develop new initiatives relevant in practice. Oliver Wyman (2017) describe how this is different from a data driven approach. As they put it:

> Research that relies exclusively on data (rather than incorporating subjective elements like empathy) may allow one to know the facts (what the customers did and when they did it), but it does not reveal the rationale and mechanisms driving these actions.

Further, design thinking is a team effort put in a stimulating environment that promotes new ideas. This also allows design thinking to include a diverse group in the problem solving – including people who may not be experts in the particular field but who bring new thinking to the process. This leads to an iterative process of inspiration, ideation and implementation.

We have not found many examples in finance although Oliver Wyman (2017) mentions cases from Capital One, Bank of America, Auckland Savings Bank and OCBC Bank, though these are not recent. One reason might be that the introduction of design thinking as a main innovation strategy necessitates a culture change towards an ongoing open ideation. Taylor and Uy (2021) go into some of the barriers that may appear as organizations add user research and design thinking to their innovation process. We will come back to these insights in Chapter 10 to discuss ways of organizing customer insights and ideas in order to combine data-driven insights with human perspectives.

Where can qualitative studies contribute the most?

Throughout the book we show how qualitative studies can help understand the complexity of human behaviour and decision-making in different contexts. In this chapter we have shared different examples of innovation or innovation potential based on taking the time to understand customer situations and needs. We have also shown how technology and data can drive innovation when based on a deep understanding of the customer communities. In the following chapter we turn to the problem of financial inclusion to show how such knowledge can be applied to people on low incomes in diverse cultures around the world.

TAKEAWAYS

- Qualitative studies provide insights for innovation that might otherwise be overlooked.
- Qualitative studies can help to innovate smartly with new technology.
- Qualitative insights can help to identify overlooked customer groups.
- Customer knowledge can come directly from customers, partners or competitors.
- One way of bringing customer knowledge into play in a digital age is through design thinking.

References

Amars, L and Blakstad, S (2018) Digitizing VSLAs: Rethinking financial inclusion for the poor, Hiveonline. www.hivenetwork.online/digitizing-vslas (archived at https://perma.cc/A5G9-96LP)

AXA (no date) Innovation to better protect our customers, AXA. www.axa.com/en/about-us/innovation#tab=axa-next (archived at https://perma.cc/ZJ9N-P279)

Broløs, A and Taylor, E (2022a) *Female Finance on the Move: Switzerland*, EWPN, Keen Innovation and Unblu. ewpn.eu/research-network/white-papers-reports/female-finance-on-the-move-switzerland (archived at https://perma.cc/E4TN-AF5E)

Broløs, A and Taylor, E B (2022b) *Buy Now, Pay Later: Understanding consumer behavior*, Filene Research Institute No 550. www.filene.org/reports/buy-now-pay-later-understanding-consumer-behavior (archived at https://perma.cc/Y8L2-NJ4S)

Broløs, A and Taylor, E B (2023) *Small Credit Union Collaboration: Sharing knowledge, services and people in a digital economy*, Filene Research Institute No 575. www.filene.org/reports/small-credit-union-collaboration-sharing-knowledge-services-and-people-in-a-digital-economy

Brown, T (2008) Design thinking, *Harvard Business Review*, June. hbr.org/2008/06/design-thinking (archived at https://perma.cc/W7WM-6LXD)

Narula, N, Swartz, L and Frizzo-Barker, J (2023) CBDC: Expanding financial inclusion or deepening the divide? Exploring design choices that could make a difference, MIT. dci.mit.edu/cbdc-fi-1 (archived at https://perma.cc/9Z45-7GRV)

Oliver Wyman (2017) Design thinking: The new DNA of the financial sector, Oliver Wyman and IESE Business School, University of Navarra. www.oliverwyman.com/our-expertise/insights/2017/apr/design-thinking-the-new-dna-of-the-financial-sector.html (archived at https://perma.cc/L8X7-28H2)

Sent, E M and van Staveren, I (2019) A feminist review of behavioral economic research on gender differences, *Feminist Economics*, 25 (2), 1–35

Servon, L (2017) *The Unbanking of America: How the new middle class survives*, Houghton Mifflin Harcourt, New York

Stewart, B (2020) A decade of rich thinking, Barbara Stewart. www.barbarastewart.ca/richthinking.html (archived at https://perma.cc/RV2A-V7M2)

Taylor, E B and Broløs, A (2022) *Money and Payments in Low Income Brazil*, Finthropology/SICPA

Taylor, E B and Uy, M T (2021) *Better Research, Better Design: How to align teams and build a human-centric company culture*, American Anthropological Association, Arlington, VA

Financial inclusion 07

Myths and workarounds

A book about customer-centricity in finance would be remiss not to discuss the important issue of financial inclusion. Indeed, so far in this book we have described a number of cases of financial inclusion research, including Lisa Servon's research in the USA and our own research in Haiti. But we haven't yet mentioned the term 'financial inclusion' or attempted to discuss it in any systematic way. Why not?

We took this approach because we believe that being client-centric means starting with people, not problems. People on low incomes do not primarily define themselves in terms of financial inclusion or exclusion. Rather, their concerns are more about making ends meet, caring for their families, planning for the future and dealing with unexpected shocks.

Financial inclusion does, however, have a significant effect on people on low incomes in particular, and so this will be our focus in this chapter and the following one. It is a critical subject for this book because it represents a collective global focus on providing better financial services to all. This is an important goal indeed, and one that the international community has been working on successfully for many decades. Mobile solutions are expanding financial reach and contributing to lower transaction costs (such as saving on travel costs), access to broader markets, or access to household items online. They also help people to build small savings and obtain some access to loans. This helps people to build financial resilience, and it supports micro-entrepreneurs. As a result, the financial inclusion agenda is broadening from just a discussion of access to a financial account to securing broader financial health and well-being for all.

We have already touched on this discussion in Chapter 4 and it is definitely a subject that merits further study.

However, there are many myths and misunderstandings about what financial inclusion can and can't do (spoiler alert: it does little to reduce poverty). There are also many issues that are not discussed often enough, such as how exactly literacy affects people's ability to access and use of financial tools, the ways people manage money collectively and the innovative workarounds people develop to navigate through complex – and sometimes unreliable – financial systems. There is often too much focus on technology as a 'silver bullet' that can resolve the financial inclusion problem, and not enough discussion of people themselves. In this chapter we address some of these myths, misconceptions and missing discussions. We draw, of course, on stories about people's behaviour in the contexts in which they live.

Financial inclusion: Background and progress

Several decades ago, Muhammad Yunus launched Grameen Bank in Bangladesh. The bank took a highly innovative approach to the problem of offering credit to people on low incomes. Since the people Yunus wanted to reach had little or no access to formal financial services, and certainly no credit scores, they relied on using informal financial services offered by people living in their communities. Sometimes these services were free or very low cost; for example, saving money weekly with a neighbour. Others, such as informal loans, could be prohibitively expensive.

Yunus wanted people on low incomes to have access to more reliable credit, and at a low cost. Based on his experience as an economist working with poor communities, he believed that very small loans could make a big difference to the poorest people. In 1976 he secured a loan to start a pilot programme to lend to people living in poverty. By 1982 the pilot had 28,000 members, and in 1983 it was renamed Grameen Bank. His new bank developed a model to give loans to groups of women rather than individuals, on the assumption that a combination of social pressure and a desire to get more loans in the future would motivate individuals to pay their loans back.

Of course, Yunus was not the first, by any means, to offer financial services to people living in poverty. We mentioned the example of Nutspaarbank in the Netherlands in Chapter 1, but there are plenty of other savings banks and credit unions that have developed in wealthier countries. However, Grameen Bank was one of the earliest to serve people living in poverty in low-income countries. His model was highly successful, and launched a massive, global microfinance industry that is still thriving today. It has changed somewhat over the years: many microfinance institutions (MFIs) are focusing less on women and more on people generally, and many are now offering loans to individuals.

Moreover, today there is a much greater range of financial services for people living in poverty, and many different kinds of companies and not-for-profits providing them. As we have discussed, the microfinance movement was followed by the development of mobile money services (which do not require a smartphone) in many countries. Now that smartphones are widespread, people on low incomes are also able to access banking apps, payments wallets, store-provided platforms and a range of apps offering financial management, insurance, transfers, investments and more. Some of these are designed specifically for people on low incomes; others are accessible to everyone.

WHAT ARE 'FORMAL' FINANCIAL SERVICES AND CASH?

Formal financial services are services provided by an organization (company, NGO, government, etc.) that is registered with the government and has permission to provide financial services to end users. There is not necessarily an official definition of formal financial services, but the description here is what is commonly used. Organizations will generally be regulated and supervised. Examples include banks, credit unions, insurance companies, payments services, pawnbrokers, payday lenders and some groups of rotating credit and savings associations (ROSCAS). Formal financial services can, however, be used in informal ways, like people using another person's account or credit card.

Informal financial services are not subject to regulation or even registration. They include loans from friends and family. Many ROSCAS belong in this category as they are started informally by local communities and are self-organized, setting their own rules and procedures. Some crypto services qualify here as well.

Cash is more tricky to define. Technically, cash is a formal financial service, since it is provided and regulated by the government. However, once cash is in circulation, people use it in very informal ways. Indeed, cash is the favoured payment mechanism of the informal economy, since it cannot be easily tracked.

There is no doubt that a combination of dedicated innovation, design thinking and hard work has had a massive impact on financial inclusion worldwide. But what does this all mean? What is financial inclusion, anyway? And has it really improved the lives of people on low incomes?

We ask this question because we feel that there is much more that financial services can do to help people who are in some way excluded or marginalized. These include not only people living in poverty, but also women, youth, elderly people, refugees and lesser-abled people. These people do not only live in the Global South – they exist everywhere. We will come back to them in Chapter 8. For now, we would like to explain the premises of financial inclusion, bust some myths that have been circulating during the past few decades, and provide a better sense of the realities of the people using services built for financial inclusion.

This rapid growth in the availability of financial services is reflected in financial inclusion figures from the Global Findex Database 2021 (adults are defined as people aged 15+). From 2011 to 2021, the number of adults who own a formal account rose from 51 per cent to 76 per cent. In 2021, 86 per cent owned a mobile phone, and 63 per cent had access to the internet. In 2021, 64 per cent per cent of adults made a digital payment, compared with 44 per cent in 2014.

Broadly speaking, financial inclusion is usually defined as the ability of people to have regular and reliable access to formal financial services, especially to save money, make payments and access credit. The World Bank defines 'financial inclusion' as follows:

> Financial inclusion means that individuals and businesses have access to useful and affordable financial products and services that meet their needs – transactions, payments, savings, credit and insurance – delivered in a responsible and sustainable way.
>
> (World Bank, no date, a)

To be accessible, financial service access points need to be within geographic reach, be affordable, be available most of the time and be reliable. This means that infrastructure is incredibly important: even if people have mobile money services on their phone, they are not accessible if people aren't able to charge their phones regularly, can't access a mobile signal, can't cash out at an agent, and so on. These issues are well-known, and the international development community, along with national service providers, have been working hard on resolving them, with considerable success (though there are still many gaps in service).

This definition of financial inclusion tends to characterize people as being either included or excluded. However, it is clear from the extensive literature on the topic, and from our own studies, that people can be included or excluded in different ways.

Unserved

There are still around 1.4 billion people without access to any kind of formal account (bank account or mobile finance). We could call this group 'unserved', and they are the ones referred to in the figures for financial exclusion. They may use remittance services or ask a family member to make a financial transaction for them, but they do not have their own accounts. They overwhelmingly transact in cash, and they probably use a range of informal financial services, such as savings associations or money lenders.

Why are so many people still excluded from formal financial services? Reasons may include:

- lack of connectivity (electricity, internet and more)
- lack of financial infrastructure, including bank branches, agents and smartphones (geography)
- lack of identity documentation
- low income and little money to manage
- living in a cash-based environment (though this is falling fast)
- services are too expensive (fees)
- services are not designed to support the needs of these groups
    - fees are too high and too frequent
    - don't go the 'last mile' where agents would often be the best solution
    - don't provide services that work for small amounts (small short-term loans and savings)
    - don't work offline
    - don't offer services for families or communities (instead of individuals)

People who are unserved tend to live in remote, rural areas, and probably have little need for formal financial services as cash fulfils most needs for payments, savings and even small loans. This group is, however, shrinking fast as infrastructure improves, mobile phones spread and services become cheaper and more reliable.

Underserved

Globally there is also a large group of people who have access to financial services but have no real use for them, as services are not designed to fit their reality. They are often called 'underserved' because traditional financial services are not really designed with their needs in mind. Similar to the unserved group, problems may include:

- fees are too high and too frequent
- services do not work for small transactions (small short-term loans and savings)
- services are aimed at individuals rather than families or communities

Such people may have access to formal financial services, but use them infrequently. For example, there are many people globally who sign up for mobile money accounts or bank accounts as they were offered an incentive to do so (such as a cash bonus for opening an account), but they soon stop using the service. Other people may not use formal financial services because they live in a society where most transactions are in cash. For such people, there is often no point in depositing money into an account, only to withdraw it again to pay others in cash. Indeed, sometimes what people lack is not financial services, but money to run through them, either in terms of depositing money or receiving it from someone. Many people in this group may well begin using formal financial services if they begin to offer benefits over cash. For example, the payments service Pix in Brazil gained widespread traction because there are no transaction fees. In other countries, people prefer paying in cash because it is free to transfer.

Poorly served

Finally, there are groups that have access to financial services and who can use them but don't feel comfortable working with existing solutions. That is to say, they use financial services such as accounts and credit cards but don't feel that the features that they want are available. We call these 'poorly served'. In our research into financial services for women, we have seen that many people who are poorly served are, indeed, women. Other groups such as young people, elderly or handicapped people can fall into this group as well. Some of the services that these groups lack are quite simple, such as the possibility to cap the spending on a card or an account. Other issues could be:

- sharing a card or an account
- ways to build a credit score without risking getting a credit card into overdraft
- ways to save or invest small amounts of money on a daily or regular basis

- sustainable solutions
- ways to learn and share the experience with others
- sharing spending or saving goals with others

But why is it that these groups are not included? As can be seen, part of the reason has been that infrastructure and connectivity have been an issue. In some countries these are improved by governments who view them as public services, but in others countries this has not happened as much. The digital and mobile transformation is helping by providing solutions to infrastructure, to smart mobile services and lower cost of services. However, there is still a need to develop suitable and inexpensive services for low-income groups who may not be profitable for traditional providers.

Most importantly for our purposes, financial inclusion highlights just how much inclusion depends equally on accessibility and design. The best-designed apps for people on low incomes will be of no use if people are not able to use them. Financial inclusion therefore demands systemic thinking as well as design thinking. This makes it even more important to understand the myths and realities we are dealing with when innovating for financial inclusion.

Myths and realities

There are several myths that have prevailed throughout financial inclusion's short history. Here we will mention a handful of them: the extent to which financial inclusion requires formal services (and, increasingly, digital ones!), the benefits of financial inclusion, the difference between access and usage, assumptions about what it takes to make the system work and myths regarding literacy. These issues are fairly well understood among professionals working on financial inclusion issues, but many are not widely discussed, and there is little written that tries to explore how these issues can be leveraged to create new innovations. This is our (perhaps ambitious) goal in this chapter and the following one.

Myth 1: Financial inclusion reduces poverty

Financial inclusion can have many positive impacts on people on low incomes, but they are not always what might be expected. Contrary to popular belief, financial inclusion has little effect on poverty reduction. In particular, access to credit – often touted as the most beneficial kind of financial inclusion – has mixed effects. An extensive review article (Duvendack and Mader, 2020) explains that while microcredit certainly provides benefits to some (such as allowing people to start a business or pay school fees) it rarely lifts people out of poverty, and indeed some people get trapped in debt cycles and end up poorer. Instead, decades of analysis reveal that microsavings (accounts designed for small deposits) provide the most consistently positive impact, since they provide benefits with few risks. Access to financial services can also help increase people's incomes, either through receiving remittances or simply by making it easier for people to pay each other.

Moreover, the World Bank finds evidence that the use of financial accounts (with a bank, MFI or mobile money provider) supports the development towards broader use of financial tools including saving, borrowing and insurance. This helps people to increase their financial resilience and counteract issues of not being able to manage aspects such as unemployment, medical bills or school fees.

We would also add that financial inclusion can substantially reduce people's stress and make their lives easier – two benefits whose importance cannot be understated. The benefits of financial inclusion for reducing 'transaction costs' (usually defined as the time a person spends completing a task) have been noted extensively by researchers working in many different countries. Our research participants in rural Brazil particularly appreciated the arrival of the payments platform Pix because it meant they did not have to travel to town to withdraw cash as frequently. Saving people time and effort can greatly reduce stress because people are often juggling many different activities and struggle to complete them all.

This is particularly evident among people who are very poor or lack basic infrastructure such as paved roads, reliable telecommunications and labour-saving devices at home. For example, in Haiti it is common for women to work as traders, selling fruits and vegetables or durable goods. They often travel extensively, perhaps hundreds of kilometres, to buy goods at wholesale prices from urban centres. Yet they are also the main caretakers for their families. We interviewed women who woke up at 5am, cooked their family's food for the day on an open fire, and spent the entire day trading. On days they were selling they returned home after dark, but when they travelled to buy good they were often absent for several days at a time, sometimes sleeping in the wholesale warehouses where they bought goods. Carrying cash induced stress as it was a security risk, and sending cash was very slow. Mobile money made it safer to carry funds and meant women could more easily receive payments for goods or remittances, or send money to their families.

Myth 2: Formal financial services are inclusive, informal ones are not

There is no doubt that access to formal financial services fosters inclusion. First, being able to use formal financial services helps include people in the broader economy beyond their own locality, for example being able to send and receive money. Second, access to financial services helps people manage their money better by providing safer savings services (in a bank rather than under the mattress), access to credit (to invest or smooth consumption), and so on. Moreover, economic and financial inclusion can also foster social inclusion by helping migrants contribute to community events back home, making it easier for family members to support each other.

However, it is often assumed that people who do not have access to formal financial services are 'excluded', full stop. The book *Portfolios of the Poor* (Ruthven et al, 2009) and countless other studies show conclusively that this is not the case. As we briefly described above, people without access to formal financial services draw on a wide range of informal services that allow them to participate in the economy and society. Indeed, there is no such thing as a 100 per cent formal banking system anywhere in the world: we (almost) all use cash, take loans from family members and provide mutual insurance (such as helping fix a neighbour's roof after a storm). Similarly, nobody is 100 per cent financially excluded. This kind of inclusion should be recognized, not discarded, because it forms an important back-stop even in places where formal financial inclusion levels are high.

Indeed, as shown in the two CBDC projects we have worked on (Narula et al, 2023; Taylor and Broløs, 2022), cash can be more inclusive than financial services, since there are no barriers to using it. In Brazil, while the new payments platform Pix has achieved widespread adoption, it does exclude some people. It is not possible to use Pix without a bank account or other payments platform account (such as MercadoPay), and to open such an account one must have Brazilian identification and a tax file number. There are still some Brazilians who lack such documentation, plus there are likely a large number of immigrants (documented or undocumented) who cannot use the system either. Cash, however, can be used by anyone. When designing CBDCs, central banks should consider how much they want CBDCs to maintain the inclusiveness of cash.

Another example comes from research we carried out in the Philippines in 2023, in which we looked at how farmers were using digital financial tools and sales tools. Although almost all of the farmers we interviewed own smartphones, they were not directly using payments systems like GCash because they either did not trust them or they found the interface too confusing. If they absolutely needed to pay someone digitally they would ask one of their children to do the transaction for them. Otherwise, they used cash for all other transactions.

Myth 3: Access is a good measure of inclusion

Fortunately, few (if any) people actually believe in this myth any more, but nonetheless it's worth mentioning because it demonstrates how careful we need to be when we try to measure things. The myth is that the best way to measure financial inclusion is to look at how many people have access to financial services. The most commonly cited figure from the Global Findex Database is the one we also cited above – how many people 'own' an account at a bank, MFI, mobile money provider or perhaps a payments platform. But this figure is misleading, since it doesn't tell us how many people actually use the services regularly. Recognizing this, the Global Findex Database added questions to their 2021 survey about frequency of use. For example, in 2021 it found that 25 per cent deposited money in a financial institution at least once per month, and 35 per cent withdrew money with the same frequency.

Another less recognized problem with measuring inclusion is the fact that there may be a substantial number of people who do not have their own formal account, but who use the accounts of other people. In 2021 the Global Findex Database included a question on this: 'No account because someone in the family has one (% age 15+, no account)'. In developing countries, 29 per cent of people without an account chose this answer. This means that many people are actually using formal financial services indirectly, and so the number of financially included people may be higher than assumed.

Throughout our research in different countries we have seen many examples of people using other people's accounts. In Brazil we encountered people selling on the street who would use a Pix account to receive payment even though they did not have a mobile phone of their own. One man selling wooden carvings would hand customers a piece of paper with his mother's Pix number written on it. They would make the transaction on their phone and then show him the 'approved' screen. Later, his mother would give him cash.

But sharing accounts isn't just done by people with no accounts and no phones of their own. Also in Brazil, we found spouses using each other's bank cards to the extent that they would forget which card belonged to which one of them. Even people who are already financially included may have a far more extensive 'financial portfolio' than we realize. Statistical measurements are very helpful for building a global picture. But if we want to understand how people experience financial inclusion, and the extent to which they use financial services, then we need to look at the micro level and particularly at how people cooperate.

Myth 4: Technology works, but people don't know how to use it

Technological innovation has played an immensely important role in promoting financial inclusion. The spread of mobile phones (analogue and smart) has allowed financial services like banking systems, mobile money and now smartphone-based apps to be rolled out at low cost to billions of people. Many of these technology-based services, such as mobile money or payment cards, have been designed to be as simple to use as possible, since they are meant to serve people who are poor and who may not be used to using technology. As more financial services are available on smartphones, interfaces are becoming more complicated, and this increases the difficulties people face in learning to use new financial services. In most cases (but not all), people tend to overcome these barriers fairly quickly. Often, young urban people are the 'early adopters' who then teach their parents and others to use technology. As described in Chapter 3, perceived usefulness and perceived ease of use are key in the adoption of new technology but in the end adoption is a question of the appropriation in a community and context – an area where we need more research.

A bigger problem than technological literacy is technological or infrastructural failure. These are not always reliable, especially in low-income countries or remote areas where infrastructure is difficult to maintain. There are many ways in which technology can fail. For example, software glitches are quite common. Many participants in our Brazil research told us stories about how they had tried to send money but had received an error message. In terms of infrastructure, telecommunications signals may be slow or unreliable, impeding transactions. In Haiti we observed long queues of people outside banks. They would sometimes spend hours waiting to be served, only to find when they got to the front of the queue that the bank had lost connection. In many low-income countries or rural regions, electricity blackouts are common, and if one occurs during a transaction then the transaction may fail.

Finally, technology may not be readily accessible, such as when an ATM is inside a shop and only accessible during business hours. In other cases, mobile network coverage may be poor, necessitating solutions that involve customers transacting with human agents (such as a mobile money agent helping a customer deposit cash in their mobile account). One example of this comes from a study of e-payment solutions in Uganda (CGAP/World Bank, 2013). The report describes a pilot to pay senior citizens a social assistance grant through a mobile network operator, MTN. Unfortunately, MTN's network coverage was limited in the areas where people lived, so agents had to travel to the field with a mobile device. Recipients had a SIM-embedded card that they inserted in the machine to confirm their cash grant was due, and then received the money in cash.

Myth 5: Literacy is a barrier to financial inclusion

Literacy is often discussed as a problem with respect to financial inclusion – and it certainly is in some ways. People with low levels of literacy are less likely to use formal financial services, and are more likely to struggle with them when they do use them. However, like financial inclusion, financial literacy is very difficult to measure. The results of standard national tests are not likely to give us much insight into what people actually struggle with in their everyday lives. A lack of knowledge of investment principles or mortgage types is not going to matter much to people who don't invest or don't have a mortgage. We therefore need to ensure that our assessments of financial literacy are relevant to people's everyday needs.

It can be helpful to differentiate between 'financial literacy' and 'financial capability', two terms that are often used interchangeably. According to the World Bank (2014), 'financial literacy' measures aptitude in understanding personal finance and awareness of key concepts. In contrast, financial capability is:

> the internal capacity to act in one's best financial interest, given socioeconomic environmental conditions. Financial capability encompasses the knowledge, attitudes, skills, and behaviours of consumers with regard to managing their resources and understanding, selecting, and making use of financial services that fit their needs.

Generally, the financial capability that people on low incomes need is similar to what everyone needs: an understanding of how to budget, the kinds of fees that can occur, how to save, rules around credit especially as these can get people into trouble the most. Often, people on low incomes are highly adept at managing their everyday finances – indeed, they have to be, since they have few resources to fall back on. In Brazil we found that many of our interviewees had got into debt when they were younger, and as a result had learned to avoid credit and plan better. They were highly knowledgeable about bank fees and the prices of everyday goods, and knew how to budget.

Our research in Haiti made it clear that it's necessary to distinguish between different kinds of literacy: financial, textual, numerical or technological. At the time of research (2010–12), many Haitians had low levels of textual literacy, but all were numerate. This meant that the design of mobile money services mattered: the easiest interfaces to use included short menus with little text. It was not uncommon for people who could not read to be able to remember the order of operations they needed to complete a transaction and undertake it successfully.

Finally, as we have discussed several times, people help each other use financial tools, especially among family members (Taylor and Horst, 2018). In Haiti, if people got stuck using mobile money they would generally ask a relative or neighbour to help them. In order for a household to achieve financial inclusion, it may not be necessary for all household members to have adequate literacy levels, although this would of course be ideal.

Human workarounds

The myths we have outlined demonstrate that the problems people face are not always the ones that we assume they face. This means that there is often a mismatch between how financial services and the systems that deliver them are designed and implemented, versus what people actually want or need.

How do people respond to this mismatch? They develop what we call 'human workarounds'. Whether dealing with software failure, inconvenient bank opening times, poor design thinking or expensive fees, people are immensely creative in making financial systems work for them. That is to say, when it comes to financial inclusion, people are skilled at including themselves in less-than-ideal systems. We could call this 'DIY financial inclusion'.

The workarounds people implement differ depending on the type of problem, the context, availability of other financial solutions, and many more factors. Different kinds of users (such as end users, merchants, FSP agents, etc.) will, of course, face different problems, and come up with different solutions. In this section we highlight some of the interesting variety of workarounds we have encountered in our own and other people's research.

Technological/infrastructural failures

As we mentioned in our myth-busting above, technology and infrastructure are not always adequate. What do people do when technology and infrastructure fail them? It isn't always feasible to wait for software bugs to be resolved or for the internet to come back online. People have bills to pay, things to buy and fees to avoid.

For example, one of our interviewees in rural Brazil explained to us that the internet service in her area is unreliable. If her credit card payment is due and the internet isn't working, she has to drive to town and go to the bank to pay at the ATM or inside the bank. Such a workaround accrues substantial transaction costs: it takes time and effort out of her busy day to resolve the problem.

In urban Brazil, several interviewees told us that they had experienced problems making transactions with Pix due to either bugs or an unreliable internet connection (Taylor and Broløs, 2022). For example, Anderson, a public servant in the countryside, accidentally duplicated a payment when transferring with Pix:

> I already had a problem with Pix. For example, I made a transfer to a supplier via Pix, the system crashed and the bank did not complete it. I logged in again and made the transfer. Within half an hour the other

> transfer had gone down and was accepted as well. So I paid double. I called the bank and said that the system crashed. I would like to resolve that. He [the bank] said that for Pix they are not responsible. I would have to call the supplier and he would refund it. But only judicially will you get any response from the bank. But there was a bank error, it can't be that way, they would have to give a return because it was a system error. It can't be that way. Accepted the double payment. They said they would have to contact the beneficiary.
>
> (Taylor and Broløs, 2022: 39)

Anderson eventually got his money back, but he had to contact the recipient directly to transfer the money back to him. This is not only a technological problem, it is also due to the fact that Pix does not have a service layer to resolve customer problems.

Service limitations

Sometimes people face issues due to a limitation of the service provided. One common issue is distance: the nearest service point of a financial service provider is a long way away. Other issues include inconvenient branch opening hours, ATMs being only accessible within opening hours, or human agents making mistakes.

Of course, technology often provides a solution to problems of distance. In our research in rural Brazil, so long as the internet and electricity were working, the ability to make transactions via Pix meant that people didn't have to travel to town. But globally there are still many people living in rural areas where services are inadequate – digital or otherwise. In many places around the world, in villages with no local remittance services it is common for one person to travel to town to collect remittances on behalf of multiple village residents (see Crucifix, 2022).

Sometimes issues of trust also affect how people handle remittances. In Mexico, Bernardo Bátiz-Lazo and Ignacio González-Correa (cited in Narula et al, 2023) conducted research on remittances from Mexicans working in the United States to their families in Mexico. They note that their interviewees often preferred cash transactions as they had had bad experiences with banks and fintech platforms. In particular, the fee structures can be confusing and change often. To keep transactions as cash-based as possible, people would deposit cash with a remittance service, and it would be withdrawn as cash at the other end.

Service issues also arise with accessing cash. In another study in Mexico, Clément Crucifix (2022) notes that in the town of El Progreso in the state of Puebla the only financial service provider available is an MFI that has limited opening hours and a limited supply of cash. If a person wants to withdraw a sizable amount of money they need to notify the MFI in advance. They overcome lack of access to cash by getting help from friends and family who regularly travel to the city, where cash is more readily available.

Lack of functionality

Another issue commonly encountered is when financial services do not meet people's needs and preferences. In our digital ethnography of BNPL services in the USA (Broløs and Taylor, 2022), we found that many customers wished to buy gift cards on BNPL, but that not all BNPL services allowed people to do so. Customers used a Facebook forum to talk with other customers and find out which BNPL services allowed gift card purchases. The gift card was itself a workaround, since customers would use BNPL to buy a gift card from one store, then use the gift card to shop in another store that didn't offer BNPL.

Back in Mexico, Crucifix gives a great example of a lack of privacy considerations that can compel people to find alternative ways to use financial services. Paola lives in El Progreso in Mexico and receives remittances from her brothers in the United States. She could easily withdraw the remittances from the bank branch in the village, but instead she prefers to travel to a neighbouring village. When Crucifix asked her why she did this, she explained that she believes the bank teller will tell others that Paola had received more money from the United States. In the absence of a digital solution, Paula prefers to expend more effort to protect her privacy.

In Brazil, people hold accounts at multiple banks to make the most of the different functionality that the banks offer:

> The interviewees actively choose to keep fees down by using cash when this gives a price reduction. They pay with Pix or card when this is easier, like Isabela, (Persona 3) who prefers to use debit cards or Pix. They transfer money between their own accounts to avoid withdrawal fees, like Maria and Isabela (Personas 1 and 3), who creatively use their different bank accounts. They use credit cards to pay in instalments for larger purchases, or to stretch funds at the end of the month, like Maria (Persona 1), for instance, who only uses her credit card when her phone breaks or there are pressing family needs.
>
> (Taylor and Broløs, 2022: 81)

While it may seem cumbersome to manage so many bank accounts, such practices are not at all uncommon. People often hold extensive 'financial portfolios' of different products to maximize the benefits of services and make money management easier, especially when it comes to cash flow.

Fees

It should come as no surprise that people go to great lengths to avoid fees. In Brazil, one of the reasons why people have so many bank accounts is because different kinds of banks charge fees for different types of transactions. Our interviewees were generally very knowledgeable about these fees and how to avoid them as much as possible. Consider the following explanation by an interviewee:

> When I need to transfer money to someone I end up transferring it through Nubank. And I don't even transfer through Banco Itaú. I transfer the money from my Itaú account to Nubank, and from Nubank to the person.
>
> (Taylor and Broløs, 2022: 24)

To reduce the amount of fees payable, this person ensures she uses her Santander card every month, withdraws cash only from digital banks and transfers money only via her account at her traditional bank. She also uses Pix, which is free.

People also rely heavily on each other, such as by borrowing from family rather than a bank to avoid paying interest: one interviewee in Brazil borrowed from his mother-in-law to buy a car. Another interviewee, facing the same problem, told us that rather than pay to withdraw money from an ATM he will transfer money to a friend using Pix and that friend will give him the cash. In this way, people are acting as human ATMs.

Similarly, a study in Indonesia (Sandbukt, 2022) explains how people top up their e-money wallets with the help of taxi drivers who work in collaboration with the wallet providers. Customers pay the taxi driver in cash, not for the ride but for the driver to top up their wallets. The driver does this from his own balance. Customers thus avoid paying a fee to top up.

Entrepreneurs also go to great lengths to avoid fees. Also in Indonesia, Mangowal (2022) studied twelve female entrepreneurs in Jakarta. She noted that all of them maintained multiple bank accounts in order to permit customers and suppliers to transfer/receive money without paying fees. She notes, however, that this creates quite a lot of work for the entrepreneurs, and that they must also keep a minimum balance in their different accounts. Entrepreneurs are increasingly using applications like ShopeePay, DANA and Flip, which allow free transfers for a limited number of transactions per day.

Contextual circumstances

The above list is not exhaustive. There are also a large number of contextual conditions that people must work around. These could be personal circumstances, political events, the weather, and everything in between. One very common issue is the need to use cash because everyone else uses cash, even if digital services are available. We found this to be the case in our research in a direct-to-consumer fruit and vegetable market in Laos: despite the widespread availability of digital payment options, customers preferred to pay in cash, and so merchants were obliged to maintain a cash float. Since they received money in cash, they would also spend in cash, such as when buying stock from the nearby wholesale market.

Another issue is access to credit. It is common for people who have a bad credit history to take credit in another person's name. We found this to be the case in Brazil, though people were wary about letting others use their name in case they got a 'dirty name' themselves. Anthropologist Marie Kolling has conducted research on digital money and credit among people on the margins of the city and the formal economy in Salvador (Kolling, 2021). Kolling explains that credit has proliferated in recent years and that people living in poverty have far more access to it. However, maintaining access takes work. When people get a 'dirty name' and are refused credit they may find someone with a 'clean name' to borrow, such as a family member. She also describes how informal sellers extend credit to their customers, arguing that this is not just good for business, but is also an act of care. When people sell to others they know, transactions transcend financial considerations and become humanistic ones.

Finally, it would be remiss not to acknowledge that human errors can cause problems. This is particularly the case in a complex payments situation, such as when travelling. An amusing example comes from researcher Andrew Crawford (2021), who experienced problems with payments when he was living in Cambodia during the Covid-19 pandemic. He describes a comedy of errors in which he had to juggle German, Australian and Cambodian bank accounts, as well as the Cambodian mobile payments platform Wing, in order to pay for university fees and the internet, withdraw cash and send a friend money.

We could develop this list of workarounds endlessly, and we are sure our readers can think of many more of their own. For now, suffice to say that the financial system is not a flawless structure that people access passively. Instead, people are constantly inventing creative ways to make financial ends meet. We all form the 'human infrastructure' that is critical to making the financial system work. This is becoming clearer as we see the development of embedded services and should be at the centre of every innovation initiative.

Issues to consider

In this chapter our main goal has been to demonstrate that financial inclusion and financial systems do not always work in the ways we think they do. The various myths about financial inclusion demonstrate this clearly, and we hope that our discussion of workarounds proves the point: that financial inclusion is realized by the people who are being included as much as by the systems and programmes that put the instruments of financial inclusion in place.

This observation generates a range of design issues. One is that we should not assume that a given solution is the only solution: people will always combine different financial tools, and come up with new ways of doing things, in order to work around failing infrastructure, obtain the functionality they need, get around personal issues like a bad credit rating, and many more.

Another is that we need to think more about what we mean by financial literacy, and consider that people are often very highly literate, not just in their understanding of practical finances but also in their understanding of how to get things done in a given financial system. This doesn't mean we should stop making apps easy to use; rather, we should explore how to design tools that capitalize on people's sophisticated practices and creativity.

Yet another insight is that people rarely operate as individuals when it comes to making financial transactions. People's money management is highly social and highly collective, even if they technically have their own personal accounts. Yet there are few tools, besides joint bank accounts, that reflect this. Why? What can we do better? It is worth further consideration.

Finally, we should not let ourselves get carried away with technical solutions. Yes, technology can do a great deal to make people's lives easier. But many people still live in a cash-based society, and many of them have little incentive to move away from this any time soon. In most countries, hybrid systems exist in which people use cash and digital money simultaneously, according to their needs. In many circumstances (though by no means always), cash is easier and more functional than digital tools. We advocate for paying attention to the reasons why people might prefer digital or cash transactions and supporting them in their preferences, rather than trying to push people into a system that they do not want and that might not work well for them. We will discuss this further in the following chapter.

> **TAKEAWAYS**
>
> - People are not simply 'financially included' or 'financially excluded'; there are different levels of inclusion.
> - Financial inclusion doesn't necessarily reduce poverty, but it can make people's lives much easier.
> - Informal financial services can be just as inclusive as formal ones.
> - Access to financial services is not the same as usage of financial services.
> - People are an important part of the 'infrastructure' that makes financial systems work.

References

Broløs, A and Taylor, E B (2022) *Buy Now, Pay Later: Understanding consumer behavior*, Filene Research Institute No 550. www.filene.org/reports/buy-now-pay-later-understanding-consumer-behavior (archived at https://perma.cc/LZ9X-K65X)

CGAP/World Bank (2013) Electronic payments with limited infrastructure: Uganda's search for a viable e-payments solution for the social assistance grants for empowerment, CGAP. www.cgap.org/sites/default/files/eG2P_Uganda.pdf (archived at https://perma.cc/83TF-ZMTA)

Crawford, A (2021) Apo-cash-alypse Now! IMTFI, 7 June. blog.imtfi.uci.edu/2021/06/apo-cash-alypse-now.html (archived at https://perma.cc/2PGP-VWUP)

Crucifix, C (2022) Challenging common assumptions about access to financial services: Reflections from rural Mexico, IMTFI, University of California Irvine, Irvine, CA. www.imtfi.uci.edu/research/2022/cbdc_mexico_crucifix.php (archived at https://perma.cc/CS3L-N3SB)

Demirgüç-Kunt, A, Klapper, L, Singer, D and Ansar, S (2022) The Global Findex Database 2021: Financial inclusion, digital payments, and resilience in the age of Covid-19, World Bank. www.worldbank.org/en/publication/globalfindex (archived at https://perma.cc/G95J-E6RR)

Duvendack, M and Mader, P (2020) Impact of financial inclusion in low-and middle-income countries: A systematic review of reviews, *Journal of Economic Surveys*, 34 (3), 594–629

Kolling, M (2021) Selling hope on credit: Women's livelihoods, debt and the production of urban informality in Brazil, *Contemporary Social Science*, 17 (3), 262–75

Mangowal, C (2022) Digital versus cash use among women urban entrepreneurs in greater Jakarta, IMTFI, University of California Irvine, Irvine, CA. www.imtfi.uci.edu/research/2022/cbdc_indonesia_mangowal.php (archived at https://perma.cc/8W2V-T9D7)

Narula, N, Swartz, L and Frizzo-Barker, J (2023) CBDC: Expanding financial inclusion or deepening the divide? Exploring design choices that could make a difference, MIT. dci.mit.edu/cbdc-fi-1 (archived at https://perma.cc/S6E6-F43B)

Ruthven, O, Morduch, J and Rutherford, S (2009) *Portfolios of the Poor: How the world's poor live on $2 a day*, Princeton University Press, New Jersey

Sandbukt, S (2022) Hierarchies of participation: Experiences with cashlessness in Indonesia, IMTFI, University of University of California Irvine, Irvine, CA. www.imtfi.uci.edu/research/2022/cbdc_indonesia_sandbukt.php (archived at https://perma.cc/4KQ6-NS8P)

Taylor, E B and Broløs, A (2022) *Money and Payments in Low Income Brazil*, Finthropology/SICPA

Taylor, E B and Horst, H A (2018) Designing financial literacy in Haiti, in A J Clarke (ed), *Design Anthropology: Object cultures in transition*, Bloomsbury, London, 179–97

World Bank (no date, a) Financial inclusion, World Bank. www.worldbank.org/en/topic/financialinclusion/overview (archived at https://perma.cc/HQ6D-L3RL)

World Bank (no date, b) Financial capability, World Bank. responsiblefinance.worldbank.org/en/responsible-finance/financial-capability (archived at https://perma.cc/A8P4-MS2E)

World Bank (2014) Financial education programs and strategies: Approaches and available resources, World Bank. documents1.worldbank.org/curated/en/901211472719528753/pdf/108104-BRI-FinancialEducationProgramsandStrategies-PUBLIC.pdf (archived at https://perma.cc/VWC2-SCM8)

Designing for people 08

Learning from inclusion initiatives

Designing for financial inclusion used to mean creating products and services for people on low incomes in the Global South. Today it means much more. These days, inclusive financial services are just as likely to be offered in the USA, India or Australia as they are in Kenya, Colombia or Laos.

Many aim to serve people who are traditionally underserved, like low-income groups, women and, in many countries, farmers. But there are an increasing number of services aiming to meet the needs of specific groups such as refugees, elderly people, children, LGBTQ communities, and so on. In the Western world this might include service meeting the needs of Black and Latino people or Muslims requiring banking without the use of interest.

By this stage of the book, the reason for this shift should be clear: it is far easier for small companies to offer tailored solutions to niche groups. Unsurprisingly, fintechs are leading the way in serving underserved groups, but banks are also following suit, especially challenger banks.

We view this shift as being overwhelmingly positive. Good design is necessary for all – and in a situation where the trend is towards more individual customer-centricity, it makes sense to discuss how qualitative data can help design for different groups. But why might it make sense to create separate financial services for specific underserved groups? Don't people on low incomes simply need access to financial services? Why should women need different features in their financial services to men?

In this chapter we take a look at financial services targeted at three different underserved groups: people on low incomes, women and refugees. We examine the features of these services to build a picture of how their designers are targeting their customers, what assumptions they are making, how the services may foster inclusion, and what the limits are of technical solutions.

Solutions for people on low incomes

Low-income customers don't only exist in low-income countries: they are everywhere. Until recently, however, few efforts were made to provide tailored services to people on low incomes in wealthier countries. Today, we find companies offering such services in all countries. They attempt to solve problems faced by people on low incomes specifically, such as the need for micro-credit at an affordable price. But this second wave of services is tackling a far greater range of issues faced by people on low incomes, and coming up with a broad range of interesting solutions. It's worth taking a look at some of these in more depth.

Before looking at the solutions, let's stop to consider some of the common problems people on low incomes face. In general terms, they struggle to meet their household's basic needs, such as paying for rent, bills transport, and education. Many people on low incomes, such as informal sellers, farmers and day labourers, have irregular incomes. The amount they earn may differ throughout the week or season, and it may be dependent on factors outside their control, such as fluctuations in tourism, weather, availability of goods and more. This makes it difficult to budget more than a few days ahead. For people with low incomes it is especially important to be paid on time, whether this means being paid immediately for goods they have sold, or paid by an employer. Lack of timely payment means people cannot pay for their basic needs.

In terms of financial issues, people on low incomes face disadvantages across the spectrum of financial activities. These include:

- Difficulty saving: Small and unstable savings results in a range of problems, including creating difficulties paying bills on time and incurring late fees as a result, which put further pressure on budgeting and can lead to even more late payments.
- Difficulty coping with shocks: When a shock occurs, such as a hospital bill, damage to housing or a death in the family, people may not have the funds to cover the cost. They must borrow from people they know, take out a loan or delay dealing with the shock.
- Credit is difficult to access or expensive: Due to their limited ability to save, people on low incomes rely on access to credit for important purchases, such as car repairs. Yet they have limited access to affordable credit, and little opportunity to build a credit score. This creates reliance on alternative lenders (which are usually expensive) and family (who might have limited resources), sacrificing important purchases, or simply 'making do'.
- Greater reliance on cash: People on low incomes are more likely to be reliant on cash, which can be difficult to manage and slow to transfer, causing delays in people's personal or commercial economic activity.
- Little to no investment for the future: Few possibilities to invest money to earn interest and grow wealth.
- Unaffordable insurance: People on low incomes may need insurance more than others due to their lack of savings, yet are less likely to be able to afford it. One global exception seems to be funeral insurance, which is widespread among low-income groups.

Being poor is expensive and stressful, and makes it difficult to plan for the short term let alone the long term. How are organizations attempting to solve these problems? As we saw in the previous chapter, there is a long history of offering products for people living in poverty in developing countries, but they tend to offer very general functionality. Recently, financial service providers have been getting much more specific when designing solutions to meet the needs of people on low incomes.

THE EUROPEAN BASIC ACCOUNT

There are other drivers of financial access than meeting the direct needs of low-income groups. For digital transformation to be complete, it will have to reach the whole of society. Access to digital identity and to a bank account or another account with a regulated entity is key. It allows payments of salaries and the distribution of public benefits to function smoothly and ensures that they reach the intended people.

In our Brazil study, we saw that many employers and state agencies actually create bank accounts for employees and beneficiaries for payments to be digital and successful. The creation of digital transaction transparency also makes taxation easier and reduces the size of the informal economy.

In Europe, the collective will to achieve financial inclusion and to drive efficiency has led to the creation of a directive on transparency in payment fees and the 'basic payment account'. If you are a legal resident in an EU country you are entitled to open a basic payment account and banks cannot refuse your application. Such an account covers standard transactions that you use in daily life, such as:

- making deposits
- withdrawing cash
- receiving and carrying out payments (for example, direct debits and card purchases)

It also includes a payment card that you can use to withdraw cash and make purchases, both online and in shops. Where available, the bank should offer access to online banking services with your account. However, they do not always have to include an overdraft or credit facility.

The directive is implemented in national law and therefore differs somewhat from country to country. In some EU countries, your bank might still charge you an annual fee for this basic payment account. This fee should be reasonable. In 2023, prices per year in Denmark ranged from 25 to 70 euros.

Before you open your account, the bank should give you a document showing the most important services offered with the account, and any related fees that you might have to pay. Member states must also provide access to comparable price information.

The basic bank account is not a panacea to the problem of serving low-income groups. The basic services it offers might not really meet people's needs, especially since there is often still a fee to be paid and banks are sometimes reluctant to offer accounts that are unlikely to be profitable.

For more information, see Directive 2014/92/EU (EUR-Lex, 2014) on the comparability of fees related to payment accounts, payment account switching and access to payment accounts with basic features.

There are a growing number of challenger banks offering digital basic services that come at low cost because of the possibility to scale. These include Revolut, N26, Starling Bank, Monzo, Atom Bank, Nu Bank and many more. They often focus on providing simple services for young people, such as savings, payments (including international payments) and cards. Though they may not particularly target low-income groups, they may prove more available to them. The US-based Varo Bank belongs in this group too. Varo was started to serve young customers but also has a specific social mission to 'make financial inclusion and opportunity a reality for all by empowering everyone with a goal to move their lives towards it'. Varo offers payments, savings and loans, as well as advice on money management and a credit card solution developed to support the building of a credit score. The Varo debit card is free and payments between Varo customers are free using the Zelle app.

Varo promotes direct deposit payments from employers to the checking account and offers an interest-bearing savings account. Varo also offers two automatic savings tools. The first lets you transfer an agreed amount of every paycheque from the checking account to the savings account. The second rounds up each checking transaction to the nearest dollar and moves the extra amount to the savings account. Loans of up to $250 that are repaid within the same month carry neither interest nor fees. Varo also partners with other mission-driven companies that seek to help people better manage their finances like bills and insurance. Varos revenue comes from interchange fees, late fees, cash withdrawal fees and fees from brand partners.

There are also new providers who offer low-cost solutions to low-income groups, taking advantage of the digital solutions to build new business models. Quite a few of these focus on different kinds of credit solutions, such as providing digital loans to people on low incomes at rates that may still seem high but are generally lower than traditional payday loans. In the following we describe a few of these and their different business propositions.

For example, US-based company Earnin takes advantage of digitalization and scaling of existing solutions to drive down cost. It offers solutions that aim to help customers meet emergency costs and pay bills on time. Its tagline is, 'You worked today. Get paid today.' Customers can request up to $100 per day within minutes of having worked to earn the money, and may request up to $750 per pay period. To do so, they must validate their employment with a work email or GPS tracking, and they allow Earnin to access their bank account so that the app can see that their employment paycheques are arriving. This means that Earnin is only available for customers with a bank account and fixed work location tracked by an electronic timesheet. Earnin does not charge mandatory fees or interest, but it encourage users to tip 10 per cent of the advanced money they received when they go to repay it. The 10 per cent tip is a default option that customers can manually change, including to zero if they prefer. Customers who don't tip may see their monthly maximum restricted, and the 10 per cent tip has been criticized for corresponding to a very high annual percentage rate (Treece, 2023). When the customer gets paid, Earnin automatically withdraws the money, including the tip. According to one news article, around 80 per cent of Earnin customers tip, amounting to $8 million in monthly revenue for Earnin (Farivar, 2019). Earnin also offers a Visa contactless charge card that requires full payment every month, rather than rolling credit that allows users to build up a debt over time.

Some FSPs have devised new ways to offer traditional loans to customers. The idea for Fair Finance took root in the early 2000s among local community organizations, housing associations and charitable agencies in East London that wanted to highlight issues of financial inclusion locally and look for solutions. The first loans were granted in 2005 with the support of existing banks like the Royal Bank of Scotland and Barclays. Fair Finance has continued its work with different organizations, including the European Microfinance Network. Today it has a large number of partners and supporters. Since 2016, Fair Finance has been authorized by the Financial Conduct Authority (FCA). It runs on a non-profit model with interest set to cover cost. Fair Finance offers 'fair' personal loans of up to £1,000 for new customers, or £3,000 for existing customers. On its website, it claims to be accessible to people who are financially disadvantaged, including migrants, people on benefits and people with bad credit scores. It states that it is more concerned with people's current financial situation than their financial history, and that it helps customers build a good credit rating. Fair Finance also offers money and debt advice.

Other providers make use of detailed customer knowledge to find ways to provide loans to people with low credit scores. One example we introduced in Chapter 6 is US-based QCash, which provides an alternative credit scoring solution to US credit unions.

Yet other providers help people to pay down their debts. In Australia, WeMoney is an app that allows customers to consolidate their debts with the goal of paying them off faster. Customers connect all their accounts (both savings and credit) to the app, which then gives them advice as to where they can save money (such as cancelling subscriptions they don't need), allows them to set goals, and pay all debts in one repayment. It also claims to help customers improve their credit score.

These are mostly examples of credit and loan services based on digital cost-saving solutions offering small loans at low or zero cost to low-income groups. You might expect there to be offers of small savings solutions as well. This does not seem to be the case, which probably has to do with the regulatory requirements to protect depositors. In most countries, you need a banking licence to receive deposits and make loans. The purpose of this is to protect depositors against losing their savings. Regulations are of course different across the world but they generally include rules of size, leadership experience, solvency, accounting requirements and a set of regulations to avoid fraud and money laundering. It is, however, possible to create closed savings circles, although we have not come across many of these. Many challenger banks offer new creative ways of supporting micro savings, as described above under Varo. We also find a number of apps offering account management systems on top of existing accounts, including ways of nudging towards savings. This could be by transferring money to a savings account instead of buying a coffee at a café. Or it could be saving towards a clearly described goal, as offered by Dreams.

Another approach to the issue is to provide ways for customers to support each other. Peer-to-peer (P2P) lenders have included Zopa, RateSetter and Funding Circle (Jones, 2021). However, after 16 years, Zopa closed down its P2P offering in 2021, citing a decrease in the public's trust of P2P lending and changes in regulations. Instead it is focusing on banking activities. RateSetter shut down its P2P service in the same year, and Funding Circle is now concentrating on making small business loans.

A different example of a new business model integrating more players than just banks and customers comes from Brazil, where employers already have a role in creating bank accounts for employees (for salary payments). SalaryFits provides a platform that allows company HR departments to interact with banks for the creation of bank accounts but also for salary advances in the form of loans and repayments. The platform also interacts with insurance companies, health care and education to offer services. Merchants can similarly connect and offer discounted services.

We set out in this section with a description of some of the issues of low-income groups and there is no doubt that many are both underserved and poorly served by traditional financial systems. As we have seen, digital development is making it possible to deliver small-scale financial services at reasonable prices with simple accessible user interfaces. This is positive. Most offers fall in two groups: challenger banks offering a full range of services including small savings solutions; and companies offering loans with less security and higher rates than traditional credit cards but still lower than 'payday-loans' and similar. We also mention that the EU is attempting a different model by requiring banks to offer a 'basic account' at a reasonable price – something that stresses that financial inclusion is practical for societal purposes. Few of the solutions that we have discussed here have worked closely with their target groups to understand the actual needs and pain points that low-income groups experience. We think that there is much to be learned in this area.

Female finance

Around the world, an increasing number of financial service offerings are designed for (and by) women. Note that, due to the scarcity of services and literature available, we have focused on traditional binary genders. We recognize that gender is, in reality, far more diverse than this.

From credit to insurance, investment to funds for female entrepreneurs, companies around the world are offering financial services specifically to women. According to our research, the number of organizations founded to provide financial services to women more than doubled in 2016–20 compared to the previous four-year period (Taylor and Broløs, 2021): in 2021 we identified 102 organizations serving women financially, and we are sure there are many more today.

Why would women need their own financial services? There are a number of reasons:

- Biased design: Financial services are not gender-neutral: they are usually designed with wealthier white men in mind, and are therefore not always appropriate to women's needs and preferences.
- Biased service: it is quite common for women to complain that financial advisers do not take them seriously and do not give them sufficient advice.
- Different needs and preferences: Due to their different social roles, women tend to engage with financial services differently to men. Women are avid financial managers: they make or influence

80 per cent of purchasing decisions globally (Miller, 1998), are more likely to manage the daily family budget (Metinko, 2017), and may even be more avid 'pioneers' of digital financial services than men (60 per cent) (Visa, 2016).

- Financial precarity: Women are also more likely to suffer financial precarity, especially during young adulthood, or as a consequence of divorce or retirement (UN Women, 2018). Men tend to do better financially over the course of their lives, retiring with more savings and facing fewer financial crises along the way (Blackburn et al, 2016).

However, there is little awareness of what companies are doing to meet women's financial needs, or whether their efforts are backed up by research. In 2019 we set out to study some of the recent services for women in credit, investment, insurance and so on, to better understand the trend towards providing women with financial services and the design thinking that goes into making them. We published a total of three reports (the Swiss study we discussed in Chapter 6 was the third report in this series).

Overall, we learned three important lessons that shape design choices to serve women better:

1. Women need financial tools that will help them develop and fulfil their social role. When women are the primary domestic money managers they depend upon tools to help them to track budgets, smooth consumption, and so on. This is why new digital tools, although designed to be used by everybody, are often popular with women (such as Afterpay and Hiveonline).
2. Women need financial tools that will help them overcome historical barriers. As we discussed, the reason why men do better than women at investing is not because they are somehow biologically better at it or because they are less 'risk averse'. Rather, research shows that women looking for professional help in the money world will often be met by stereotypical expectations and may have lower confidence. Today, apps such as Ellevest make investment easier by providing an interface and content that are specifically designed for women.

3 Women's preferences for design and aesthetics are different to those of men. As seen in Figure 8.1, successfully marketing any product to women means making different design decisions than if that same product were designed for men. Financial service providers have recognized this for decades, but until recently their approach to the female market was to 'pink it and shrink it' – that is, make the product look feminized rather than actually building in any features specifically for women. As we discuss later in this report, this is not a very sophisticated approach, and it completely fails to take advantage of the buying power of women.

We see indications that across cultures and nationalities women face similar challenges (legal, economic and social) and look for similar characteristics in their financial solutions. Women tend to focus on goals rather than profit, on trust and transparency, as they also look for financial tools that make an impact in society – local or global, on climate and on inclusion, among others. And they like to do this as part of a network or community (see also Zakrzewski et al, 2020).

Digital financial services, especially those provided by fintechs, are beginning to both benefit this market and profit from it (McKinsey, 2020). While women around the world share a similar structural position, they are also highly diverse. The benefit of digital financial tools is that they can be designed to suit women's particular contexts and needs, rather than following a 'one size fits all (women)' model. Compared with traditional financial service providers, fintechs tend to focus on a specific customer pain point, such as making investment easier, choosing insurance, increasing the ability to track household budgets, encouraging savings behaviour and helping women to pay for purchases more easily. In order to attract customers from traditional providers, they must provide solutions that are attractive, accessible (mostly through mobile phones), user-friendly (such as easily navigable apps) and affordable. Most importantly, these products can be designed specifically to meet women's financial needs.

One example of a money management app designed for women is US-based company Nav.it. The company was founded in 2019 by CEO Erin Papworth and boasts an all-women executive team. It partners with financial planning, investment and insurance companies to offer a bundle of services to women. Users can download the app

Figure 8.1 Designing financial services for women

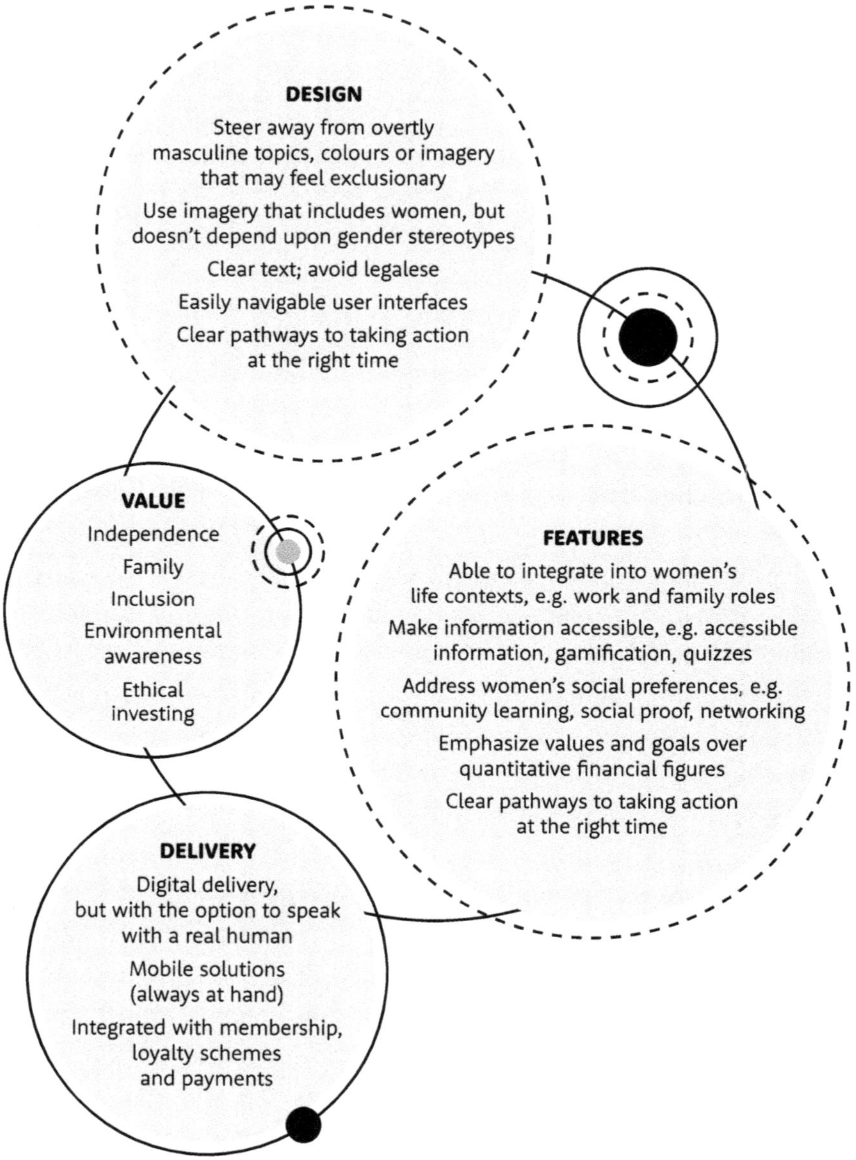

SOURCE Broløs and Taylor, 2020

from Google Play or the Apple Store and link it to their bank accounts to gain an overview of their finances. There is a free version, which includes a range of features focusing on spending, saving, community engagement, education and support. These include helping users to pay down debt, automate savings, track spending and investments, setting spending limits, setting trip funding goals and creating savings goals with friends. The free version also allows users to take quizzes, check their 'money mindset' with daily mindset check-ins, and engage with the app's user community. An interesting feature of the app is its focus on well-being and mental health.

Women can also have specific needs or preferences in the area of insurance, including things like health insurance and car insurance. AXA is a French multinational insurance company with operations in 60 countries around the world. AXA products include life, health, property and casualty insurance, as well as investment management. In 2018 its annual revenue was €104 billion (AXA, 2018). In Mexico, AXA developed a combined health and life insurance product, Mujer Única, for women who are diagnosed with cancer. According to Liza Garay-de Vaubernier, Global Head of Women's Market for AXA, women's cancers are the leading cause of death for women between the ages of 25 and 44 in Mexico but only 8 per cent of women have life insurance (Garay-de Vaubernier, 2019). The idea behind Mujer Única is to make insurance accessible for the things women are likely to need it for. It is a very specific product that only covers the most relevant health issues. This should therefore lower premiums, since women aren't paying for things they are unlikely to need. It should also improve communications: the product should seem more relevant to potential customers, and the product information should be easier to understand. The product takes into account that women with cancer need a range of services, not just ones that are cancer-specific or even health-specific. AXA provides not just insurance payouts but also comprehensive medical, legal and nutritional support.

Of course, investment is a well-known area where women fall behind. There are many apps that aim to serve women in this area. One example is Ellevest Inc., a robo-adviser service providing savings and investment services to women based on knowledge of their career paths, income and life expectations and with regard to preferences for sustainability. The company was established in 2014 in New York by Founder and CEO Sallie Krawcheck, who has an impressive background in traditional investment banking. The Ellevest website explains how Krawcheck realized that most investment services were created by (over 50 years of age) men and for men. She decided that 'it was time to do better' and founded Ellevest together with technology entrepreneur Charlie Kroll. According to the company's website, Ellevest was built on the basis of anthropological research, including 200 hours of interviews with women from different age groups who provided input not only on knowledge and expectations, but also design and aesthetics. Ellevest also has male customers and provides these services based on their working experience and education. The company does not disclose customer numbers (Perez, 2019). Like most investment products aimed at individuals, the basic Ellevest solution, Ellevest Digital, is a mobile app allowing customers to enter (and change) basic information such as personal details, pay, family and savings goals, time horizons, impact preferences, and so on. Ellevest then suggests an investment profile for each goal, including a forecast of the profit they will make and the taxes and fees they will pay. This means that investing is directed toward obtaining goals, rather than on documenting a risk-based profile with regard to market revenue.

Most of our examples are from the Global North, and most are 'By women, for women' solutions. This means that most of the companies that we studied were developed to solve pain points experienced by women in traditional finance, such as being poorly served. Some, like Ellevest, included communities and events as a source of customer insights. As we have often pointed out when presenting our studies, it might well be that the solutions that better meet women's needs actually might also serve men better.

Migrants and refugees

Migrants and refugees are two different but interrelated groups who face financial issues. We discuss them together because they often face similar challenges. These include:

- Lack of access to financial services: Migrants often lack documentation such as passports or residency documents needed to access financial services like bank accounts.

- Difficulties accessing credit: Being a new resident in a country can be a disadvantage when applying for a loan, due to lack of a credit score or employment history.
- Difficulties managing money across borders: The cost of remittances can be a disadvantage for people who rely on sending or receiving money to other countries, especially if the transactions involve small amounts of money. The cost and complexity of exchange rates can also be an issue.
- Difficulties receiving benefits: Lack of access to financial services can make it difficult to receive benefits for migrants and refugees, such as those offered by governments and NGOs.
- Insufficient knowledge of the financial system: New residents may lack knowledge about important information about the financial system of their host country, making it difficult to navigate and leaving them vulnerable to mistakes or fraud.

In some ways, migrants have long been financially served. As we mentioned earlier, many remittance services developed to serve the vast number of low-income labourers who travel to distant countries and who wish to send money back to their families. However, access to services that allow one to send internationally doesn't guarantee that migrants have the services they need domestically. Many migrants (especially 'irregular' ones) lack the identity documentation or local residency status needed to open a bank account or use domestic payments service (Consumer Finance Protection Bureau, 2022). Sometimes a lack of a passport is the problem, but not always. Migrants may not have the right to register as a resident, or get a tax file number or other official document, and this can impede access.

This can be true of any migrant, not only low-income or 'irregular' ones. One of this book's authors, Erin, remembers that when she migrated to the Netherlands it took a while to get registered in the local municipality, and in the meantime she could not open a bank account. Since many shops in the Netherlands do not accept cash or credit cards, there were places Erin could not shop until she got a Dutch bank account, thereby becoming a 'financial citizen' of the Netherlands.

In Erin's case, the struggles were short-lived. But many migrants go through a far longer, and more stressful, process to access financial services in their new country. Some governments and international organizations have set up programmes to help them. Italy, for example, has a National Observatory for the Financial Inclusion of Migrants, which helps migrants integrate into the financial system and learn about entrepreneurship. In the USA, an app called MAJORITY allows migrants to open a bank account without a social security number (Hall, 2023). They need to provide an international government-issued ID and proof of US residence. The company's website states that the app was created 'by migrants, for migrants'. It includes a number of features that we have seen designed into apps for people on low incomes, including no overdraft fees and the possibility to have your wages advanced to your account two days early. Features more targeted at migrants include free international transfers and good rates on international phone calls.

There are also many fintechs offering cheaper services in specific areas, such as international payments or remittances. These include Remitly, Wise and TransferGo. Remittance services like these developed historically to cater for international migrants who wanted to send money home, often people on low incomes. In 2023, remittances are projected to reach $840 billion globally (Migration Data Portal, 2023). However, according to Bátiz-Lazo (2022), though such organizations may offer 'free' transfers the solutions may sometimes actually be more costly than traditional solutions.

It should be noted that many fintech companies offer services with no fees to attract new customers, charging exclusively through the exchange rate. While this sounds very attractive and the sender may, in principle, face a lower cost, this is not guaranteed. It is perfectly possible that the price of the remittance through the exchange rate is so high that it is higher than an average market commission of $10 and the exchange rate cost of a 'remitter'. Therefore, it is essential that customers identify the costs associated with sending remittances and do not end up paying more for falling within the scope of the 'no fees' offer. In addition, there are other offers from many fintech companies looking to expand their clientele. A joint promotion is to give away a number of dollars, for example $15, if a user recommends the fintech service to a person who is not a client (referrals). When this new client operates with the fintech firm, $15 are charged in favour of the referring client.

Refugees (forcibly displaced persons, or FDPs) in particular tend to face enormous obstacles with respect to financial inclusion. They may have had to flee their country in haste, and may lack documentation altogether. Often refugees spend months or years in a sort of residency limbo, without the right to reside in the country they have fled to, but with no option to travel elsewhere either. They may receive a regular allowance from a government body or international organization, but have no account in which to store it to make transactions. They may not be able to receive remittances from family members overseas due to lack of identity documentation.

Identity is a critical component in financial services. This is particularly so with respect to digital transformation, risk of digital fraud and increasing requirements for FSPs to comply with 'know your customer' (KYC) rules. A (digital) ID will most often be a prerequisite to obtaining a simple bank account. Even if a person has documentation such as a passport this may take time. With no proven records refugees – and particularly irregular refugees – experience difficulties. Once an ID is issued, it can still be a problem to find a financial solution that may be necessary to receive government benefits or wages.

Part of the problem is that identities are generally national solutions. They can either be government-issued or privately issued according to government requirements, but they will most often not be accepted in a new country. Several attempts have been made to solve this problem. The EU is introducing a requirement for all member countries to offer ID wallets with the aim of introducing ID compatibility, and private companies have developed solutions based on blockchain-based self-sovereign identities that would in principle work across borders – indeed, across the globe.

In 2016, an entrepreneur launched an app called Tagqnu to help both migrants and refugees obtain a digital identity that would be sufficient to open a bank account (Peters, 2017). The app tracked data on the user's smartphone, including their social media accounts, to build their identity. Users could also build their reputation by asking family and friends to vouch for them. The service was closed in 2022 due to market complexity and differences between regulations.

Having an ID is a first step towards financial access. The next issue is often to find a financial solution that fits. The OECD (2016) cites several barriers to their financial inclusion, including underdeveloped financial infrastructures in their home and/or host country, cultural and social attitudes, and knowledge, skills and access to services. It views financial education as a critical part of overcoming these issues. It notes that managing money can be more complex for migrants and refugees due to the fact that they live their financial lives across borders. It says:

> Even if most transactions are undertaken in cash it is beneficial to understand and know how to calculate exchange rates, to know how to budget and make effective use of financial resources, how to keep records of money sent and received, and how to smooth irregular cash flows.
>
> (OECD, 2016: 3)

Additionally, migrants and refugees need knowledge on issues like fees, inflation, taxes, credit and more. The OECD calls for more education for refugees and cites research indicating that such education does have a positive impact.

In many countries, the UNHCR provides cash grants to refugees. In a 2020 report, the UNHCR describes how it has been working to find ways to deliver these incentives digitally, such as through bank accounts or mobile money accounts. It states that whereas, in 2016, digital delivery of cash grants was only possible in a few countries, by 2020 it was possible in 47 countries. It describes how, during the Covid-19 pandemic, the Jordanian government made it possible for refugees to register for a mobile money account using only their official refugee registration number (see also Giz, 2022).

The UNHCR has also developed a digital identity solution and a blockchain-based wallet. In 2017 the programme Building Blocks began delivering cash grants to Syrian refugees in Jordanian camps using this system. It allows refugees to receive their money in a wallet, and to pay for groceries in a supermarket located on the outskirts of the camp by simply showing their iris to a camera. Such a system could potentially make it much easier and cheaper for the UNHCR and other UN organizations to disburse cash payments. However, it is not yet clear what benefits it is bringing to refugees. Between 2017 and 2019, anthropologist Margie Cheesman carried out research in four women's centres in two refugee camps in Jordan, including 40 in-depth focus groups with around 300 women in cash-for-work schemes. The women told her that the new digital system made it difficult for them to track their money. It was not easy to identify which work period each payment was for, so they did not know whether they were still owed money for work they had done. The only transaction records they were able to access were the paper receipts handed to them by the supermarket. This meant that they had to keep their own paper ledgers tracking work hours and cross-checking receipts against the ledger. It created far more work than getting paid in cash, and reinforced the use of paper rather than reducing it. Additionally, women were concerned that the eye scans they were required to perform to make transactions would damage their eyes. Cheesman (2022a) concludes:

> Ultimately, having a digital wallet to manage money cannot solve the root problems of abject poverty and oppression. Responsible, just, and mindful innovation is a matter of understanding people's concerns, subjectivities, resources, relationships, and choices. Humanitarian agencies and their corporate and government partners promote big data technologies, high-tech infrastructures, and the insights, targeting, and optimization they facilitate. But refugee women workers' perspectives show that sometimes the optimum technology is a humble envelope or a folded up receipt.

It is clear that, while digital services may well assist with the financial inclusion of refugees, it is important that the design and implementation of such services matches the realities of refugees' lives. In their roadmap for the financial inclusion of refugees, Giz (2020) recommend that researchers do the following to better understand the financial inclusion issues facing refugees:

- Develop case studies highlighting global best practices in the distribution of services and the management of financial infrastructure.

- Understand the experience of FDPs and other vulnerable communities with existing infrastructure to highlight gaps and to help policy-makers and the private sector prioritize needs.
- Support the testing of innovative solutions to ongoing infrastructure challenges including agent liquidity.
- Support the private sector, government and humanitarian organizations in mapping infrastructure capabilities before and after crisis situations.

There is a long way to go before we have solved the issue of financially including migrants and refugees: indeed, given that a substantial part of the solution is bureaucratic, it is likely that systems will always need to be in place to work with refugees especially on a case-by-case basis. However, technology promises to lighten the administrative load and speed up the process.

Designing for people

In the last two chapters we have focused on the fact that many people across the globe still do not have access to adequate and affordable financial services. We have discussed Global South rural farmers, migrants and refugees, as well as Global North low-income groups and women. We have illustrated how these people struggle with bigger problems of managing jobs, housing and health – and, particularly for refugees, issues of personal identification.

We have shown that mainstream financial services do not serve the financial needs of marginalized or underserved groups, such as small-scale savings, low-cost accounts, cards and access to credit without a traditional credit score. Most of these people are very well aware of the pain points of existing solutions (including the fact that they would rather have basic services available at low prices than extended services for fees they can't afford).

There is a growing body of initiatives to provide financial services to such groups. But it is clear that financial inclusion isn't just about delivering well-designed services – that is just half the story. People also financially include themselves either by deciding to adopt services or by finding ways to make unreliable/inconvenient ones work. They also use them in ways not envisaged by the designers.

Unfortunately, there are few organizations – whether new or old – doing customer studies to understand how to better design financial services to reduce the burden on customers of making services usable and to serve their customers' needs in terms of financial well-being. This is particularly an issue with regard to marginalized or underserved groups, since they often face very specific problems accessing and using financial services, and have particular needs. Indeed, much discussion of financial inclusion focuses on education, financial literacy and teaching people money management. This is definitely both important and relevant, but the relatively few qualitative studies of customers' use of financial services illustrate the need to bring knowledge of the underserved in contact with knowledge of financial services.

This is not just an issue regarding excluded groups. We argue that it is true for all customer groups. The lesson that we take from this is that customer-centric solutions – for any group of customers – cannot be developed without understanding customer behaviour in different cultures, societies and communities. This is absolutely key when working with new solutions in times of change, such as digital transformation.

We will witness this more in the future, as financial services become part of developing embedded solutions that are easily accessible, integrated in daily activities and sustainable. This will be the general demand of future generations as part of their financial well-being. There will also be an increasing need to understand how Web 3.0 and virtual communities change people's interactions, including finance, and to study this in new environments. Thus the following chapter discusses how and why it is possible to learn from existing customers to build for the future.

TAKEAWAYS

- Marginalized and underserved groups such as people on low incomes, women and refugees have specific needs and preferences for financial services.
- New financial service providers are developing innovative solutions to meet the needs of these groups.
- However, these groups often face problems that cannot be solved with technical solutions only, such as the need for identification.
- In-depth, qualitative research is necessary to understand the problems marginalized and underserved groups face and develop solutions that take into account personal, social, governmental and technological considerations.

References

AXA (2018) Registration document 2018: Annual financial report, AXA. www-axa-com.cdn.axa-contento-118412.eu/www-axa-com%2F913d1869-3d11-4eb2-b013-4caedb747fab_axa-ddr2018b-en.pdf (archived at https://perma.cc/UM3Y-U4FN)

Bátiz-Lazo, B and Gonzalez-Correa, I (2022) The journey of a remittance in the US–Mexico corridor: From my salary to my family, 17 August. ssrn.com/abstract=4192932 (archived at https://perma.cc/JA4H-3M7L)

Blackburn, R M, Jarman, J and Racko, G (2016) Understanding gender inequality in employment and retirement, *Contemporary Social Science*, 11 (2–3), 238–52

Broløs, A and Taylor, E B (2020) *Female Finance: Digital, mobile, networked*, EWPN and Keen Innovation. ewpn.eu/female-finance-digital-mobile-networked (archived at https://perma.cc/PW4S-MG6D)

Cheesman, M (2022a) Blockchain for refugees, Ammon News, 9 June. en.ammonnews.net/article/58859 (archived at https://perma.cc/C25Q-BQH5)

Cheesman, M (2022b) Infrastructure justice and humanitarianism: Blockchain's promises in practice, University of Oxford. www.ora.ox.ac.uk/objects/uuid:3a375a60-85b2-4953-bc04-5cae34021df1 (archived at https://perma.cc/YJT9-LFSM)

Consumer Finance Protection Bureau (2022) Identifying and addressing the financial needs of immigrants, CFPB, 27 June. www.consumerfinance.gov/about-us/blog/identifying-and-addressing-the-financial-needs-of-immigrants (archived at https://perma.cc/NCP9-WY7U)

EUR-Lex (2014) Directive 2014/92/EU on the comparability of fees related to payment accounts, payment account switching and access to payment accounts with basic features, EUR-Lex. eur-lex.europa.eu/legal-content/EN/TXT/?uri=CELEX:32014L0092 (archived at https://perma.cc/4YPT-ENFZ)

Farivar, C (2019) Millions use Earnin to get cash before payday. Critics say the app is taking advantage of them, NBC News, 26 July. www.nbcnews.com/tech/internet/millions-use-earnin-get-cash-payday-critics-say-app-taking-n1034071 (archived at https://perma.cc/3WJU-AL9G)

Garay-de Vaubernier, L (2019) Why do we need a specific approach for the women's market? AXA. www.axa.com/en/news/why-do-we-need-a-specific-approach-for-the-womens-market (archived at https://perma.cc/4UB2-YHZJ)

Giz (2020) Roadmap to the sustainable and responsible financial inclusion of forcibly displaced persons, AFI Global. www.afi-global.org/wp-content/uploads/2020/07/Roadmap_FI-of-FDPs_122019_0.pdf (archived at https://perma.cc/RT54-3LJB)

Giz (2022) Financial inclusion of refugees in Jordan: Knowledge note, Giz, 17 November. www.giz.de/en/downloads/giz2022-en-financial-inclusion-refugees-jordan.pdf (archived at https://perma.cc/MY54-KJ3E)

Hall, C (2023) Majority, a digital bank for US migrants, grabs $9.75m amid expansion in Texas, TechCrunch, 14 June. www.techcrunch.com/2023/06/14/majority-digital-bank-migrants-9-75m-fintech (archived at https://perma.cc/3699-K6D9)

Jones, R (2021) Zopa exits peer-to-peer lending focus on banking, *Guardian*, 11 December. www.theguardian.com/money/2021/dec/11/zopa-peer-to-peer-lending-p2p-money (archived at https://perma.cc/G799-B3RQ)

McKinsey (2020) Diversity wins: How inclusion matters, McKinsey. www.mckinsey.com/~/media/mckinsey/featured%20insights/diversity%20and%20inclusion/diversity%20wins%20how%20inclusion%20matters/diversity-wins-how-inclusion-matters-vf.pdf (archived at https://perma.cc/73XA-R6HT)

Metinko, C (2017) Women are the new CFO of the household, The Street, 19 April. www.thestreet.com/personal-finance/women-are-the-new-cfo-of-the-household-14089470 (archived at https://perma.cc/8UEZ-JVJH)

Migration Data Portal (2023) Remittances, Migration Data Portal, 2 August. www.migrationdataportal.org/themes/remittances (archived at https://perma.cc/TZ4W-WJA3)

Miller, D (1998) *A Theory of Shopping*, Cornell University Press, New York

OECD (2016) Responses to the refugee crisis: Financial education and the long-term integration of refugees and migrants, OECD Directorate for Financial and Enterprise Affairs, February. web-archive.oecd.org/2016-02-02/386437-Financial-education-long-term-integration-refugees-migrants.pdf

Perez, S (2019) Investment platform Ellevest raises $33m from Melinda Gates Pivotal Ventures and Valerie Jarrett and PayPal, TechCrunch, 28 March. www.techcrunch.com/2019/03/28/investment-platform-ellevest-raises-33m-melinda-gates-pivotal-ventures-valerie-jarrett-paypal (archived at https://perma.cc/KQK8-NJ7M)

Peters, A (2017) This app helps refugees get bank accounts by giving them a digital identity, Fast Company, 4 October. www.fastcompany.com/40403583/this-app-helps-refugees-get-bank-accounts-by-giving-them-a-digital-identity (archived at https://perma.cc/6WJN-JS9M)

Reset (2018) How Finland is using the blockchain to revolutionise financial services for refugees, Reliefweb, 10 May. reliefweb.int/report/finland/how-finland-using-blockchain-revolutionise-financial-services-refugees (archived at https://perma.cc/SS86-QEU7)

Taylor, EB and Broløs, A (2020) Financial technology and the gender gap: Designing and delivering services for women, in T de Waal Malefyt and M McCabe (eds), *Women, Consumption and Paradox: Towards a more humanistic approach to consumption*, Routledge, Abingdon, 103–28

Taylor, E B and Broløs, A (2021) *Female Finance in Figures*, EWPN, Keen Innovation and Bank Cler. www.ewpn.eu/research-network/white-papers-reports/female-finance-in-figures (archived at https://perma.cc/NS5L-95CG)

Treece, K (2023) Earnin app review 2023, Forbes, 4 August. www.forbes.com/advisor/personal-loans/earnin-app-review (archived at https://perma.cc/MB5K-NA6X)

UN Women (2018) Turning promises into action: Gender equality in the 2030 Agenda for Sustainable Development, UN Women. www.unwomen.org/en/digital-library/publications/2018/2/gender-equality-in-the-2030-agenda-for-sustainable-development-2018 (archived at https://perma.cc/V87W-Z745)

UNHCR (no date) Financial inclusion, UNHCR. www.unhcr.org/what-we-do/build-better-futures/livelihoods-and-economic-inclusion/financial-inclusion

UNHCR (2020) Digital payments to refugees: A pathway towards financial inclusion, UNHCR. www.unhcr.org/media/digital-payments-refugees-pathway-towards-financial-inclusion (archived at https://perma.cc/K5FN-GXWM)

Visa (2016) Visa RFi group payments report 2016: Driving engagement and differentiation, and the rise of the digital customer, Visa. www.visa.com.au/dam/VCOM/regional/ap/australia/global-elements/Documents/2016-visa-and-rfi-report.pdf (archived at https://perma.cc/L3X3-TJEQ)

Zakrzewski, A, Newsom Reeves, K, Kahlich, M, Klein, M, Real Mattar, A and Knobel, S (2020) Managing the next decade of women's wealth, Boston Consulting Group, 9 April. www.bcg.com/publications/2020/managing-next-decade-women-wealth (archived at https://perma.cc/HL5A-VW8W)

The future is in the field

09

Insights for services that don't exist yet

So far in this book we have discussed the fast-paced digital change that is occurring in society as a whole, and in finance in particular. We have illustrated how new technologies can change not only financial products, but in fact the whole industry structure, including regulation and infrastructure. Digital transformation is affecting all parts of society, from public services to media, transport and health, to communities and relations. People increasingly expect instant and mobile solutions. We have illustrated how people adapt their behaviour to new services and technologies – sometimes very fast.

At the same time, we know that it may take time for new realities to become new norms. In finance it is worth recalling that it is not so many years ago that cash, cheques and passbooks were widely used. The development of access to smartphones has been critical for a global uptake of digital payments, shopping, bill payments and investments. Corporates and SMEs are quickly becoming used to open API environments that allow them new ways of interacting with financial services.

While this is still settling – while market standards, privacy, fraud management and regulation are still catching up – a new wave of change is on the horizon. Web 3.0 has the potential to introduce much more customer influence on finances and financial services. Getting used to partly virtual interactions including virtual assets, virtual spaces, digital twins and avatars may once again completely change financial infrastructure, financial intermediation, financial services and customer expectations.

When it comes to innovation, we argue that in times of an uncertain future it is even more important to understand customer development. In this chapter we discuss a question that we have often been asked when suggesting fieldwork in innovation. How can spending time with customers who may not even know about technology throw light on future innovations? We start by elaborating on the changing field of finance. We particularly dive into the changes that have taken place in relation to customer knowledge, customer roles and the interplay between financial service providers and customers – including consumers, SMEs and corporates. We then move on to describe some examples of the introduction of innovations and new technology. These examples differ in both approach and effect. Examples are of both successes and failures, as we want to illustrate how we can learn from both. We finally discuss what we need to be aware of when doing qualitative customer research in the future.

The field is changing: Why start with customers?

As we saw in Chapter 3, innovation is always about both the future (what is new) and the present (why customers will buy the new solution). But why might it be a good idea to study existing customer behaviour (among consumers, SMEs and corporates) to develop innovative solutions for the future? And how can existing behaviour point forward? Would customers not be stuck in old habits – like wishing for 'a faster horse'? The answer is simple – gaining insights from customers will always be a combination of several elements:

- The key is **understanding the issues, pain points and dreams of those involved** (both individuals and groups). This also requires understanding the success of existing products. Why are they chosen, how are they used and where are they supplemented with other solutions?
- In times of uncertainty about the future, it is just as **important to understand the drivers of changes in behaviour**, including trust and

customer networks – both real and virtual. FSP's ca choose to join customer network, and to offer new networks for customers to share comments and ideas for use and innovation.

- **The foundation for putting customer knowledge to use is of course a good understanding of changes in technology and their potential.**
- And finally we must understand how new technologies can make a difference to existing customers and/or new or underserved markets.

This illustrates how qualitative studies can help gain deep insights into customer pain points and how these can add to an understanding of technology potential to build successful innovation. An example of this, Hiveonline, was discussed in Chapter 5. Their successful offer to village savings and loans associations was built on qualitative observations and interviews in African villages undertaken in collaboration with local experts that enabled them to provide a modern digital solution based on a blockchain platform that can support existing savings and loan solutions. On top of this, the digital solutions help to provide a new type of credit scoring.

The existing field

Before we turn to the argument for why we should start with customers, let's come back to how financial innovation is currently taking place. As discussed in Chapter 2, both incumbent organizations and entrepreneurs spend time following the development of technology and the way that others see their potential business value. Part of this dialogue is related to the potential of data management and AI to build data-driven solutions and offers directed at very specific customer groups or even individual customers. Customer-centricity has seen a new upturn in interest. Companies also work with partners, consultants, fintechs and regulators to understand development potential. This will naturally lead to ideas for the development of new products, services and processes, with the aim of providing quality services to customers and to build efficient and low-cost processes throughout the value chain.

As we saw in Chapter 3, this knowledge and innovation may well be developed without customer involvement and instead be based on the TAM model of how customers can and will adapt new technologies, and how best to help them become familiar with it. As we shall see, this may work in some environments and be irrelevant in others.

Are we saying that innovation models are of poor quality? Not at all – although perhaps they could be even better. We have seen many examples of fintechs that develop more or less successful solutions to perceived customer pain points. Some such innovations may be grounded in customer observations, some in personal experience and some in response to learning from other fields of digital change. Other solutions may come about through a trial-and-error process, with customer response determining their success or failure – in the latter case, leading to company closure or mergers. Studying many-such examples may lead to the following description of different strategies for innovation:

- Some base the development of new solutions on digital analysis of the transactions of existing customers as a proxy for changing behaviour – the ultimate aim being customer-centricity based on a 1:1 solution.
- Others build a business model on services for specific customer groups as discussed in Chapter 8, whether this is to work for financial inclusion or to provide services for special purposes, such as venture capital, saving for your dream or investment solutions for the wealthy.
- Some base innovation models on surveys leading customers to identify themselves in particular customer profiles that relate to personas creating digital customer segmentation. The software company Oxford Risk does just that in its solutions for investment companies.
- A very particular solution is offering the opportunity to copy the behaviour of successful people, for instance in investments like eToro (as described in Chapter 3).

It is clear that working with customers in their own context is not often used as a way to build innovation. Yet there are excellent reasons for doing so.

Understanding the new field

We called this chapter 'The future is in the field' because we still think that solutions for people are best built upon understanding people's needs and pain points in context. But, as we see, the context is changing, moving people into digital spaces. This means that while some customer groups may not be familiar with AI or IoT, other groups may already be experimenting with digital finance in digital spaces.

One example, of course, is social media, where financial ideas can be shared, discussed or copied. In Chapter 3 we saw companies in investment setting up business models based on customers offering their investment profiles for others to copy. eToro is a good example of this set up as a business. We have also seen a widespread growth in financial influencers who offer their investment profiles with the promise of high gains. In some of these cases, the business model has been for the influencers being paid by the number of members who follow them and set up accounts with (non-regulated) investment platforms. In both cases, some customer groups are already experimenting in new financial spaces.

Another example covers embedded contexts of financial services, like BNPL apps in which credit and shopping experiences come together, as described both in Chapter 3 and Chapter 8. Including finance in shopping spaces makes it possible for companies to offer cheaper financial solutions to some customer groups, based on a higher degree of customer loyalty in shopping. As we have shown in recent research (Taylor and Broløs, 2022), customers can be very adept at taking advantage of these solutions – using them when they offer the cheapest credit or the best shopping offer.

As we saw in Chapter 3, insurance is another field in which some customer groups are already changing financial behaviour in the light of new digital insurance offers. Micro-insurance involves unbundling existing insurance concepts by offering insurance cover for specific assets, specific risks and a limited period of time. Car insurance for a rented car during the rental period is an example. The insurance policy can cover the individual user or the car fleet owner. Since such insurance is part of a rental package, it can be considered to be an embedded service. The capability to collect, share and analyse large amounts of data is also changing business models towards more precise offers. Hippo Insurance, for instance, offers home insurance with a lower premium package based on the collection of data from water, smoke and intrusion sensors. Along similar lines, car computers can share driving data (speed, acceleration, braking, etc.) or personal health data (exercise, eating and sleeping habits, weight, etc.). The ethical issues such services raise are still in question.

And, of course, large customer groups – particularly young people – are already active in video games, resulting in large developing digital spaces where participants can create their own characters and (of course) build impressive assets in game results. To some extent, excellence in games already rests on the ability to build or buy virtual assets. We already see connections between game currencies and real world currencies. As virtual spaces develop, we see a movement toward the metaverse as interconnected virtual worlds. The metaverse offers an obvious space for new services in payments, credit, investment and insurance. Most existing financial players are working on establishing and maintaining their brand in the metaverse. For instance, J P Morgan (no date) describes its Onyx community on its website and mentions that it sees virtual worlds as parallels to the existing global economy with currencies and digital assets where banking core competences and customer knowledge can play a major role. Following customers into the metaverse entails new innovations and infrastructures including tokenization and digital identity.

This means that many customers are already present in the 'future' – making this a great space to study customer behaviour for future innovation. We will come back to how in Chapter 10. It also means that some customers may already be experimenting with developing their own financial solutions. This shows that not only can you study customer behaviour in a changing field; you can also study changing customer roles for the future. A recent example of a customer building their own financial innovations was discussed by Dave Birch, Principal at 15MB Ltd. and Global Ambassador for Consult Hyperion in a Forbes article:

> Mike, who is both an entrepreneur and a fintech nuts and bolts man (and a very nice guy), has been doing some tinkering and built a plug-in to link

> ChatGPT to his bank account using the UK's open banking APIs. The plug-in, called 'BankGPT', can tell you your balance, find transactions, discuss your budgeting and even make payments... He wasn't demonstrating a minimum viable product (MVP), he was demonstrating how simple it is to connect AI and open banking... ChatGPT is a window into the future of financial services: while no-one will deliver a consumer service using ChatGPT and open banking as they are now, AI and open finance will change retail financial services beyond measure. What Mike's experiment showed is just how easy it is to connect the two: He's built the powered drone, now we can start thinking about what we will do when we can all fly.
>
> (Birch, 2023)

This is just one example of how customers may take on new roles in future innovation.

Changed behaviours in the new field

Considering solutions for the future means considering how pain points may be met for different customers, ranging from those who will be setting up their own financial solutions looking to share a learning experience in networks or to copy the acts and choices of a peer or a group of peers to those who would still just like to feel assured that their money matters are handled securely and professionally.

When studying the most active financial users, there is information to be learned from gaming environments. We already know that gamers spend much time in gaming communities and that they are often willing to share tips, tricks and workarounds with others. We also know that many successful gamers are impatient for an optimal experience and will share complaints and discontent both with other users and with game developers. This can go as far as suggesting new storylines or changes in the games. In a study of the Polish game environment, Klimas and Czakon (2022) identify four distinctive roles in the co-creation process (direct value creation, supporting value creation, encouraging entrepreneurship and leadership) and five stages of contribution (co-discovery, co-development, co-deployment, co-delivery and co-dissemination).

Their aim is to identify how various actors contribute to co-innovation in innovation ecosystems, and more specifically to establish the various types of actors (who?), the distinct roles (what?), the different stages (when?), and the diverse engagement in co-innovation processes (how?).

An interesting example of co-customer development is Roblox. This game developer for children build their game with ideas from gamers and they share the revenue from such solutions with the users providing the ideas. In their studies, they include both development companies (which for financial services might be compared with fintech partners) and game users (like financial customers). They find that many different actors can contribute to both direct development and supportive development but that professional developers are more likely to contribute to leadership and entrepreneurship. A particular result of these findings is that the gaming innovation ecosystem is not necessarily managed by a single leader but becomes collectively orchestrated.

These findings on roles and co-innovation in gaming are similar to the many studies of open source (IT) development describing how communities contribute to ideation and development based on their documented skills (meritocracy). Other community members may contribute by fixing bugs or answering questions from users, thus reducing the pressure on support teams (von Hippel, 2007).

While financial companies rarely interact directly with consumers and other private customers in the development of new solutions, there is another space where changes in the roles of both corporate and SME customer roles can already be studied. These are the many developer communities emerging from open banking and open finance initiatives that most incumbent players are carrying out. In these environments, banks or insurers share customer data through APIs – either for free as required following the revised Payment Services Directive (PSD2) regulation in European payments, or at a premium. These environments allow customers (mostly corporates and SMEs) to build their own customized integration mechanisms or to integrate with different partners. The communities also (to some extent) allow them to share solutions or ideas. The payment provider InnoPAY publishes a yearly overview and ranking of these solutions with regards to functionality, usability, documentation and community support (Peter et al, 2023). This represents a clear new field of observation that is growing even wider as open banking changes into open finance.

Through the discussion of changes in customer behaviour, customer knowledge about technology and customer participation in innovation, we have established it is both relevant and important to study customer behaviour now to build innovations for the future. First, customers' behaviour in the existing environment can give important insights into the way new solutions can help overcome pain points and better meet customer needs. Second, some customers may already be using new tools and technologies and be able to provide their own ideas on how they could be used to build new services. As has so often been said, 'the future is already here, it is just not evenly distributed' (originally attributed to William Gibson).

We have also substantiated that the current wave of change is considerably more complex than many earlier changes. One thing is the pace of change. We have several times described it as fast, but just how fast the adoption will develop is difficult to anticipate. On the customer side, this is likely to depend on several factors. One is what we already described in Chapter 3 as the perceived usefulness of solutions for different user groups. This relies on the convenience, the value and the experience of control in the financial environment.

Another element is trust in financial intermediaries. Trust both with regard to the perceived security and compliance of services and trust with regard to the advice given. Regulation and the development of standards will play a key role here. The ability to reach communities is important, too, as we have already seen many examples of customers following their peers in the choice of solution (quite apart from the network effect of many financial solutions). A third issue is where the development will actually take us – an open question of the balance between digital and analogue (or human) and the balance between central and decentralized.

For now, let's turn to some examples and experiences of introducing new technology in financial solutions for broader groups of customers.

Learning from innovation in payments

Finding good examples of how qualitative studies can help innovation based on future technology is not easy. In the following section we have gathered a few examples, mostly from the payments area. They are different in time, in goal and introduced by different organizations. They also include both successes and failures, taking into account that we can learn from both.

More importantly, the examples represent different ways of involving customers. We try to understand how customers have been or can be involved in developing the 'right' solution, focusing on differences between technology adoption (learning new behaviour), the expression of wishes and the actual pain points. We realize, of course, that successful innovation relies on many other factors like company strategy, competition, the existence of infrastructure and standards, regulation and more.

Customer perspectives on the introduction of Mondex

We start our examination of the future by looking into the past. The example of Mondex goes back to the 1990s and was not successful. It was, however, a large-scale introduction of entirely new technology and a digital payment solution targeting a broad group of customers. In this respect, the story is similar to the existing considerations of introducing CBDCs. Contrary to many introductions of payment solutions, Mondex was introduced with consumer tests, interviews with merchants and a large-scale pilot. Yet the initiative failed. We study the learning from the project and point out how customer and participant suggestions to include whole ecosystems and local initiatives were not acted upon.

Mondex was an electronic purse, a prepaid payment instrument based on a secure chip, and was introduced in the 1990s. The chip was integrated in a smart card, allowing peer-to-peer transfer directly between the card and offline. In the words of Dave Birch (2017: 28), 'people could pay each other without going through a third party and without paying a charge. It was a true cash replacement.'

The solution was developed by Tim Jones and Graham Higgins working for NatWest Bank and later spun off as Mondex International with a large number of banks and Mastercard as shareholders. The solution was implemented in a number of countries in the late 1990s including the UK, the US, Canada, Hong Kong and more, but it never fully caught on. Mondex was fully acquired by Mastercard in 2001, and the last solution was replaced in the mid-2000s.

The solution allowed users to make transactions by inserting their cards into a device which would facilitate the transfer of funds and record the transaction onto the card. Shops needed special point-of-sale machines to accept the cards and a special device for the customers to unlock and lock their card with a PIN.

Cards could be topped up using an ATM, at a bank branch, or in several stores and businesses with compatible hardware. There was also a special Mondex phone developed that let you top up the card by phone. Depending on the country where the system was implemented, Mondex cards were accepted at a variety of businesses – supermarkets, department stores, public transport, taxis, car parks, vending machines, restaurants, cafés and many more. Interestingly, the card could be used internationally as it could manage up to five currencies that could even be changed.

According to Bátiz-Lazo and Moretta (2016) and Consult Hyperion (2015) the early prototypes of the solution underwent substantial consumer research, including trials in canteens. During the market research, customers stressed that the solutions should be close to cash (no central record of transactions), that it should be possible to lock the card, and that it should be possible to use the card everywhere. The first was part of the model, the locking device was developed, but in the major UK trial of Mondex the card could not be used throughout the whole ecosystem, meaning that several means of payments were always needed. The UK trial was for two years, and was conducted in Swindon. It included 700 shops, restaurants and large retailers, as well as many of Swindon's buses and car parks. Over the trial period this only led to its adoption by 15 per cent of customers, and the trial was deemed a failure.

The failure can be put down to several reasons. First, internet payments were introduced before the project was finished, changing the potential of the model. Second, users found the processes for getting a card and topping it up with money far too complex. Third, the fact that not all parts of the ecosystem (like all car parks) were included was a drawback leading to continued use of cash. This last point was probably key. A trial in a number of university campuses was more successful. Here the card was used for all relevant aspects of student life.

Birch gives some good explanations of what happened from the points of both retailers and customers: 'Many of the retailers were enthusiastic because there was no transaction charge' (2017: 28). It also cut down the cost of handling cash despite the need for POS machines and lock/unlock devices. Interestingly, customers never used some of the service's features, but they turned out to be useful in unexpected ways:

> As it turned out, customers never bothered locking their cards and never used the lock or unlock stations, but it was the fact that the lock existed and that the lock/unlock stations were visible that gave them confidence in the system.
>
> (Birch, 2017: 28)

But, Birch explains, the card was difficult to obtain:

> It was a pain to get hold of – I can remember the first time I walked into a bank to get a card. I wandered in with 50 quid and had expected to wander out with a card with 50 quid loaded onto it but it didn't work like that. I had to set up an account and fill out some forms and then wait for the card to be posted to me. Most normal people couldn't be bothered to do any of this so ultimately only around 14,000 cards were issued.
>
> (Birch, 2017: 29)

And the solution to top up the card wasn't well thought out:

> The way that you loaded your card was to go to an ATM. Now, the banks involved in the project had chosen an especially crazy way to implement the ATM interface. Remember, you have to have a bank account in order to have one of these cards and so that meant that you also had an ATM card. So if you wanted to load money onto your Mondex card, you had to go to the ATM with your ATM card and put

> your ATM card in and enter your pin and then select 'Mondex value' or whatever the menu said and then you had to put in your Mondex card. Most people couldn't be bothered. If you go to an ATM with your ATM card then you might as well get cash, which is what they did.
>
> (Birch, 2017: 29)

Along the same lines, it was a problem that although many retailers and some car parks and buses accepted the Mondex card, there was not full coverage (as wished for by customers in the first place) and people in the pilot city still needed to carry cash for some car parks and some types of travel. This ties in nicely with the view from Bátiz-Lazo and Moretta (2016):

> The one big exception and where Mondex was indeed successful had been the six British university campuses using the electronic wallet and in particular that of Exeter, which is very much self-contained and the card was really universal as, regardless of their choice of bank, every single student and staff member was issued with a NatWest Mondex card. It then became not only their debit card but also their student union card, ID card, photocopier, library, bars inside and outside campus, payphones, buses, etc., at the point of replacing every other card the student had.

Both also point out that it was probably a mistake not to bring the solution to the internet or mobile, and in general not to follow up on ideas from users:

> There were many people who came to the scheme with innovative ideas and new applications – retailers who wanted to issue their own Mondex cards, groups who wanted to buy preloaded disposable cards and so on. They were all turned away. I remember going to a couple of meetings with groups of charities who wanted to put 'Swindon Money' on the card, something that I was very enthusiastic about. But the banks were not interested.
>
> (Birch, 2017: 30)

The story of Mondex is a great example of how difficult it is to understand how new technology may catch on in existing environments. In the words of Bátiz-Lazo and Moretta (2016), 'Consumers don't always know what they want. So be wary of consumer research.' But, this is exactly where we would argue that it is important not to stop at asking customers 'what they want'. Rather, the importance is to observe behaviour and pain points, and analyse how technology can help overcome them. In this respect the story of Mondex provides valuable information:

- When doing such an extensive pilot of a new solution it would be useful to let anthropologists observe and document the actions and experiences alongside the uptake numbers. This would surely have led to an understanding of the difficulties in getting a card and topping it up.
- The observation about the need to cover whole ecosystems was stated, but overlooked. Customers reacted against having to carry several different payment methods for parking. We normally consider choice an advantage, but here is a message about the need to take time to consider which kind of payment will work. We saw similar reactions in Indonesia when analysing material for a study on CBDCs and financial inclusion (Narula et al, 2023). There were so many digital wallets available that people would need for different purposes. Particularly, cab drivers explained how they would need to use workarounds when a customer did not have the relevant means of payment (see the description in Chapter 7).
- Finally, time and work was spent on developing a locking mechanism at the request of customers – a solution that caused issues for merchants and was little used. This is a reminder that listening to customers may not need to be literal. When customers say that they want to be able to lock a payment device, the broader message is that they need to trust the providers and to understand the risk they are dealing with.

Coming back to our earlier question of why it is important to do customer research, the story is a good example of the importance of designing good research, combining customer wishes with other insights and being willing to act to overcome specific pain points.

Pix, the Brazilian instant payment success

Our next payment example is far more recent and very different in the type and amount of customer attention. The introduction of the payments system Pix in Brazil illustrates that an understanding of customer needs can develop through other means than direct customer observation or interviews. In Chapter 5 we mentioned employees as a source of information. In the example of Pix we see a combination of learning from previous solutions, merchant representation and input from customer organizations, resulting in a success. The Brazilian instant payment solution gained an uptake of 67 per cent of the adult population in just 15 months.

As early as 2016 Brazil's central bank, the BCB, set a strategic payments agenda which has since been updated in 2019 and 2020 to include six pillars (inclusion, competitiveness, transparency, education, sustainability and excellence) and initiatives like open banking, financial education and instant payments like Pix.

Pix was introduced by the BCB in 2020 as part of the financial inclusion agenda. The instant payments solution is free for individuals and entrepreneurs but has a fee for merchants and corporations. It helps merchants and consumers make instant payments via telephone based on their phone contacts, their personal tax number (CPF), and a random key code or a QR code. Pix is based on an account, which could be a bank account or an account with a payment service provider participating in Pix. The account can be a current deposit account, a savings account or a prepaid payment account. This, of course, means that an account with a bank or a payment provider offering the Pix solution is necessary. However, in 2021 the Global Findex Database found that 84 per cent of people in Brazil have either one or the other.

By April 2023 there were just over 800 financial institutions offering Pix, including banks, digital wallet services, and retail stores. By the end of May 2023, 138 million individuals, or 80 per cent of the Brazilian adult population, had either made or received a Pix transaction. The majority of Pix transactions by number are peer-to-peer.

At the end of 2021, the first part of the third phase opened, which supports payment initiation services (PISPs) via Pix, meaning that Pix can be used to initiate a payment in another financial institution (bank) when authorized by the customer, that is, without using the bank's own banking app. Since the end of 2021 it has been possible to use Pix to withdraw cash in shops and stores, either as a specific amount, 'Pix Troco', or as the difference between the total transaction and the amount spent in the shop, 'Pix Saque'.

The introduction of Pix hasn't been without its teething problems. In particular, Pix became the target of crime, with robbers forcing people to transfer money to them using Pix. In response, the BCB implemented upper limits on transfers, particularly at night when most robberies take place. One of the issues raised during our fieldwork (Taylor and Broløs, 2022) is that there is no customer service if a Pix transaction goes wrong. Once the transaction is confirmed the only way to change it is through negotiation with the counterparty. This function is available on Pix.

In this way, Pix resembles cash. Unlike cash transactions, though, Pix transactions are automatically documented with an electronic receipt provided to both payer and payee. Financial providers are required to keep a log of transactions. Our sense is that people appreciate the fact that they can go into their banking app and view their Pix transactions among their other ones.

Pix has attracted attention across the world for the success in adoption (World Bank, 2022; Duarte et al, 2022). As mentioned by Duarte et al (2022), the success is based on the combination of the overall central bank strategy and previous experience with the double role of the central bank as regulator and infrastructure provider as well as the fact that Pix was mandatory to adopt for the major banks.

As far as we have been able to find, no customer research has been conducted in Brazil. However, according to Duarte et al (2022), 'The BCB approached Pix product development with a user-centric perspective, focusing on the concrete needs of households and businesses in their payment habits, and gaps in the current system.'

Since the initiation of the project in 2018, the BCB has worked with a forum called the Pix Forum, including a long list of market participants, experts, consultants and representatives from user organizations (Banco Central do Brasil, no date). From the very start of the work, they identified a range of use cases, such as P2P, P2B, electronic bill pay and deferred payments. The Pix Forum is still active in the discussion of adjustments and expansions of Pix.

BCB also supported the rolling out of the solution by communication measures, In the words of Duarte et al (2022):

> For instance, to support public awareness and adoption, the BCB ran an extensive communication strategy with PSPs, individuals, businesses, media and other stakeholders. The rollout required complementary policies to increase digital literacy, particularly for the most disadvantaged and for older users, who are less comfortable making digital payments.

Many of the interviewees in our Brazil study mentioned the extensive TV campaigns for Pix. But nobody talked about educational initiatives. Rather, most of the more vulnerable groups mentioned that they had learned from friends and family. Particularly, many older people had learned from their children. We expected that the Pix uptake would be lower in the rural area of study, but in fact particularly for the elderly it was the opposite. The reason was that access to cash is more difficult in the rural areas with ATMs, which are often only available in major cities, necessitating a weekly visit for banking, shopping and bill paying. Here Pix was a great help.

The global challenge of replacing cash: Adoption of CBDCs

As already mentioned in Chapter 3, the probable introduction of CBDCs in many countries is perhaps one of the most discussed innovations in payments and indeed in financial intermediation. It can be seen as a simple replacement of cash with a digital payment system but in reality this has broader implications. For each country there are issues of macroeconomic independence, support of trading and cross-border transactions, financial intermediation, data storage and privacy as well as financial inclusion. The introduction of a CBDC represents a case of the kind of complexity discussed at the start of the chapter. Field research may need to be undertaken in several fields and contexts, and each country will have to find its own solution. And probably not only a one-time solution but also a digital path forward.

The Bank for International Settlements (BIS, 2022) published the study mentioned above to discuss what drives consumer needs and adoption of CBDCs. Its angle is that of a government needing to understand consumer needs in a new financial ecosystem. The analysis is based on existing experience and knowledge about consumer adaptation of new means of payments, like mobile P2P solutions. It also considers market conditions in general. The report does not only look at immediate needs, but also tries to anticipate consumers' future needs. The report identifies drivers such as reduced cost of payments and access, including the customer's option to not change their current device and the possibility to conduct offline transactions. The report also points to the importance of network effects. Though CBDCs may be designed to reach non-included groups or target poverty, implementing a CBDC as a comprehensive initiative will generally be dependent also on a broader use of the currency among other groups of consumers, as well as merchants and public institutions (Taylor and Broløs, 2022). The report identifies drivers like safety of funds, reduced costs, offline functionality, security, privacy and accessibility. It also identifies a number of use cases for different consumer groups. Since this report focuses on consumers, these include well-connected consumers, consumers with limited internet access, unbanked persons, disabled users, users with high privacy concerns and small merchants at the POS.

Narula et al (2023), on the other hand, focus on describing design possibilities that will ensure financial reach and inclusion. They combined 13 field studies of low-income payment behaviour in four different countries spanning experiences of rural payments, small merchant needs, freelance workers, shopping, religion and cross-border payments (remittances). These studies provide rich descriptions of access, difficulties, fraud and workarounds, often including the help of friends, family or community. These insights help identify differences between intermediated and non-intermediated currencies (cash) with regard to inclusion:

> Crucially, we argue, any digital currency is only as good for inclusion as the intermediaries through which people use it. Designing a CBDC that merely replicates the features of existing digital payment systems would not make a meaningful difference for financial inclusion.
>
> (Narula et al, 2023)

Important points to consider when designing and before choosing technology are:

- custody (whether you hold money yourself, e.g. cash, or have access through a deposit in an account)
- access (whether a device, a connection, ID, etc., are necessary to use money)
- finality (whether a transaction can be reversed)
- data (whether there is a data trail and who can access it)
- distance (how to transact over a distance)

The report also points out that the level of trust in different stakeholders is crucial.

Following these insights, we hope to see a wide array of fieldwork studies initiated in the area of CBDCs as countries move from the decision to research the area toward the design and launch of solutions.

The introduction of the eNaira

Only a few CBDCs have been introduced so far, making it a good example of developing for the future. We use the example of Nigeria because of the launch in 2021 and because of the country's inclusion in a recent study of CBDCs and financial inclusion (Narula et al, 2023).

Though most countries research the issue of CBDCs and though many mention financial reach and inclusion as a potential benefit of CBDCs, there has been little research into consumer and merchant adoption of a solution (BIS, 2022). The authors' participation in a central bank CBDC conference in 2022 with presentations from a large number of banks showed much mention of customers, but little research into customer needs.

Nigeria launched the first phase of the eNaira in October 2021, making it one of the first countries, and the first African country, to implement a retail CBDC. There were several goals of the eNaira, including financial inclusion, empowerment and poverty reduction.

The eNaira is accessed through the eNaira wallet. At the launch, the download and use of the wallet was open for users with either a bank account and bank identification or a mobile phone number in combination with a simple personal ID. This was meant to offer broad access but did not lead to broad adoption. In response, the government introduced a lower level of activity open to customers without a bank account, requiring no ID and simply a mobile phone. In August 2022 the Central Bank introduced a second phase of the eNaira with the goal of reaching eight million users (Central Bank of Nigeria, 2022) and at the same time announced the adoption with 840,000 downloads and 270,000 active users in August 2022. Of the active users, 252,000 were consumer wallets and only 17,000 merchants.

As far as we know, no targeted research of consumer behaviour or consumer needs was undertaken prior to the introduction of the eNaira. But the research in Nigeria in 2022 as part of the study on CBDCs and financial inclusion (Narula et al, 2023) brings a few insights that could have been used to help the new currency reach its target. These studies clearly illustrated both the lack of trust in the government and the central bank and the lack of consumers with bank accounts. Particularly the last information was readily available and could have been considered before the launch (or alternatively with a launch in phases).

A specific goal of the launch was the reduction of the informal economy (including corruption). This had already led to low trust in government institutions and was furthered by the ban on investment in cryptocurrencies in February 2021 (Central Bank of Nigeria, 2021). (Nigerians had been among the most active worldwide investors in cryptocurrency following high inflation and currency depreciation.) Narula et al (2023) found that many of the Nigerian interviewees identified lack of trust in government and banks as a reason for the low uptake of the eNaira.

As can be seen from the numbers of active users, there was not only a problem of uptake among low-income groups. Interviewees also mentioned that they had difficulty finding merchants who would accept payments with eNaira. Just as in the case of Mondex, a new means of payments needs to be introduced in the whole ecosystem to be a success (see also BIS, 2022).

Finally, there was an obvious lack of prepared communication for the eNaira launch. Interviewees tell stories of lack of knowledge about the new payment solution, not only among consumers but also with the banking partners (Narula et al, 2023). This is very much in contrast with Brazil's introduction of Pix.

Learning for the introduction of CBDCs

The examples described above illustrate the value of understanding customer behaviour and pain points as well as possible when introducing new solutions. They also illustrate that different participants in the financial ecosystem need to prepare in different ways to reach customers of the future with their innovations. This means that the angle of a customer insight project will be different for a government introducing money, a company introducing a payment solution, an NGO building a first overview of design and technical infrastructure or a technology provider preparing to develop the security systems of the future.

As described in Chapter 7, the Finthropology study in Brazil was undertaken by the technology and security provider SICPA and aimed to understand low-income and particularly rural payment behaviour with a view to develop and support an inclusive CBDC solution for countries in the Global South. The study focused on creating an understanding of customer use of cash and other payment instruments, including how they combine tools, manage finances and interact with customers and family members. The study further focused on understanding the uptake of the newly introduced Pix, as described above. The report contains a wide variety of insights, particularly regarding the ways in which people make payments, how they combine payments tools, manage finances with others (especially family members), and issues of trust, some of which focus on the differences between the urban and rural locations. We have described a wealth of examples throughout this book and particularly in Chapter 7. These insights were helpful for SICPA's further work on supporting central banks in the introduction of CBDCs – not necessarily in Brazil, but generally.

Researching for future innovation

We set out in this chapter to answer the question of why it might be a good idea to study existing customer behaviour to develop innovative solutions for the future. We have seen that a deep understanding of customer needs, dreams and pain points can lead to innovation where new technologies are put to use to improve and reinvent basic financial solutions. We have also seen that such understanding can start in different ways, including customer observation and interviews, personal experience of challenges to be overcome, front-end employees with strong customer understanding, and the input of customer organizations. The example of Mondex particularly explains that those insights always need to be seen in context.

We have made the important point that though customers in general may not be technological experts at the level of FSPs they may still be able to share insights into future customer behaviour. Some customers may already have great digital and virtual experience, for instance, from social media or from gaming. Also, customer roles will be changing, allowing more interaction – even in finance. In this area we can find much inspiration from the digital community roles where customers may come up with ideas, identity faults and malfunctions and even to some extent act as supporters or teachers.

We have not yet discussed how this changes the way we do qualitative research. Most of the examples in this book have been based on traditional physical observations and interviews. But, of course, the development towards digital environments is also changing anthropological methods. We need to observe payment behaviour in digital spaces and do interviews that can throw light on differences in choice. We need to interview people about their preferences between virtual and real, and relations to personal identity and characters. It will also be interesting to observe customer roles in digital spaces and in API platforms, and to discuss with customers how focused they are on creating their own solutions and how willing to share ideas.

In Chapter 10 we take a next step to discuss how such work can be integrated into research for innovation.

TAKEAWAYS

- Innovation starts with listening to customers and understanding.
- Understanding in a context means understanding the ecosystem including network effects.
- Innovation can be built on removing pain points or avoiding them altogether by changing the context. Technology can help to do that.
- The field is changing. You may need to listen to new groups of customers or partners – and to listen in new environments.
- And you will need to listen in new ways as customer roles are changing.

References

Banco Central do Brasil (no date) The Pix forum, BCB. www.bcb.gov.br/estabilidadefinanceira/forumpagamentosinstantaneos (archived at https://perma.cc/PE3B-YW5X)

Bank for International Settlements (2021) Central bank digital currencies: User needs and adoption. www.bis.org/publ/othp42_user_needs.pdf (archived at https://perma.cc/NSP3-E7LW)

Bátiz-Lazo, B and Moretta, T (2016) Mondex and VisaCash: The first (failed) attempt at an electronic purse, in B Bátiz-Lazo and L Efthymiou (eds) *The Book of Payments: Historical and contemporary views on the cashless economy*, Palgrave-Macmillan (Springer Nature), London, 177–86

Birch, D (2017) *Before Babylon, Beyond Bitcoin: From money that we understand to money that understands us*, London Publishing Partnership, London

Birch, D (2023) The impact of ChatGPT and open banking cannot be underestimated, Forbes, 27 May. www.forbes.com/sites/davidbirch/2023/05/27/the-impact-of-chatgpt-and-open-banking-cannot-be-underestimated (archived at https://perma.cc/H4UB-A2M5)

BIS (2022) CBDCs in emerging market economies, BIS paper 123, 30 April, 89–94

Broløs, A and Taylor, E B (2020) *Female Finance: Digital, mobile, networked*, EWPN and Keen Innovation. ewpn.eu/female-finance-digital-mobile-networked (archived at https://perma.cc/U4JV-HD32)

Broløs, A and Taylor, E B (2023) Appendix: Fieldwork contexts, in N Narula, L Swartz and J Frizzo-Barker, *CBDC: Expanding financial inclusion or deepening the divide? Exploring design choices that could make a difference*, MIT Digital Currency Initiative, MIT Media Lab and Maiden Lab

CapGemini Research Institute (2023) World property and casualty insurance report 2023, CapGemini. www.capgemini.com/insights/research-library/world-property-and-casualty-insurance-report (archived at https://perma.cc/6NWT-X694)

Central Bank of Nigeria (2021) Cryptocurrency trading: CBN orders banks to close operating accounts, CBN. www.cbn.gov.ng/out/2021/ccd/volume%203%20number%202%20cbn%20update%20february%20 2021.pdf (archived at https://perma.cc/MN83-8Y7V)

Central Bank of Nigeria (2022) Emefiele flags-off second phase of eNaira project, CBN, August. www.cbn.gov.ng/FeaturedArticles/2022/articles/eNairaHackathonStory.pdf (archived at https://perma.cc/XJH6-9BD5)

Consult Hyperion (2015) It was twenty years ago today, Consult Hyperion, 7 July. chyp.com/2015/07/07/it-was-twenty-years-ago-today (archived at https://perma.cc/7VZV-J6WZ)

Duarte, A, Frost, J, Gambacorta, L, Wilkens, P K and Shin, H S (2022) Central banks, the monetary system and public payment infrastructures: Lessons from Brazil's Pix, BIS Bulletin, 52, 23 March. www.bis.org/publ/bisbull52.pdf (archived at https://perma.cc/S2WN-738B)

J P Morgan (no date) Transforming the way money, information and assets move around the world, J P Morgan. www.jpmorgan.com/onyx/index (archived at https://perma.cc/EF8R-WMEN)

Klimas, P and Czakon, W (2022) Gaming innovation ecosystem: Actors, roles and co-innovation processes, *Review of Managerial Science*, 16, 2213–59

Narula, N, Swartz, L and Frizzo-Barker, J (2023) *Expanding Financial Inclusion or Deepening the Divide? Exploring design choices that could make a difference*, MIT Digital Currency Initiative/Maiden Lab, Cambridge, MA

Peter, T, Cortet, M and Tsovillis, J (2023) A sneak preview of the InnoPAY Open Banking Monitor Q1 2023: The old guard are embracing new opportunities, InnoPAY, 11 May. www.innopay.com/en/publications/sneak-preview-innopay-open-banking-monitor-q1-2023-old-guard-are-embracing-new (archived at https://perma.cc/4PPR-UEX3)

Ree, J (2023) Nigeria's eNaira, one year after, IMF Working Paper no WP/23/104. www.imf.org/-/media/Files/Publications/WP/2023/English/wpiea2023104-print-pdf.ashx (archived at https://perma.cc/A8FR-SX8L)

Taylor, E B and Broløs, A (2022) *Money and Payments in Low Income Brazil*, Finthropology/SICPA, The Hague, Netherlands

Thompson, S (2023) *Green and Sustainable Finance: Principles and practice in banking, investment and insurance*, Kogan Chartered Banker Series, Kogan Page, London

Von Hippel, E (2007) Horizontal innovation networks – by and for users, *Industrial and Corporate Change*, 16 (2), 293–315

World Bank (2022) World Bank fast payment toolkit case study: Brazil, World Bank. fastpayments.worldbank.org/sites/default/files/2022-07/WorldBank_FPS_Brazil_%20Pix_Case_study.pdf (archived at https://perma.cc/YP5J-BPQV)

World Bank (2022) the Global Findex Database

World Economic Forum (2023) Demystifying the consumer metaverse, World Economic Forum in collaboration with Accenture, January. www.weforum.org/publications/demystifying-the-consumer-metaverse (archived at https://perma.cc/A8CV-P32P)

Zunino, A (2023) The future of real estate: Tokenization and its impact on the industry, Forbes, 22 May. www.forbes.com/sites/forbestechcouncil/2023/05/22/the-future-of-real-estate-tokenization-and-its-impact-on-the-industry (archived at https://perma.cc/V9NM-ZRXW)

Organizing for customer-driven innovation 10

Analysis, tools and resources to use for innovation

Throughout this book, we have argued that innovation for customers should be based on insights into customer pain points, needs and dreams. The foundation for this is an understanding of human behaviour as often irrational, quickly changing, and very social. Digital transformation is very much driven by the introduction of new technology, not only with regard to infrastructure but also in the development of customer innovation. We have given many examples of how turning this around to focus on customer needs can lead to successful adoption of new solutions. Customer-centricity is not only about the analysis of customer transactions but should also dive deeper into customer environments – whether these are analogue or digital, real or virtual.

We realize that many financial organizations are unfamiliar with this type of research. This is a practical chapter that provides advice on how to begin collecting, analysing and using qualitative data in innovation and how to integrate such work into innovation processes, from ideation to customer testing.

We start by discussing what applied research is and how it relates to existing user practices. We then give practical advice on how to start integrating systematic research in innovation. We advise companies to begin by drawing upon their existing resources; that is, who in their organization already has experience of customer research, and how they connect with the company strategy and company's work with digital transformation. We suggest creating a pilot project to base further work on a practical story. We share an overview of different qualitative tools to understand customer needs. We discuss how to build a research culture and how to integrate this in the company's customer-centricity and innovation culture, and how to relate to partners. We finally discuss how valuable customer insights can be part of the company development of future scenarios or 'future preparedness'.

Doing user research in your organization

We have often encountered the view that research is both long-term and difficult to integrate into company practices. Organizations expect such knowledge generated by research to trickle 'down' from universities to financial institutions over time, often with the help and understanding of consultancies or technology providers. However, research comes in many forms. Stokes (1997), for example, argues that some research will be purely driven by theoretical curiosity, some will be driven by potential application and some may result from a combination of theoretical and application curiosity, as in the development of penicillin by Louis Pasteur who also did practical company research.

Applied research fits well in companies. It can include long-term initiatives or short-term projects, for instance in relation to innovation. It can be carried out to understand future trends and scenarios to help form future strategy. It can help to develop ideas for how to apply new technologies within company strategy, whether to enhance processes or to support customer innovation. Indeed, the potential of research to contribute to innovation and strategy is often overlooked:

> One of the most common complaints we have heard from user researchers over the years is that their colleagues think that user research involves only basic research or solutions-centred research. There is little awareness that researchers can also set about discovering the unknown and putting their insights to work for the company overall.
>
> (Taylor and Uy, 2021: 11)

User research is already undertaken in most larger organizations in the form of market research, analysis of customer activity, user tests or even listening to employee comments on customer behaviour or complaints (like the case of QCash in Chapter 6). However, such research often remains within a lab setting, with few excursions into real-life contexts. How can organizations break with this habit and venture into the places where people live, work, and play – whether face-to-face or digitally?

USER RESEARCH

'User research' can mean many different things. Taylor and Uy (2021) define user research as 'any kind of systematic investigation of how people… use and experience products and services'. They mention that user research can be applied for different purposes, ranging from general understanding of customers over users' tests of products and solutions to the development of strategy. 'People' can be individual customers or consumers, or they can be employees in organizations (corporates, SMEs or others). User research can be both qualitative and quantitative and it can involve customers directly – or not. Seen in this broad light, it follows that most organizations, even small ones, do some kind of research. In the following, we explore qualitative user research focused on the perspective of the customer in a context. We also relate it to the more common quantitative research where insights are based on data about customer groups.

How to get started

As we discussed in Chapter 2, many organizations see digital transformation as a road to achieving customer-centricity with the purpose of innovating both services and business models. We also pointed out that many experts seem to see digital data as the main path towards the development of hyper-personal solutions for customers.

Most experts (Camp et al, 2020), however, agree that customer-centricity requires the introduction of a customer-centric culture throughout the organization to make sure that all teams focus on serving customer needs and that this effort is aligned with company strategy. Here we focus on how to start doing customer research. We divide the process into three steps: (1) a user research pilot; (2) mapping research knowledge; and (3) building a research culture and metrics. Depending on your organization, (1) and (2) could be reversed.

A user research pilot

There are several reasons why a natural initial step would be a user research pilot. The first and foremost is that a successful project creates a great narrative to use in the continued development of a user research culture. The second reason is that it will contribute to the organization's understanding of what is needed to do good user research, the necessary skills, the tools that work, how to communicate both internally and externally, and what key elements might go into metrics that measure the success of the work.

Such a project should be anchored in the company strategy and target areas where innovation is important for key customers or important niche groups. Given the current rate of change, it would be a great idea to choose an area where you already know that your company needs to build new knowledge; for example, the younger generation's experiences in virtual environments and their expectations about future financial services. Depending on company size, existing skills and the innovativeness of company culture, there is a variety of possibilities to get started and to learn:

- Contact a researcher to work with you on the planning and analysis of the pilot project.
- Identify an internal employee with relevant experience to drive the project – with full leadership support and possibly access to assistance. If the company culture already supports interdisciplinary work, bringing marketing, IT, customer support and business development resources together, the project could be anchored in a project group. This could also include external partners.

- Another possibility is to reach out to a local university and set a challenge for a group of Masters students. Best projects could be invited to write their thesis in-company and supported by the company data. They should also be invited to present tools and ideas in groups of company employees.
- Different combinations can of course come into play.

No matter how the pilot is done, it is important to ensure that the process and results are communicated across the company and partners so that the lessons (positive and negative) can be taken forward.

Mapping research in your organization

The pilot project should set you up with a good innovation story to start the next step, which would be to identify research and knowledge resources across the organization. The larger the organization, the more difficult it is to know about all research done or knowledge collected by different departments:

> In large organizations research and data collection tend to be done in different departments. Nobody has an overview of all the knowledge being created, and it is rarely brought together… people with a formal research role aren't the only ones who collect, analyze, and manage data. You might find that your company has more researchers than you thought.
>
> (Taylor and Uy, 2021: 28)

So, if you have not already done so, then take some time to map out your organization's knowledge competencies and gaps:

- Identify who in the organization is involved in customer-centric work. They could be placed in digital development, R&D, marketing, customer service, strategy, data analytics or UX. And they could be partners from outside the organization.
- You should further consider how data and insights are brought about and by whom. How are they analysed and used, and how are insights shared throughout the organization?

- A natural next step is to map out how the different groups interact, with a specific view to how they serve your customer-centricity goals and your innovation processes.
- Create an overview of the skills and competencies involved as well as what seems to be missing.

This will provide you with a good overview of how customer knowledge is built in your organization and how well this knowledge is integrated towards customer-centricity. It will also identify gaps in knowledge and gaps in communication.

In small organizations, this exercise can likely be managed more easily by bringing people together in a meeting or event. Small organizations may, however, need to bring external expertise to undertake systematic research work.

Mapping existing and potential customer involvement

An overview of company research is just the beginning. For innovation to be relevant to customers, customer comments need to be taken into account. To do this, you should map your customer touchpoints. You should pay particular attention to human ones that may not be digitally recorded or part of quantitative data that is automatically collected. This may include, for example, contact between customers and customer service representatives.

You should identify who in your organization is directly involved with customers, and how. You should also identify and describe how well the organization picks up on insights from front personnel. These might include insurance brokers and sales personnel, advisers in branches or customer service centres, as well as personnel managing complaints or damage. As we have described earlier, employees can be a great source of customer information – though they may not necessarily be able to analyse how best to provide customers with innovation.

This means that the mapping should consider how well frontline customer data is interacting with quantitative customer data. The mapping should consider how customer interaction is changing with the development of virtual spaces, customer communities and social media influencers, as well as customer interaction in open finance interfaces like open APIs. What new customer touchpoints are appearing and how do they connect with existing customer services?

Building the culture

Mapping your organization's customer knowledge is a good starting point for understanding how your customer insights fit into your company's overall strategy, and particularly how it fits into innovation processes and the company's customer-centricity culture. As with any other transformative initiative, the support of company leadership is crucial. Top management recognition of the need to understand customers actions and decision-making in their communities and environments is necessary to create time and space for research as a new way of working. This includes the whole process, from hiring to competence-building to integration of research into goals and company communications. McKinsey describes the process of achieving customer-centricity like this:

> Culture is often overlooked, but is a critical foundation in a distinctively customer-centric organization: an organization where all employees collectively and individually prioritize customer needs in everything that they do every day.
>
> (Camp et al, 2020)

The need to create a customer research culture is similar in many ways. However, little has been written on how best to do this in finance. Some important elements of a user research culture are the following, mainly from Taylor and Uy (2021):

- Curiosity as a key value. This is an element that relates well to innovation. It is a value that should be encouraged, not only among researchers but across all employees. Often the knowledge of a customer pain point will already be registered in some part of the organization. The story behind the building of QCash (Chapter 6) is a good example of how an employee wondering about 'strange' actions can lead to a research process, and later to innovation.

- Building interdisciplinary trust and teams is another key issue. Your knowledge-mapping exercise will probably show how resources are placed in different departments where their work may be directed by different and possibly contradicting key point indicators of activity and result. It is key to creating a broad understanding of how research supports company goals and why contributing to data collection and data analysis can generate better services and results. This can only happen if researchers' roles and importance are broadly described and accepted. And it is perhaps a more important issue because research skills are quite different from traditional financial skills. They may require both hiring differently and helping bridge gaps between different employee backgrounds. Learning about the need to listen with an open mind can prove very useful throughout the organization. There are many ways of going about this, such as creating interdisciplinary teams and projects as well as letting researchers describe research projects and insights in workshops and events.
- Working with partners. It is important to involve partners and customers in this work wherever it resonates with company processes.
- Building capacity. Of course, it is important to improve the company's capacity with respect to relevant research skills and competencies, and integrating them across the organization will be necessary to ensure results. This can come through hiring, education or through external assistance or through a combination of all three. We should mention that retention of employees is important here, including the potential of people moving between different roles in the company. This may appear self-evident for key knowledge workers, but should be taken seriously.
- Communication. Creating a common way of communicating about customer services and customer insights is important and should include not only information about projects, but also the celebration of insights and the ways they contribute to innovation.
- Metrics and indicators. If metrics and key point indicators are important parts of company practices, you should consider how user research can be fitted into these. It is not easy, as research will

never have outcomes that can be specified in advance. You can, however, create metrics on customer research activity and communication as well as customer involvement in different projects and processes.

Building a research organization

Building a research organization to offer continuous customer or user research within a customer-centric culture should be reflected in company organization. By 'research organization', we mean an organization where customer services are built on customer insights and customer research, and in which research is viewed as a core company activity. We do not think of a designated research and development department doing research on their own. In a customer-centric organization all activities will be focused on serving customer needs in the best possible way, and customer research should be an integrated part of innovation. We would, however, like to stress that qualitative research can provide great leverage, not just for testing prototypes or building customer innovation but also to contribute to company strategy. Qualitative customer research can play an important part in understanding how new technologies can best serve changing customer needs in a digital future.

A natural part of product development and innovation

User research should be a natural part of product development and innovation. Users include a diverse group of contacts, spanning:

- individual customers using products in traditional ways
- customers participating in digital communities
- corporate customers or SMEs designing interfaces, and solutions through open banking platforms
- partners connecting their services to FSP solutions

They also include both internal and external participants providing market scans and technology trends.

Customers can be involved throughout the whole process, from market search to ideation, development, testing, implementation, troubleshooting and customer group support when the solution is introduced. As described above, undertaking customer studies that take place within a customer's own environment is a great way to start when entering new markets, offering services to new customer groups, or introducing new or changed solutions or technologies. Such studies allow you to gain insights into the way customers consider technologies, how they engage with them, how they use them alongside other tools, and what role a community plays in this work. At the same time, it is possible to gain a deeper understanding of customers' views on changes in services or technology.

In the pre-development phase, it also makes sense to involve existing knowledge of customer questions and complaints. This could be either from customers directly, for instance in digital communities, or through interviews with employees who handle customer interactions. This will often throw light on pain points – but not necessarily point out a direct way of overcoming them.

In the innovation development phase, it is a good idea to consider whether customer or partner co-creation is a possibility. Partner co-development and development in API environments are obvious areas of co-creation. But it is also possible to do this in broader customer communities. Participants can suggest ideas for new features or solutions – or even make them if you share an open environment with them.

Later in the development process, customer communities and customer focus groups can provide ratings of suggested changes in solutions. They can also be part of testing. And depending on the communities, they can even be helpful in sharing views or advice on tech glitches and more, like our examples from buy now, pay later communities in Chapter 7.

A key part of strategy development

Qualitative research can also provide great leverage for the development of company strategy. This can clearly be a great advantage when targeting new markets or new customer groups. Asking customers to talk about their financial habits, how they learned about money management, and how they would like to be able to save or have access to credit, can provide new insights to understand the potential in new markets.

From a different perspective, there is potential in sharing some kind of learning environment with users, partners and even regulators to co-create an understanding of the complexity of future finance. This could be with the goal of identifying long-term considerations and market scans of trends to build into potential scenarios. This kind of learning leads to 'future-preparedness', making it easier to make fast strategic decisions when new developments show. And as companies are likely to have different purposes and cultures, they are likely to make different decisions, making collaboration less of a threat.

Building a user research organization is likely to take some time, and will also require a process that includes occasional failures. During this period of digital transformation, it is, however, likely to provide valid input both in the short and long term. For now, let's dive into some practical possibilities in the toolbox.

The toolbox

Academic research uses qualitative research to gain new knowledge and there is a large body of literature describing how to make sure such research meets scientific standards. As we discussed in Chapter 4, all kinds of biases and assumptions can affect the quality of research data, and so it is necessary to make extensive consideration of the research questions we pose, how we go about investigating them, and the conclusions we reach from our analyses. This is also the case when doing customer research.

But how do we collect data? Throughout this book we have described many research projects – our own and other researchers' – and the method used in them. In this section we describe some of these methods in more detail, focusing especially on their uses in finance research. Most importantly, as mentioned in Chapter 9, research methods are changing and becoming more digital as customer contact moves online. This presents new opportunities in terms of how we can reach research participants, but also challenges in terms of ensuring research remains both scientific and ethical.

In terms of remaining scientific, for example, researchers need to ensure that their sampling makes sense. Just as qualitative researchers tend to carefully select a research site and participants in the analogue world, researchers need to ensure that any sample of online customers is cohesive. For example, when studying buy now, pay later solutions, we conducted digital ethnography of a small number of user fora. We analysed posts in a selected time period in each of the fora rather than cherry-picking posts across many fora.

Ethical issues always arise when you work with people – particularly when collecting data on sensitive questions like emotions about finances. Before starting work, we recommend that you think about the general requirements to consider participant rights and protection. This is particularly the case when doing online research, as it is sometimes too easy to collect data on people without their consent. Generally, participants should always be informed about the purpose of the study and be allowed to refuse to participate at any time. You should make sure that you have participants' consent. Participants should be allowed confidentiality and also be allowed to refuse audio or video recording. Also, data should be managed in accordance with agreements and regulations like the General Data Protection Regulation (GDPR) in Europe.

Before we dive into the different ways of collecting data, we would like to draw the attention to the fact that this is only part of the research work. To achieve usable customer insights it is equally important to be able to analyse collected data to draw relevant insights from them. Tools can be helpful in this process but most important is the research experience in describing and combining data to build new knowledge. As we have described before, customer research is not only about asking customers what they think they need but understanding what is needed from the practices and workarounds described and observed.

When building knowledge from interviews, there is a hurdle in transcribing, coding and analysing the insights. There are plenty of digital tools available to help with that, so we won't go deeper into this.

Figure 10.1 Persona of Anna Gomes, the rural entrepreneur

ANNA GOMES

TYPE A rural entrepreneur

DEMOGRAPHICS

Location Ipiabas | **Gender** Female | **Age** 54
Education Primary school
Family Partnered, 2 children, 2 grandchildren
Job Small business owner

BACKGROUND Anna runs a grocery store in the centre of Ipiabas. Anna was able to open the store because she received a small inheritance from an aunt. Her business soon started going well because the other grocery stores in the area are very small; hers has a better range of stock. She said that business dropped a little during the pandemic, but not by much, because people still needed to buy basic goods. Mostly the drop in sales was in more expensive items, such as alcohol and premium dairy products. Her children and grandchildren have all worked in the shop over the years. Now she hires a young local woman to help in the store. Her husband works as a manager on a nearby farm that now offers tourist services such as accommodation and meals.

ITEMS CARRIED

Location:
Debit cards
Store credit card
Loyalty cards
Cash

Non-financial items:
Bag
Keys
Phone
Wallet
Face mask
Headscarf
Paracetamol

PAIN POINTS

Access to cash (distance to ATM/bank)
Carrying cash
Getting change for cash
Lining up at the bank
Cost of transactions

FINANCIAL NEEDS

Receiving money for sales (POS, Pix, cash)
Paying employees
Paying bills
Shopping for groceries
Shopping for personal needs
Buying larger items like phone or furniture
Buying stock for business/production
Saving

FINANCIAL CHOICES

Anna's primary financial concerns involve running her business. She accepts payment in her store via whichever method her customers prefer: cash, card and Pix. She also lets some customers buy groceries on credit, but only if she knows them well and trusts them. Every Monday she rides her scooter to Barra do Piraí to do her banking. She always goes on Mondays because sales are greater over the weekend and she wants to deposit her cash takings as soon as possible. Anna is confident doing her banking online, using both her mobile phone and laptop, but she is unable to stop going to the bank because customers still pay her using cash. Anna and her husband manage the household expenses jointly. Usually she is in charge of the groceries because she runs a shop, and she usually also pays the bills. She is more comfortable using digital banking than her husband.

SOURCE Taylor and Broløs, 2022

Another way of analysing input from qualitative studies is through the creation of 'personas'. This is a well-known way of working with insights and helps condense the many different inputs by creating fictive persons with a background including age, job, family situation and more and examples from the core of the study. In our Brazil study (Taylor and Broløs, 2022) we created a number of personas to illustrate ways of paying and finding workarounds (see Figure 10.1).

Based on our 63 interviews, we created six different personas:

- a mother who works in precarious jobs
- a father who works as a vendor in a market
- a student
- an elderly person in the countryside
- a rural entrepreneur
- a rural farmer

Our aim in this section is to give examples of the most relevant data-collection tools in customer user research, including short descriptions and references. We will try to include possibilities for the use of digital approaches too. We include a series of examples to illustrate the use and the results that can be derived from the use. We also add a description of how combinations of different tools can create great insights. We recommend that you work with specialists in-house or externally to do this type of research.

DATA COLLECTION AND ANALYSIS HAS MANY FLAVOURS

- interviews
- observations, in real or virtual environments
  - work or household environment
  - customer spaces
  - customer interaction
  - open API platforms

- financial diaries
- focus groups
- workshops
- portable kit studies
- drawing money relationships
- user testing
- personas
- coding tools

Ethnography

Ethnography is a method of studying people in the places where they live or where the action is taking place. This can be either in a real or in a virtual setting. The cornerstone of ethnography is participant observation, which involves learning about people's experiences by doing activities with them and recording observations in extensive field notes. This could be a village, a neighbourhood, a workplace, or an online environment (such as an internet forum).

Ethnographers complement participant observation with data obtained in other ways, including recording interviews, analysing documents and deploying questionnaires and surveys. Such data is used to record actual behaviour (what people actually do) as well as reported behaviour (what people say they do). Ethnography is particularly useful to understand how consumers adapt to changing products or economic conditions, and how people's financial behaviour is influenced by their social environment.

Doing ethnography in virtual communities like user groups or gaming communities is most relevant when users communicate in digital spaces, such as internal company sites or public user groups. In our study of BNPL in the USA (Broløs and Taylor, 2022a), we used digital ethnography to study user behaviour in four different BNPL user groups and review fora. We collected and analysed several months of posts consumers placed on each of these sites, including text and images, and other users' comments on them. We examined the language and sentiment consumers used to discuss the services, to build a picture of consumers' overall impressions as well as specific issues. One of the first things we observed was that the vast majority of the groups' members were women. Digital ethnography helped us understand how these groups provide a mutual support group for women who are trying to meet shopping goals and smooth consumption, but are running into pain points. In the near-absence of fast customer service, members turn to each other for help, often successfully.

We used in-person ethnography extensively in our research on payments in Brazil (Taylor and Broløs, 2022). While our main data source was the 63 interviews we carried out across two sites, we also used participant observation in public markets to observe payment behaviour. Throughout the entire period of fieldwork we conducted observations and recorded them in the form of field notes. We spent time in public places in several locations in each fieldsite, watching how people made payments, paying particular attention to interactions between vendors and customers, and the extent to which people seemed to feel comfortable handling items like cash, cards and their phone in public. We also conducted 'participant observation', paying for things ourselves using various methods to test processes and, in particular, asking all shops and vendors if they accept Pix (whether we were intending to pay with it or not).

The value of these kinds of observations is not to be underestimated as they serve as a reliable way to cross-check findings from the surveys and interviews. Observations are a core method of ethnographic research. They are an excellent way to discover how people actually use services rather than relying on people to tell us what they do. For example, when reading the interviews one could be left with the impression that people are very afraid of theft and are exceedingly careful with how they manage valuables in public places. While this is to some extent true, our observations indicate that people are not as careful as they say they are. In the São Paulo market Rua 25 de Março in particular, a site where people say they must be very careful to avoid theft and fraud, people were openly using their phones, standing with their cards in their hands for long periods and communicating their CPFs (Brazilian personal tax number). Our analysis of the interview data is tempered, and improved, by our observations.

Interviews

Interviews are a standard method in qualitative research. They may seem simple, but training in interview techniques is recommended. The main types of interviews are structured interviews and unstructured/semi-structured interviews. In structured interviews, interviewers ask exactly the same questions of each interviewee. The purpose of this is to avoid bias. In unstructured/semi-structured interviews, interviewers adapt their questions as the interview progresses. This allows interviewees to explore topics as they arise and ask new questions in order to elicit deeper information from the interviewee. There are also many sub-types of interviews, including life histories and video interviews. Interviews can, of course, take place either in-person or online.

People's descriptions of their own behaviour can tell us *why* they behave in certain ways and also what they think motivates their behaviour. This can provide a great complement to quantitative data that is often valuable in telling us *what* people do, and also to observational data which tells us what people actually do.

A great example of using interviews to understand financial behaviour comes from design company Is It A Bird (www.isitabird.dk), which carried out a study for Danske Bank on the pains families experience with regard to pocket money in a cashless society. The research team carried out ethnographic interviews with 20 families in Denmark and Sweden 'to explore their thoughts, routines, challenges and motivations in relation to pocket money'. Part of the process involved asking participants to 'act out' activities associated with pocket money, such as storing it and budgeting for it. The insights showed the need for families to have a proper, dedicated solution for handling pocket money and a way to teach children about money in a cashless society. Ultimately, the research contributed to the development of a digital piggy bank solution, the Lommepenge app.

Interviews can be used to understand broader pictures and obtain general insights. In our study on small credit unions in the USA (Broløs and Taylor, 2023), we conducted a series of interviews with credit union leaders and experts. The semi-structured interviews were conducted digitally and were based on introductions by our research partner, Filene Research Institute. As the interviews progressed, we also included new interviewees suggested by the participants. This technique is known as 'snowballing'. We generally asked open-ended questions about the potential and challenges of credit unions. We also asked for examples of solutions including collaboration with different types of partners. The insights and examples from the interviews allowed us to develop a framework of different types of collaboration, spanning from very loose contacts to mergers. It also helped build the story of small credit union strength and potential for the future.

Another very interesting application of interview techniques is their incorporation into social network analysis (SNA). SNA is usually a highly quantitative method, with specific software used to analyse the data and map nodes and connections in social networks. But qualitative interview data can be used to explain what drives social networks. For example, Sibel Kusimba and her colleagues conducted a study of mobile money in Kenya, where at least 60 per cent of adults are unbanked (Kusimba et al, 2015). They used interview techniques to find out information such as why particular connections exist, how they are maintained, and how they have changed over time. In other words, they used qualitative data to explain what they were seeing in the quantitative data.

The Portable Kit Method

In object-centred research, participants are invited to engage with a particular object or with their environment. Researchers may ask the participant to talk about something they can see, hear, or feel. One example of an object-centred method is the Portable Kit Method. This method was originally developed by Ito et al (2009) in the 'Portable Kit Study', which examined the use of objects by young urban professionals living in Los Angeles, Tokyo, and London.

Portable kit refers to the things people carry with them on a daily basis when away from home.

One of the greatest advantages of this method is prompting conversation in a way that generates rich discussion and bridges online and offline worlds. This is often key when asking questions about money and money management, as people often find answering difficult or even shameful, as they sometimes think they should know more. We have used this in a number of studies mentioned in this book – most often to talk about payments starting with the money-related items that interviewees use every day: cash, cards, receipts, apps on their phones, and so on (see Taylor et al, forthcoming). In our Swiss study of female finance (Broløs and Taylor, 2022b) we conducted 14 portable kit interviews digitally because of the Covid-19 pandemic. The women showed us the content of bags and phones during the interviews and shared the photos of the content with us digitally, giving almost the same impression as in a face-to-face interview. The portable kit interviews are recorded using an audio device. We take photographs of the items people carry, anonymizing them beforehand by sticking bits of paper over identifying details.

The process begins with asking background questions about the interviewee, their life and their work. Then the researcher asks interviewees to take all of the objects they carry with them out of their bags, pockets and wallets, and display them on a flat surface. This includes objects related to consumer finance (currency, cards, receipts) and other items (identity documents, photographs, pens, notebooks, etc.). In our studies, we usually ask them to divide the objects into two piles: one of objects that they must carry with them every day, and a second pile of objects that could be left at home. The interviewees are asked to explain why some items were more important than others. This step is useful for identifying what people felt they needed in order to navigate their everyday lives. As the interviews progress, the interviewers formulate questions that shed light on how different objects are involved in personal and household finances.

Once the items are divided we generally begin by asking questions about interviewees' non-financial objects so that we are able to develop a sense of the person. Interviewees are invited to discuss the objects generally. We often begin by asking about the bag or wallet itself: where it had been purchased, why they chose that particular item, and whether they own other bags that they switch between depending upon their plans for the day. The benefit of this initial step is that it gives participants a chance to relax and provides an opportunity to build rapport.

We then ask people to talk to us about all their possessions that relate to financial transactions: cash, debit cards, credit cards, store cards, receipts and tokens. We ask people to show us what apps and websites they use on their mobile phones to do financial transactions. Finally, we ask questions about how people feel about the role financial services play in their lives, and are likely to play in the future.

Asking people to talk about the objects they carry can be easier and more rewarding for both interviewer and interviewee. Interviewees may find it easier to walk the interviewer through how they make a mobile payment than to recall it. The method also provides the researcher with an opportunity to ask about objects that the interviewee has overlooked. This is especially true of financial apps on the phone, as interviewees often do not remember all the apps they have or associate them all with financial management or economic activities (especially shopping apps). Prompting conversation can generate benefits beyond the practical: many interviewees find the experience of being able to talk about their money valuable and go away with new ideas and more confidence. The Portable Kit Method can assist in opening up dialogue and creating trust. Money and money management are very much a means to an end in a very concrete way of survival. As a result, asking questions about cash kept in different pockets and bags or several different bank cards will prompt an explanation that might otherwise be difficult to obtain. This is particularly important when working in areas where people's trust in institutions is low.

Financial diaries

Financial diary studies are a method of collecting data on financial behaviours by using a 'diary' to record transactions. For example, the European Central Bank (2020) in collaboration with national central banks uncover the use of different payment methods with the use of diaries. Users are asked to answer a set of qualitative and sometimes quantitative questions at regular intervals, for instance every week or every two weeks over a period of time. Questions can be designed to ask respondents about both formal and informal financial activities, and how these fit into the context of a participant's life. They can, of course, be combined with other data collection methods such as interviews. Diaries may be recorded on paper, using a mobile application, or directly into a digital database. They can be implemented in person or using online software.

Financial diaries are great for collecting data for a broad range of financial uses, particularly over longer time periods. The format can be creative and interactive, allowing for drawings and comments and the expression of individual feelings. A potential side effect of financial diaries is that they may help participants to become more aware of their financial behaviours, leading them to make changes in their lives.

While she was a Research Fellow at Pitney Bowes, Alexandra Mack conducted financial diaries as part of a study of financial communications management in the United States. Mack was interested in how 'financial communications' impacted financial management within a household (Alexandra Mack generously told us about her work in personal communications; the full description appears in Taylor and Lynch, 2020). The financial diaries were an opportunity to dig into issues such as how financial management varies by life stage, and factors that impact attitudes toward new technologies for managing finances.

The study took place entirely online. Participants were recruited through a recruiting firm and offered a small remuneration for the participation. Participants were introduced to the study and asked to keep a financial diary. They consented to participate with a daily login to complete a variety of activities. They were generally able to record their diaries in their own time over the course of a week. Activities included answering questions, keeping logs of some financial interactions, and having group discussions with other participants. Participants would also take pictures using their digital camera or camera phone and post them to the project site.

Mack found the method to be suitable to create a broad picture of people's financial behaviours, the products they use, and their financial communications. While not longitudinal, she was able to ask questions about changing practices, and what prompted individuals' shifts in their own behaviours. Because the interactions lasted over several days, Mack could query the subjects on different topics that might have felt disconnected if asked back-to-back in an interview. What began as a study of financial communications evolved based on participant responses into a larger project around financial management.

Drawing money relationships

Along similar lines as the Portable Kit Method, you can ask interviewees to express their feelings about money and money management in drawings. Danish academic Kirsten Bonde Sørensen (2013) carried out research in customer workshops. She asked bank customers to develop collages of their experience with money. As in the case of the Portable Kit Method, she asked them for examples of their experiences and feelings about money both as adults and as children. She next invited them to reflect on how they wanted this relationship to be and to express that in collages and personal statements. In her particular case, she had the opportunity to interview the people six weeks later and generally found that they had used insights from the first workshop to increasingly take control of their money management and the position of money in their lives. Seen from the perspective of understanding customer needs and wishes, this method reveals not only customer reactions to existing services but also enables them to express a potential of what new services might look like. The use of art to understand emotions is perhaps most often used in healthcare and education. Anthropologist Sibel Kusimba (Kusimba, 2018) did, however, use the drawing of financial self-portraits and financial networks to understand monetary practices in Kenya. More on the use of this technique within organizations can be found in methodology descriptions such as Ward and King (2020).

COMBINING TOOLS

We have described tools as single interventions, but of course it makes a lot of sense to consider combining different ways of understanding customer behaviour. It also makes sense to combine knowledge from user research with knowledge built from the analysis of customer data. A great example of combining tools is a study of gender roles in informal money management in Kenya (Kusimba, 2018).

The study used:

- a diary exercise with eight women who shared information about their money transfers, digital credit, and other financial services, taking place over twenty-two weeks
- an exercise where the same eight women drew network self-portraits to illustrate how they participated in financial and social relationships
- ethnographic interviews with sixty men and women who used money transfers and digital credit
- informal conversations and observations with the same sixty men and women

The combination of documentation of actual payment transactions, descriptions of family and community networks and the ethnographic interviews revealed a new understanding of gender roles.

Whereas development economics often expects that creating financial access for women as individuals will change gender norms, the alternative research methods showed that Kenyan women and men use digital finance not to seek individual control of their money but to grow as participants in a financial community.

Similar results could arise in other environments as the result of studying not only customer transactions, but also how such transactions are part of human relations.

Research culture-centricity

Throughout this book, we have illustrated how working with customers and customer insights is an important key driver of innovation. Customer-centricity is often related to the increased capacity to gather and analyse quantitative data in what people often call 'data-driven innovation'.

This approach often misses the most important insights about customer behaviour and customer needs for a number of reasons. For example, transaction data of different kinds reflect what the customers chose to do using their accounts. However, it does not reflect the choices customers considered or the workarounds they felt it was necessary to use to avoid fees or obtain promotions. It does not show if someone else used the account because they asked the account holder or cardholder to make a purchase or because they borrowed a credit card. In this respect, it does not show what kind of relations customers are part of – or what role they play in their community, whether this be a family or a group of friends. These are all elements that are key to developing a customer-centric-organization.

As we discussed in Chapter 4, there are competing theories about how people make financial decisions, but it is clear that people do not behave like 'economic man'. Rather, people's decisions are driven by their desires, biases, social relations and cultural practices. As a result, financial practices always include both qualitative and quantitative elements, making it important for researchers to build a good basic knowledge of methods outside their own area of expertise.

In this chapter we have taken a practical approach to the work and to describe how it can fit into an organizational focus on customer-centricity and innovation. We argue that any organization, despite size or focus, can start experimenting with customer research, what steps might be useful, and what method and tools to work with. We are well aware that most financial organizations are already working with some kinds of user research, including the important work of designers and user interface developers. We have not had the space to touch upon these tools, apart from the short mention in Chapter 2. Instead, we have chosen to focus on qualitative customer research, particularly the ethnographic kind that is undertaken in the places where people live, because this context is so important for deeply understanding customers, and particularly their future needs.

Of course, the qualitative methods we describe can be combined with other methods. From an academic perspective, much research is done using mixed method approaches, combining quantitative methods like surveys and social network analysis with insights from interviews and ethnographic studies. Similarly, it is clear that applied user research done in companies will easily be combined with quantitative data from customer surveys and transaction data. We hope to see companies doing many more such collaborative, mixed method studies in the future.

Creating a customer research culture is critical to building a customer-centric organization. Both reflect the need to start with customers and bring all parts of the organization together to build new insights with the aim of serving customers better. A deep understanding of existing customer needs is the foundation for future innovation. Customers can be part of the innovation process – not only by being part of customer research, but also through contributions to product development, testing and implementation. Creating a customer research culture requires a combination of integrating stakeholders and working with customers throughout the innovation process. We must conceptualize research as a larger process of collaboration.

In the book's conclusion we come back to the question of what it means to create a financial system fit for humans, and expand on the role of research-centricity and customer-centricity in achieving this goal.

TAKEAWAYS

- You can do applied user research in your organization.
- Start by doing a pilot to get a feeling of results.
- Map your research knowledge.
- Remember to include partner resources.
- Build the culture.
- Get familiar with usual tools.
- Integrate the research in innovation.

References

Broløs, A and Taylor, E B (2022a) *Buy Now, Pay Later: Understanding consumer behavior*, Filene Research Institute No 550. www.filene.org/reports/buy-now-pay-later-understanding-consumer-behavior

Broløs, A and Taylor, E (2022b) *Female Finance on the Move: Switzerland*, EWPN, Keen Innovation and Unblu. ewpn.eu/research-network/white-papers-reports/female-finance-on-the-move-switzerland (archived at https://perma.cc/YE85-KXFY)

Broløs, A and Taylor, E B (2023) *Small Credit Union Collaboration: Sharing knowledge, services and people in a digital economy*, Filene Research Institute No 575. www.filene.org/reports/small-credit-union-collaboration-sharing-knowledge-services-and-people-in-a-digital-economy

Brown, T (2008) Design thinking, *Harvard Business Review*, June. www.hbr.org/2008/06/design-thinking (archived at https://perma.cc/8HRZ-DHKE)

Camp, A, Fanderl, H, Jain, N, Sternfels, B and von Difloe, R (2020) The human touch at the center of customer-experience excellence, McKinsey, 8 October. www.mckinsey.com/capabilities/operations/our-insights/the-human-touch-at-the-center-of-customer-experience-excellence (archived at https://perma.cc/V8YT-HB3J)

European Central Bank (2022) Study on the payment attitudes of consumers in the Euro area (SPACE), European Central Bank. www.ecb.europa.eu/stats/ecb_surveys/space/html/ecb.spacereport202212~783ffdf46e.en.html (archived at https://perma.cc/M5ND-E4JA)

Gibbs, G (2018) *Analyzing Qualitative Data*, Sage Publications, New York

Is It A Bird (no date) What is pocket money in a cashless society? Case study: Danske Bank, Is It A Bird. www.isitabird.dk/cases/danske-bank (archived at https://perma.cc/UA3N-RJQM)

Ito, M, Okabe, O and Anderson, K (2009) Portable objects in three global cities: The personalization of urban places, in R Ling and S Campbell, eds, *The Reconstruction of Space and Time: Mobile communication practices*, Transaction Books, New Jersey, 67–88

Kusimba, S (2018) 'It is easy for women to ask!' Gender and digital finance in Kenya, *Economic Anthropology*, 5, 247–60

Kusimba, S, Yang, Y and Chawla, N V (2015) Family networks of mobile money in Kenya, *Information Technology in International Development*, 11 (3), 1–21

Sørensen, K B (2013) Designing for self-leadership, Nordic Design Research Conference, Copenhagen–Malmö

Stokes, D E (1997) *Pasteur's Quadrant: Basic science and technological innovation*, Brookings Institution Press, Washington DC

Taylor, E B and Broløs, A (2022) *Money and Payments in Low Income Brazil*, Finthropology/SICPA

Taylor, E B and Lynch, G (2020) *Consumer Finance Research Methods Toolkit*, IMTFI, University of California Irvine, Irvine, CA

Taylor, E B and Uy, M T (2021) *Better Research, Better Design: How to align teams and build a human-centric company culture*, American Anthropological Association, Arlington, VA

Taylor, E B, Broløs, A and Horst, H A (forthcoming) How to talk about money: The portable kit as a research approach, in N Rangaswamy and S Venkatraman (eds), *Digital Qualitative Methods: Studies from the Global South*, Springer, New York

Ward, J and King, D (2020) Drawing out emotion in organisational life, in J Ward and H Shortt (eds) *Using Arts-Based Research Methods*, Palgrave Macmillan, London, 15–40

Watchravesringkan, K (2008) Financial behavior of Hispanic Americans, in J Jian Xiao, ed, *Handbook of Consumer Finance Research*, Springer, New York, 271–85

World Bank Group (2020) Understanding people's perspectives on identification: A qualitative research toolkit, Identification for Development ID4D, World Bank. id4d.worldbank.org/sites/id4d/files/WB-ID4D-Understanding-Peoples-Perspective-on-Identification-A-Qualitative-Research-Toolkit.pdf (archived at https://perma.cc/4HUE-7K2K)

Conclusion

A human financial world

We began this book by arguing that finance is inherently human. While it has, of course, many technological and quantitative features, the whole point of finance is to support human activities in trading, purchasing, sharing and so on. Since humans are social animals, these activities are always underpinned by social goals. This means that, before we can quantify people's behaviours, we must first understand the social qualities that underpin them. Thus any study of people, no matter how quantitative, always has qualitative considerations at its core.

Recognizing the qualitative nature of human behaviour is one thing. Ensuring that we incorporate such an understanding into financial innovations is another. Most financial service providers do this to some degree, using methods such as user experience (UX) research, service design research, and design thinking to ensure that products and services are usable and appropriate to people's needs. Indeed, as we have discussed throughout this book, many companies apply human insights in highly creative and laudable ways.

But there is more to be done. Indeed, more *must* be done, given the changing nature of financial services. The explosion in consumer choice and emergence of new technologies like AI and Web 3.0 present a whole host of challenges for business and society alike. On the business side, staying ahead of customer trends and designing future services will require strategic foresight and solid research. On the societal side, there is a need to understand people's practices within and across jurisdictions to improve public programmes and regulation. There is, of course, also the issue that the perpetual nature of change in financial services means that all of us – end users and professionals alike – need to engage in lifelong learning about finance.

It is clear that we need to balance the human side of finance with the particularities of the implementation of the financial system. Technology and design will not be less important in a human financial world; indeed, they will be *more* critical to meeting people's needs. But human activities and workarounds show that the financial system is built on, dependent on and operated by humans as much as anything else. Thus we need to ensure that a qualitative understanding of people is built into our efforts to reach people with financial products, programmes and policies. We need customer-centricity that takes the generation of human insights seriously.

In this conclusion we first summarize the main themes of the book. We then ask what financial services might look like if they were built to support customers' needs and dreams – taking into consideration that people are so very different. We finally identify possible next steps for incumbent financial players, fintechs and regulators.

A short summary

This summary touches on the main themes that we have discussed throughout the book: the transformative digital change that we are going through, the relationship between customer focus and customer behaviour, and finally the usefulness of qualitative research to help us move forward.

Digital transformation

Digital transformation is more than just new technology. It changes how we act, work and communicate. It changes society and culture. It also changes the ways that companies innovate. Digital transformation has the potential to change financial intermediation. Blockchain, tokens, DeFi, virtual communities, the introduction of CBDCs and new ways of solving cross-border payments can lead to a much broader financial intermediation structure than we have been used to. On the financial company side we see new competitors, new business models, new partnerships in open banking and open finance.

Customer focus

The power to collect and manage very large and detailed amounts of customer data creates the impression of deep customer knowledge and leads to a focus on customer-centric innovation. In this context, customer-centricity is derived from digital customer data. The innovation it entails is often called data-driven innovation. However, data reflects only the actual transactions, not the reasons why people undertook the transaction, whether they are the result of a workaround, or whether they represent the least damaging solution/transaction.

Throughout the book, we have shared examples about people's financial behaviour in their everyday context – most often insights that would not be captured by data on the actual financial transactions.

Most people do not find finance in itself very interesting, but it is a very important means to an end – or perhaps to most 'ends' including housing, entrepreneurship, education and everyday financial well-being. We know that people do not make rational decisions. We also know that people make decisions within a context, such as a community (family and friends), in the situation (such as being out with friends, having left without a purse, etc.). Understanding these issues would lead to real customer-centricity in financial innovation.

Customer behaviour

The complexity and irrationality of human behaviour and decision-making are key to understanding customer needs. We have argued that we need to start with customers to build good financial solutions.

We discuss the importance of taking into account people's feelings and emotions about money and explain how complex decision processes are. It is also important to take culture into account, including issues like trust.

We argue against the often-expressed view that customers just need to be educated in finance and in technology to be able to use the solutions offered. We show how most people manage quite well without a deep understanding of finance or technology. We also present examples of how technology is letting people down. Apps and devices designed with people's needs in mind, and more reliable infrastructure could take some of the pain out of people's attempts to achieve financial goals.

There are, however, many financial services that try to overcome customer pain points, whether because these pain points were experienced directly by the start-up's leaders or whether they were professionally researched and developed.

Future solutions can be built from research into existing customer behaviours – for several reasons. A behaviour may illustrate a need or a pain point, even if it is not addressed. Convenience, seamlessness, economic control and value are key. And customers can help organizations to understand new trends (like virtual communities) and suggest the best future solutions. Indeed, in some cases, customers already are more experienced in these new environments.

How can qualitative research create insights?

Our stories about people's choices and use of financial tools help to explain the value of qualitative research in uncovering customer needs, wishes and pain points. In Chapter 10 we tried to illustrate how a company can build a research culture that can support both customer innovation and customer-centricity. We stressed that qualitative data can be used in combination with quantitative data.

Customer observations and insights can create innovation for the future. Making sense of customer pain points and combining these with knowledge about technology development can lead to new ideas.

An important potential lies in working directly with customers, moving from observations and interviews to co-creation. There is also great potential in the development of broader partnerships for collaborative research in ecosystems of innovation.

What would happen if...?

In this short section, we ask some of the questions that spring from our prior discussions about understanding people's behaviour and the role that emotions play in everyday financial decisions and well-being. We ask ourselves – and you, the reader – what differences we might see in the financial ecosystem as a consequence.

What would happen if emotions had a more prominent place and role in financial advice and decision-making? We have shared some examples but much is still to be explored. Throughout this book we have given many examples of how money decisions are based on emotions, regardless of gender, age group, income group, or profession (remember our professor of finance from Chapter 4). Some people carry unhappy experiences from their childhood all their lives that make them hate seeing a bill or making decisions about debt or investments. From our studies of women, and particularly of financial services designed specifically for women, we have shown that the creation of learning communities and financial advice that start with the customers' pain points can lead to changes in people's attitudes towards finance. We think that this is probably not only valued by women but indeed by most people.

WHAT WOULD HAPPEN IF...

... we understood how emotions can affect everyday financial decisions and well-being?

... we could design, develop and deliver financial solutions that take account of customers' emotions?

... we could learn to understand the connections between emotions and finances, and to treat emotions as a valid part of financial lives rather than something that must be buried?

... we could learn not just to be financially literate, but also *emotionally* financially literate?

... we included financial health, literacy and emotions in the upbringing of children to understand money – instead of merely focusing only on interest rate calculations, contractual terms and 'spreadsheets'?

... we developed – and regulated – financial services to meet people's needs and dreams?

... we developed solutions to work in communities of people – not only for individuals?

... we could create a culture of money that recognizes emotions and different personal perceptions of financial potential and troubles?

... the culture of money reflected that financial health is different for different groups of people?

And what would the financial ecosystem look like if it was built on a money culture that included emotions and was built to help different customers manage their finances in ways that suit them? We find this a very interesting and important question as we move into a new digital era. How will the introduction of CBDCs, the development of virtual worlds and the potential of decentralized finance answer – or challenge – these questions? Will they help build different money cultures, or will they merely provide modern infrastructures?

WHAT WOULD THE FINANCIAL ECOSYSTEM OF THE FUTURE LOOK LIKE?

Would it...

... take account of customers' feelings as much as figures?

... include more learning opportunities for customers?

... provide different tools to work with financial decisions – like games, drawings, storytelling or mood ratings?

... involve more customer dialogue to complete insights gained from AI and transactional data (because the last only explains 'what' and not 'why')?

... focus on families or groups of people more than individuals?

... include more focus on diversity and societal impact?

Where to next?

Customer-centricity has perhaps never been more in focus. A very large amount of detailed customer quantitative data is in the hands of financial suppliers – young and old – to innovate in the digital future. In this book we have argued that it is just as important to understand why customers make the decision about money that they make. Why do they prefer one solution over another, and why might they listen to some advisers rather than others? Collecting qualitative data about customers as they discuss money and make decisions in communities is a great way of learning. Listening and learning can help create open spaces and opportunities for co-creation with customers of all types. Responding well to complaints and suggestions is a very simple way. Involving customers in development processes is another. A third is to take advantage of the open banking and open finance environments created to learn and develop together with (predominantly corporate and business) customers.

Collecting qualitative data can also help us to understand why and how it might be possible to take advantage of quantitative data to develop financial solutions to serve many different groups of customers well. This is the case in the traditional development of solutions. More interestingly, it is very much the case in the developing areas of future finance where all financial participants, whether customers, financial professionals, fintech or partners, need to learn. Qualitative data can help us to understand how different groups of people might respond to things like decentralized finance, assets and payments in virtual worlds and new types of technological infrastructure, including CBDCs and digital IDs. It may also help build more sustainable solutions.

These are all areas where it makes sense for financial players of all sizes to learn alongside employees, partners and customers – and, in so doing, take advantage of the knowledge that these bring to the table. As we have discussed, customers in general may not know much about financial technology, but some people may already be well versed in digital money such as in a gaming setting.

We have shown that qualitative research in customer behaviour is just as natural and as important a part of financial innovation initiatives as is quantitative data analysis. We think that the two together can take solutions to a next level, regardless of the customer groups. We know that this is already the case in many organizations, and where it is not we would argue that just now is a great time to start. This is also true for regulators and central bankers in charge of building digital money, updated financial intermediation systems and frameworks for customer and investor protection in the future.

Enjoy the journey.

APPENDIX

List of company examples

Acorns	www.acorns.com
Amelia Insurance	www.ameliainsurance.com
Dreams Technology	dreamstech.com
Earnin	www.earnin.com
Fair Finance	www.fairfinance.org.uk
Ellevest	www.ellevest.com
eToro	www.etoro.com
Female Invest	www.femaleinvest.com
Go Henry	www.gohenry.com
Hippo Insurance	www.hippo.com
hiveonline	www.hivenetwork.online
Is it a Bird	www.isitabird.dk
Lemonade	www.lemonade.com
Majority	majority.com
L'Osservatorio Nazionale sull'Inclusione Finanziaria dei Migranti	www.migrantiefinanza.it
Moneypenny & More	moneypennyandmore.dk
Mujer Única	cotiza.axa.com.mx/mujer_unica_axa
Limitless	www.limitless.app
Nav.it	www.navitmoney.com
Oxford Risk	www.oxfordrisk.com
Pixpay	www.pixpay.fr
Roblox	www.roblox.com
Salary Fits	www.salaryfits.com.br

The Camp	www.thecamp.io
Varo	www.varomoney.com
WeMoney	www.wemoney.com.au
Zelle	www.zellepay.com

GLOSSARY

artificial intelligence (AI) AI is a machine's ability to perform the cognitive functions we associate with human minds, such as perceiving, reasoning, learning, interacting with an environment, problem solving and even exercising creativity.

behavioural finance Behavioural finance theory takes psychological considerations as an essential feature of the security markets. It attempts to explain and increase understanding of how the emotions and mental mistakes of investors influence the decision-making process. It focuses on four key themes: overconfidence, cognitive dissonance, regret and prospect theory.

behavioural science The study of human behaviour. A behavioural scientist uses scientific methods to learn why people do the things they do and how they react to different treatments. It is possible to use behavioural science to predict future behaviour.

blockchain A secure distributed ledger technology that allows secure sharing of data across a network of participants, where up-to-date information is available to all participants at the same time.

central bank digital currency (CBDC) Digital currencies issued by central banks either as a wholesale solution, similar to cash, or directly to end users in a retail solution.

decentralized finance (DeFi) A general term for decentralized applications providing financial services on a blockchain settlement layer, including payments, lending, trading, investments, insurance and asset management. DeFi services typically operate without centralized intermediaries or institutions, and use open protocols that allow services to be programmatically combined in flexible ways.

decentralized autonomous organizations (DAOs) Entities whose rules are defined and enforced in the form of smart contracts.

digital platforms A platform can be defined as a set of institutional arrangements that brings together two or more different types of economic agents and facilitates trade between them. In financial services, digital platforms can for example include borrowers and savers on a fintech app, or retail clients and financial service providers on social media, search or e-commerce platforms.

digital transformation Also known as 'digitalization', digital transformation is concerned with the changes that digital technologies can bring about in a company's business model, products, processes and organizational structure.

digitalization Reframing solutions to fit a digital environment.

digitization Digital automation of processes.

financial inclusion Generally defined by the World Bank to mean that individuals and businesses have access to useful and affordable financial products and services that meet their needs – transactions, payments, savings, credit and insurance – delivered in a responsible and sustainable way.

fintech An umbrella term for innovative technology-enabled financial services and the business models that accompany those services

generative AI Generative AI is perhaps the latest use of AI in a model that generates content in response to a prompt. The best examples are the open source or proprietary solution of search machines or problem solvers trained on internet data, like ChatGPT.

machine learning (ML) Machine learning is a form of artificial intelligence based on algorithms that are trained on data. Deep learning is a specific form of machine learning based on neural networks.

metaverse The metaverse can be described as an interoperable network of real-time, 3D virtual worlds with an unlimited number of users. Users can be people with traditional identities, avatars or 'things' like your car.

tokenization The process of transforming ownerships and rights of particular assets into a digital form. By tokenization, you can transform indivisible assets into token forms.

user research Systematic investigation of how people use and experience products and services.

Web 3.0 Web 3.0 is envisioned to be a 'decentralized web ecosystem' in which users can retain ownership of their data through blockchain rather than relying on single servers and centralized databases.

INDEX

Page numbers in *italic* denote information contained within a figure.

A/B tests 106
ABN Amro 48
academic research 10, 105, 241
  see also qualitative data
accessibility 126–27, 145, 148, 151–54, 157, 160–61, 171–72, 175–76, 178–79, 185
  see also financial inclusion
Acorns 127
actual behaviour 231
actual norms 75
Afro-Trinidadians 79
Afterpay 26, 46, 60, 174
agent networks 82, 103, 105, 154
AI (artificial intelligence) 4, 19, 20, 21, 46, 56, 197, 255, 256
  see also machine learning (ML)
Airbnb 26
Alibaba 23–24
alternative data 20
Amazon 23–24, 26, 27
Amelia Insurance 21, 253
America *see* United States (US)
Anse a Foleur 98
Anse-à-Pitres 95, 98–99
anthropology 71, 75–76, 77, 93, 106, 107, 108, 109, 110
Apple 23–24, 27
Apple Store 177
application programming interfaces (APIs) 25, 47–48, 191, 197, 198, 226
apps 8, 73, 83, 87, 119
  see also Afterpay; Ellevest; Lommepenge; MAJORITY; Money Missions; Nav.it; WeMoney; Zelle
aspirations 77–78
Aspire 132
ATMs 82, 113, 153, 160, 201, 202–03, 207
Atom Bank 169
Australia 26, 82, 109, 165, 171
automation 20–21, 45
avatars 33, 191
Axa 133–34, 177
AXA Next 133, 134
backend processes 17, 49
Baidu 23–24
Banco Central do Brasil (BCB) 110, 205, 206–07
bank deposits 35
Bank for International Settlements (BIS) 32, 33, 35, 208, 210
banks 2–3, 17, 24–26, 31, 32–33, 49, 82, 121–22, 171
  account ownership 28–29, 145–48, 168–69
  apps 83
  fees 159–60
  Haiti 93, 97–98, 102, 104
  see also ABN Amro; ATMs; Atom Bank; Banco Centro do Brasel (BCB); bank deposits; Bank for International Settlements (BIS); central bank digital currencies (CBDCs); central banks; challenger banks; digital banking; Grameen Bank; open banking (finance); savings accounts; Varo Bank
Baptiste, Dr Espelencia (Espelencia) 95, 97
Barclays 171
basic bank payment accounts 158–69
'Beautiful Girls Thrifting' 46
behaviour 56–59, 69–92, 199, 231, 247–48
behavioural economics 72–74, 75–76, 84
behavioural finance theory 71, 255
behavioural science 70–71, 88, 126–28, 255
Belle Anse 99
Benin 54
bias 109–11, 173, 240
big data 56, 183
Bill and Melinda Gates Foundation 94–95, 98
BIS (Bank for International Settlements) 32, 33, 35, 208, 210
bitcoins 32, 33
'black swans' 74
blockchain 32, 33, 55, 135, 181, 182, 193, 246, 255

Brazil 8–9, 10, 36, 81, 86, 107–08, 110–11, 112, 128, 211–12
financial inclusion 168, 172
human work arounds 155, 159–61
see also Banco Centro do Brasil (BCB); Pix
Building Blocks 182–83
business concept innovation 43–44
buy now pay later (BNPL) schemes 26, 27, 30, 46, 60, 122–24, 158, 195, 231–32

CAM 98
Cambodia 84, 109, 161
capability, financial 154–55
capacity building 154, 224
car insurance 59, 195–96
Caribe Express 99
cash 29, 86, 88–89, 144, 145, 151, 157–58, 159–60, 162, 167
cash incentives 111
cash transfers 96–101
see also cross-border payments
central bank digital currencies (CBDCs) 34–35, 84, 121, 151, 204, 207–12, 255
central banks 11, 34–35
see also European Central Bank
challenger banks 165, 169, 172
see also Starling Bank; Varo
charity sector 8
chatbots 20, 21, 60
ChatGPT 20, 47, 197
Check Center 2
children 55, 127, 198, 233
China 8, 21
Citi Money Gallery 104
City Ventures Studio 134
cloud technology 7–8, 19, 49
co-creation 45–49, 197, 226, 227, 251
cognitive dissonance 71
collaboration (partnerships) 22, 24–27, 50, 52, 132–34, 193, 224
communication 113, 207, 224, 237–38
see also informal conversations
company strategy 226–27
complexity 22, 75–76, 88–90, 161
contribution stages 197–98
control 82–83, 88
convenience (transaction costs) 81–82, 88, 118–22, 141, 149, 156
cooperatives 6, 7, 55
Copenhagen Fintech 25
corporate customers 31, 46, 48, 129, 225
Covid-19 119, 129, 182, 235
credit 21, 149, 160–61, 167
credit cards 17, 21, 24, 30, 77–78, 81, 88–89, 103, 119
credit unions 122, 126, 129–32, 143, 234
cross-border payments 17, 30, 36, 53, 157–58, 179, 208, 246
see also cash transfers
crowdfunding 22, 27
crowdsourcing 48, 49
cryptocurrencies 32, 57, 125, 144, 211
cultural capital 77
culture 16, 29, 31, 52, 78–79, 88, 223–25
Cumulus Card 81
curiosity 218, 223
customer onboarding 20–21, 22, 26, 53
customer pain points 22, 54, 122–23, 178, 184, 192, 223, 229, 248
see also ATMs; customer onboarding
customer preferences 60–63, 173–74, 175
customer workarounds 155–61, 162, 209, 240
cyber crime (security) 21, 22, 59

DANA 160
data-driven innovation 20, 45–49, 52, 105–06, 133, 136, 193, 222–23, 240, 247
see also big data; employee insights; qualitative data; quantitative data; data management 4, 19, 58, 59, 193
data privacy 80, 102, 104, 158, 208
data protection 21, 228
day traders 57
death insurance 6
debit cards 81, 119, 127, 169, 203
decentralized autonomous organizations 47, 255
decentralized finance (DeFi) 32–34, 36–37, 47, 58, 255
decision-making 72, 74, 76, 80–89
deep learning 20, 256
demographics 20, 109, 110, 128, 229
see also Generation Z; Millennials
Denmark 29, 121–22, 168, 233
design thinking 137–38
desk research 108
developing (emerging) markets 28–29, 53
diaries 113, 236–38, 239
diffusion of innovation 44
Digicel 84, 94–95, 100, 102, 103, 104, 112
digital advisory services 45
digital banking 53
see also fintechs
digital ethnography 114, 123–24, 158, 228, 231–32
Digital Finance and Farming 109
digital identity 36, 151, 168, 178, 179, 181–83
digital payments 8, 144–45, 160, 200, 207–08, 209

digital platforms 26–27, 63, 256
digital transformation 15–41, 48–49, 59, 246, 256
see also AI (artificial intelligence); machine learning (ML); tokenization; virtual reality
digital twins 34, 191
digital wallets (electronic wallets) 9, 30, 36, 81–82, 121, 160, 182–83, 203–05, 210
digitalization 16, 170, 256
digitization 16
Diners 17
Directive 2014/92/EU 168–69
dispositions 52
disruptive innovation 44
distributed ledger technology *see* blockchain
Dominican Republic 94, 95, 96, 97, 99, 104, 110
Dreams 25, 55, 134, 172, 253

e-commerce 26, 30
see also Amazon; eBay
Earnin 170
eBay 23–24
economics 7, 71–77
El Progreso 158
electronic (digital) wallets 9, 30, 36, 81–82, 121, 160, 182–83, 203–05, 210
Ellevest 57, 174, 177–78, 253
Ellevest Digital 178
embedded finance 26
emerging (developing) markets 28–29, 53
emotions 86–87
employee insights 121–22
eNaira 209–11
encounters 52
enterprise resource planning (ERP) systems 31, 46
Ericsson 27
error 109–11, 161
Espelencia (Baptiste, Dr) 95, 97
ethics 228
ethnography 75, 78, 93, 113–15, 122–24, 158, 228, 231–33
eToro 57, 194, 195, 253
European Central Bank 30, 236–37
European Microfinance Network 171
European Union (EU) 53, 168–69, 181
experimentation 9, 34, 50, 71, 72, 73–74
see also field experiments (fieldwork)

face-to-face interviews 113, 235
face-to-face transactions 30, 62, 113
Facebook 26, 46, 125, 158
Fair Finance 170–71, 253
fees 159–60
Female Invest 57, 253
females (women) 85–86, 124–25, 147, 150, 173–78
field experiments (fieldwork) 73, 75, 93–115, 121, 191–215
field notes 106
Filene Research Institute 122–24, 234
finance, evolution of 5–7
financial capability 154–55
financial choice model 60–63
financial cognitive dissonance 71
Financial Conduct Authority 171
financial diaries 113, 236–38, 239
financial inclusion 141–89
see also accessibility
financial literacy 21, 86, 128, 154, 162, 179
financial portfolios 88, 152, 159
financial precarity 174
financial service providers 15, 27–28
see also banks; cooperatives; fintechs; incumbents; insurance companies
financial tour method 112–13
fintechs 4, 10, 20, 22–27, 30, 52–56, 132–34, 180–81
see also Acorns; Dreams; GoHenry; Pixpay
Finthropology 24, 52, 211
Flip 160
focus groups 55, 71, 183, 226
form-filling 81
formal financial services 143–44, 150, 152
see also banks; credit unions; insurance companies, payday lenders
fraud management 21, 26, 59, 191
free transfers 160, 180–81
freelancers 18, 36, 208
functionality 158–59
Funding Circle 172
funeral insurance 6
fungible tokens 32
future preparedness 13, 37, 137, 218, 227

game theory 72
gaming 33, 58, 59, 127, 196, 197–98, 212, 231, 251
Gates Foundation 94–95, 98
GCash 151
General Data Protection Regulation 228
Generation Z 30–31
generative AI 20, 256
Ghana 54
gift cards 111, 123, 158
global financial crisis 1–2, 74
Global Findex Database 144, 151–52, 205

GoHenry 127, 253
Google 23–24, 27
Google Pay 119
Google Play 177
Google Wallet 9, 77
government sector 33, 36, 72–73, 76, 83–84, 106, 148, 179, 180–84, 210–11
Grameen Bank 7, 142–43
group affiliations 78–79
Guatemala 1–2, 10

Haiti 82, 84, 93–105, 111–14, 150, 153, 155
Handelbanken 37
heuristics 85
HIFIVE competition 94–95, 100–01, 103
Higgins, Graham 201
Hippo Insurance 59, 196, 253
Hiveonline 55–56, 134, 135, 137, 174, 193, 253
home tours 112–13
Horst, Dr Heather 95
human error 109–11, 161
human workarounds 155–61, 162, 209, 240
hypotheses 105

Icebreaker 35
ID wallets 181
  see also digital identity
ideal norms 75
ideas as capital 46–47
inclusion 141–89
  see also accessibility
incremental innovation 43, 49
incumbents 49–54
India 36, 165
individual decision-making 88–89
Indo-Trinidadians 79
Indonesia 113, 121, 160, 204
influencers 57, 195, 223
informal conversations 97, 99, 100, 239
informal financial services 144, 145, 150–51
infrastructure 153, 156–57
  see also technology
ING 76
Innopay 198–99
innovation 44
innovation development phase 226
Innovation Hub (BIS) 35
innovation labs (hubs) 35, 133
innovation networks 47, 48
Institute for Money, Technology and Financial Inclusion 95
insurance companies 17, 19, 21–22, 24–25, 29, 34, 48–49, 58–59, 73, 167
  car insurance 195–96
  death (funeral) insurance 6
  evolution of 6–7
  see also Axa; Hippo Insurance
Intel 76
internet 4, 18–19, 32, 36, 103, 119, 121, 144, 156, 201–02
interviews 97, 107–08, 109–14, 228, 232–39
investments 34, 56–58, 82, 124–25
Is It A Bird 233, 253
Italy 20, 86, 180

Jacmel 95, 96, 99
Jones, Tim 201
Joseph, Michael 103

Kahneman, Daniel 72, 85
Kaye, Joseph 112–13
Kenya 8, 95, 165, 234, 238, 239
Kickstarter 8
Klarna 26, 46
'know your customer' rules 181
Krawcheck, Sallie 178
Kroll, Charlie 178

Laos 3, 109, 160, 165
Le Borge 98
learning communities 46
Lemonade 21, 253
Level 39 54
Limitless 25, 57, 133, 253
liquidity pooling 33
literacy 155
  see also financial literacy
Living Labs 48
lock-ins 27
Lommepenge 233
loss aversion 85–86
low income customers 2, 78, 83, 85, 95, 100, 128, 166–73, 180
  see also financial inclusion
loyalty programmes 34, 81, 88, 119, 137

M-PESA 8, 60, 94–95
machine learning (ML) 4, 19–20, 21, 46, 256
Mack, Alexandra 113, 237–38
MAJORITY 180
Malawi 73
Marche en Fer 100, 101
Marigot 99
market research 105, 201, 219
Mastercard 17, 127, 201
Maurer, Bill 95

mental health 16, 86–87, 177
MercadoPay 151
Mercy Corps 101
meritocracy 47, 198
metaverse 33–34, 58, 196, 256
metrics 220, 224–25
Me2Me transactions 102–03
Mexico 9, 157–58, 177
micro-insurance 58–59, 195
microcredit 149
microeconomics 71–72, 76
microfinance 1–2, 7
microfinance institutions (MFIs) 28, 143, 149, 152, 158, 171
microsavings 149
migrants 178–84
Millennials 25, 26, 30–31
Miss Moneypenny 46, 57, 125
ML (machine learning) 4, 19–20, 21, 46
mobile network operators 53–54
mobile phones 4, 8, 17–18, 27, 82, 93–104, 119, 141, 153–54
  accessibility 28–29, 53–54, 144–45
  see also smartphones
MobilePay 27, 50, 62, 126–27
mobility 21, 30
MonCash 103
Mondex 200–04
Monese 30
monetary policy committees 11
Money Missions 127
money relationship drawings 238–39
MoneyGram 98
monopolies 27
Monzo 169
multi-sided platforms 26

National Observatory for the Financial Inclusion of Migrants 180
native tokens 32
Nav.it 175, 177, 253
Nebaj 1–2
Netherlands 7, 74, 87, 179
new entrants 22–24
Niger 135
Nigeria 209–11
Nissan 76
non-fungible tokens 32
non-life insurance 58
non-native tokens 32
norms 75
not-for-profit organizations 3, 22, 105–06, 143
N26 30, 169
Nu Bank 169
nudges 72–73
Nutspaarbank 7, 143

observation 97, 100, 106, 135–36, 204, 230–33, 239
onboarding 20–21, 22, 26, 53
Onys 196
open banking (finance) 25, 30, 31, 46, 47–48, 63, 197
open innovation (co-creation) 45–49, 197, 226, 227, 251
open science development 47
open source development 47, 198
Orange 27
overconfidence 71
Oxford Risk 194, 253

pain points 22, 54, 122–23, 178, 184, 192, 223, 229, 248
  see also onboarding
Pap Padap 103
participant observation 232
partnerships 22, 24–27, 50, 52, 132–34, 193, 224
payday lenders 2, 83, 126, 130
payment initiation services 206
Payment Services Directive 198
PayPal 27
Pedernales 95, 99
peer-to-peer (P2P) 22, 50, 54, 127, 172, 207, 208
pensions 49, 53, 73, 74, 82, 125
Peralta, Dr 109
Peredo 99
personas 194, 229, 230
Philippines 111, 151
pilot studies 220–21
Pix 24, 84, 88–89, 108, 147, 149, 151, 152, 156–57, 159, 205–07
Pix Forum 207
Pix Saque 206
Pix Troco 206
Pixpay 127, 253
platforms 26–27, 63, 256
point-of-sale (POS) transactions 29–30
poorly served populations 147–48
Port-au-Prince 94, 95, 96, 97–98, 99, 100, 101–02, 103, 112
Port-de-Paix 98
portable kit method 95, 112, 234–36
poverty, and financial inclusion 149–50
pre-development phase 226
primary research questions 106
problem framing 105–07
process management 17, 49, 51

product development 225–26
propositions 52
proprietary solutions 16, 20, 47, 256
prospect theory 71
psychology 70–71, 72, 73, 79, 84
P2P 22, 50, 54, 127, 172, 207, 208
Pulp Fiction 81

QCash 130, *131*, 171
qualitative data 4, 9–11, 71, 93–115, 136–39, 192–93, 225, 227–31, 248, 251
quantitative data 4, 10–11, 71, 96, 105–07, 108, 109, 222–23
question formulation 105–06, 110
questionnaires 110–11

radical innovation 43–44
Raisin 30
Ratesetter 172
rational choice theory 85
realism 78
Recherche du temps perdu (Proust) 118
recruiting companies 110
recruitment 110–11
'red envelopes' 8
refugees 178–84
regret 71
regulation 24, 26, 29, 33, 35, 171–72, 228
relational data 20
Remitly 180
reported behaviour 231
research 79–80, 218–19
  academic 10, 105, 241
  desk 108
  market research 105, 209, 219
  primary 106
  see also qualitative data; quantitative data
research mapping 221–23
research organizations 225–27
responses 52
retail sector 26, 34–35, 119, 137, 197, 201–02, 203, 205
retirement 30, 72–73, 74, 174
  see also pensions
returns processes 124
Revelation 113
Revolut 30, 169
risk 21, 84–86
risk assessment (analysis) 58, 59
risk aversion 85–86, 174
risk awareness 86
risk preferences 76–79, 84–85
RiteCheck 2
Roblox 198, 253
robotic process automation 20–21, 45
rotating credit and savings associations (ROSCAS) 143–44
Royal Bank of Scotland 171
Rua 25 de Março 232–33

Safaricom 103
Saint Marc 101
SalaryFits 172, 253
sampling 10, 93–94, 107–09
sandboxes 37, 54
'sanity checks' 109–10
São Paulo 86, 88, 232–33
Save More Tomorrow scheme 81
savings accounts 55, 76, 103, 126, 167, 169
scenario planning 37, 137, 218, 227
Scottish Widows Association 7
security certificates 50
semi-structured interviews 97, 112, 233, 234
service design research 106–07, 122
service industries 44–45
service limitations 157–58
Servon, Professor Lisa 2–3, 9, 10, 83, 126
ShopeePay 160
Shopify 27
SICPA 211–12
small and medium-sized enterprises (SMEs) 23, 31, 44, 53, 55, 126
Smart 30
smart contracts 32, 33
smartphones 18, 143, 151, 153, 181, 191
snowballing 110, 234
social media 10, 19, 20, 46, 181, 195
  see also Facebook
social network analysis 234
social relations 8–9, 15–41, 60, 62, 89, 98, 114, 152
social transformation 15–41
'socioeconomic humans' 88, 114
sociology 10, 70, 71, 77, 79, 110
SogeXpress 98
South of Sahara Telecommunications Solutions 53–54
'spaces' (Starling Bank) 55
specific insurance policies 59
SSL security 50
stablecoins 32
Starling Bank 55, 134, 169
start-ups 22–23, 125, 133
  see also fintechs
StartUp Weekend 22
statistics 74–75, 85, 105, 108
Stoll, David 1–3, 9, 10
Storebrand 25

strategic decision-making 72
  see also game theory
strategy 226–27
stress 87
Stripe 27
sub-questions 105, 106
Sub-Saharan Africa 28–29, 53–54, 55–56
supervised learning 20
sustainable finance 16–17, 31
Sweden 233
SWIFT 17
Switzerland 5, 9, 48, 57, 62, 81–83, 118–20
Syrian refugees 182–83

Tagqnu 181–82
taste 77
tax culture 79
tax mentality 79
TchoTcho 102
technology 4, 7–9, 17, 52, 58, 62, 153–54, 156–57
  cloud 19, 49
  testing 49–50
  see also AI (artificial intelligence); blockchain; chatbots; ChatGPT; digital transformation; digitalization; digitization
technology acceptance model (TAM) 51–52, 194
Tencent 23–24
testing, A/B 106
Thaler, Richard 72–73, 76, 81
'thick description' technique 75, 93, 97–104, 108, 114, 117
Tikkie 87
tokenization 32, 57, 196, 236, 256
transaction costs (convenience) 81–82, 88, 118–22, 141, 149, 156
transactional data 20
TransferGo 180
Trinidad 78–79
trust 60, 62, 83–84, 199, 224
Tversky, Amos 72, 85
Twint 119
two-sided platforms 26

Uber 26
Uganda 154
underserved populations 44, 146–47, 165–66, 172, 185
United Nations 135
  UNHCR 182–83
United States (US) 1–2, 10, 29, 83, 112–13, 122–24, 234, 237–38
  credit unions 126, 129–32
Unitransfer 98
University of California Irvine 95
unserved populations 145–46
unsupervised learning 20
USAID 94, 98
user communities 46
user research 219–41
utility maximization 71–72
UX researchers 106–07

value 80–81, 88
Varo Bank 169–70, 172
Varo Money 76
village savings and loan associations 135
virtual assets 58, 59
virtual cards 55
virtual reality 33–34, 55, 58, 59, 196
  see also gaming
Visa 17, 170
Voilá 94–95, 100, 112
volume, variety, velocity and veracity 19

Washington State Employees Credit Union 130
Web 1.0 (internet) 4, 18–19, 32, 36, 103, 119, 121, 144, 156, 201–02
Web 2.0 32
Web 3.0 4, 32–33, 47, 191
WEIRD research subjects 110
WeMoney 171, 254
Western Union 98, 99
'white label' fintech 25, 55, 130, 133
Wise 30, 180
women (females) 85–86, 124–25, 147, 150, 173–78
workarounds 155–61, 162, 209, 240
workshops 122, 224, 238
World of Warcraft 8

young people 30–31, 133, 147, 169, 196
  see also children; Generation Z; Millennials
Yunnis, Muhammad 7, 142–43

Zelle 169, 254
Zopa 172
Züricher Kantonalbank 48

Printed in the USA
CPSIA information can be obtained
at www.ICGtesting.com
JSHW072059040424
60587JS00012B/58

9 781398 613874